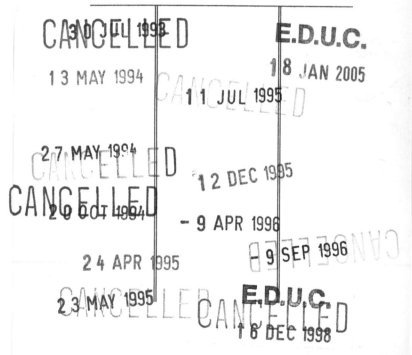

Empowerment
through
Experiential
Learning
Explorations
of Good Practice

EDITED BY

JOHN MULLIGAN AND COLIN GRIFFIN

KOGAN
PAGE

First published in 1992

Kogan Page Limited
120 Pentonville Road
London N1 9JN

© John Mulligan, Colin Griffin and named Contributors, 1992

British Library Cataloguing in Publication Data

A CIP record for this book is available from the British Library.

ISBN 0 7494 0680 1

Typeset by DP Photosetting, Aylesbury, Bucks
Printed and bound in Great Britain by
Clays Ltd, St Ives plc

Contents

List of Contributors

Professor Betty Anderson, Foundation Dean and Head of School of Nursing & Health Studies, University of Western Sydney, MacArthur, Australia.

Bruce Anderson, Lecturer in Electronic Systems Engineering, University of Essex, UK.

Dr Paul Barber, Staff Tutor, Human Potential Resource Group, Department of Educational Studies, University of Surrey, UK.

Inspector J A Bartrop, Training Department, Leicestershire Constabulary, UK.

Dr Shane Blackman, Research Fellow, Department of Educational Studies, University of Surrey, UK.

Professor David Boud, Professor of Adult Education, University of Technology, Sydney, Australia.

Dr Alan Brown, Senior Research Fellow, Department of Educational Studies, University of Surrey, UK.

Norman Evans, Director of the Learning from Experience Trust, London, UK.

Dr Colin Griffin, Senior Lecturer, Staff Tutor, Department of Educational Studies, University of Surrey.

Jane Henry, Lecturer, IET, The Open University, UK.

John Heron, Founder of the Human Potential Resource Group, Consultant and Facilitator, Podere Gello, Italy.

Dr Joy Higgs, Head, Physiotherapy School, Cumberland College of Health Sciences, Sydney University, Australia

Grethe Hooper-Hansen, Teacher of English as a Foreign Language, University of Macerata, Italy.

Cathy Hull, Lecturer, Goldsmiths' College, University of London, UK.

Susan Knights, Senior Lecturer, Department of Community and Aboriginal Education, University of Technology, Sydney, Australia.

Professor Margaret McMillan, Former Associate Professor, School of

Nursing and Health Studies, University of Western Sydney, MacArthur, Australia.

W M Mak, Lecturer, Department of Management, Hong Kong Polytechnic, Hong Kong.

Dr Iain S Marshall, Director of Work-Based Learning Projects at Napier Polytechnic, Edinburgh, UK.

Dr Judith Marshall, Senior Lecturer, School of Management Studies, University of Bath, UK.

Margaret Mill, Researcher, Napier Polytechnic, Edinburgh, UK.

John Mulligan, Senior Staff Tutor, Human Potential Resource Group, Department of Educational Studies, University of Surrey, UK.

Anna Paczuska, BP Access Project Coordinator, Division of Continuing Education, South Bank Polytechnic, London, UK.

Ranjan, Lecturer, School for Independent Study, Polytechnic of East London, UK.

Sharon Redhead, Community Education Worker and Action Research Worker, Manchester Open College Federation, Manchester Polytechnic, UK.

Professor Anthony Richards, Co-ordinator, Youth Research Unit, Dalhousie University, Nova Scotia, Canada.

James Anthony Saddington, Senior Lecturer, Department of Adult Education and Extra-Mural Studies, University of Cape Town, South Africa.

Pamela Tate, President of the Council for Adult and Experiential Learning, USA.

Ian Taylor, Evaluator of the Enrichment Programme, Education Department, University of Liverpool, UK.

Dr David Walker, The Centre, Randwick, Sydney, Australia.

Dr Sue Webb, Development Officer, Manchester Open College Federation, Manchester Polytechnic, UK.

Foreword

Empowerment and Experiential Learning. How the world has changed!

Take a month in 1992. At the Learning from Experience Trust (LET) in Britain. We took seminars on accreditation of prior experiential learning (APEL) for masters degree programmes in universities. We did consultancies in both higher and further education institutions on introducing APEL as part of their provision. We took seminars and workshops for nurse and midwife tutors, course and agency providers of a Diploma in Social Work – all to do with aspects of APEL. We conducted an APEL seminar for the development of employees in small and medium-sized businesses as a way of improving the skills of the workforce and company profitability and were consulted by some Training and Enterprise Councils about similar schemes. We wrote articles asked for by a variety of journals and publications. There were chapters for books to be written. Another LET publication was underway if not completed. A series of seminars on different aspects of APEL was on offer to further education colleges. There was an LET national conference, 'From Mission to Action', which revolved round APEL. We made presentations at other national conferences. And all the time a stream of phone and letter inquiries came in about experiential learning from an ever widening range of backgrounds and professional interests, most of them buying LET publications. Overseas visitors appeared asking the same range of questions.

All that went on against the background of several funded projects concerned with APEL in higher education, further education, employment and the professions. And every one of them was a first in Britain.

That is 1992. Go back to 1980, when I first convened a small group of British academics (which included Colin Griffin) to puzzle out where, if at all, the assessment of experiential learning might fit into higher education and if anywhere, how we could set about it. The group was sceptical about turning idea into action, and for good reason. At that time no one in higher education – let alone further education or employment – had considered possibilities; in any case, the idea itself was 'suspect'.

The Trust is only one of the players. Others can tell the same story. So what has happened in the intervening 12 years? A combination of demography and mounting anxiety about the state of the economy has forced attention on a number of issues about which experiential learning has something to say. They all concern a dreadful waste of human talents: wider participation by young people and adults in post-secondary education and training; retraining and skill enhancement; rising unemployment. Take experiential learning seriously and the connections are obvious: every one of them involves empowerment in one form or another.

So it is hardly surprising that in summer 1991 some 160 people from many parts of the world thought it worthwhile to spend three days in a conference on empowerment through experiential learning. As the contributions which follow show, there were differing interests, interpretations and preoccupations. But a common theme is evident: a belief in the power and potential of the concept of learning from experience.

There are two comments to make about this growing interest. Both concern societies as a whole. The first is that many democratic societies are experiencing disquiet about the present structure of public institutions and the service they provide for the tax payers who fund them. Education fits into that general disquiet. Many practitioners and institutional leaders see experiential learning as an additional route towards a better relationship between potential learners in post-secondary education and institutions as facilitators of learning. But that is tricky. I've always seen experiential learning as potential dynamite for the curriculum and academic organization. You cannot send the message, 'We value what you bring with you. Let's see what it amounts to and then plan the best learning programme for you', which is where experiential learning takes you, without raising inconvenient questions about course content and how it is offered. Those who are impatient with the way things are, especially those who are affronted by the sheer waste of human potential which is the result of some present education arrangements, can take to experiential learning as easily as ducks to water.

The second point is that the growing interest in experiential learning by both employers and educators draws attention to the fact that employing organizations are increasingly becoming places of learning. More and more employers have to do that to stay in business. Many education institutions may find they need to take experiential learning seriously to stay in business too. Experiential learning serves notice that learning is not confined to classrooms. It points to a convergence between formal education and the workaday world of earning a living and leisure as sites where people learn and hence to the need to recognize learning whatever its source.

Explicitly or implicitly, all the contributors connect with these two implications of experiential learning. With their differing approaches to the topic, and indeed because of them, they amount to a rising chorus. Many more will sing the same tune. This book is a celebration of that song's theme. Interpret it as you will – empowerment through experiential learning.

Norman Evans
Director, Learning from Experience Trust
April 1992

Introduction

Background to the conference

Interest in a major British conference on experiential learning had smouldered quietly in the collective minds of a small group of academics from third-level educational establishments for some years before it eventually became a reality at Surrey University in 1991. This small group, who later helped form the conference organizing committee, had met at the two earlier International Conferences on Experiential Learning in London 1987, and Sydney 1989 and continued to meet sporadically in the intervening period with the broad intention of promoting experiential learning within the United Kingdom. In 1991 the group supported an offer from the Human Potential Resource Group to host the conference at Surrey University, as part of their 21st anniversary celebrations. The conference planning was under way and the Learning from Experience Trust, which had made a major contribution to the field, was invited to join the organizing committee.

From the outset it was the intention of the conference committee to design a conference which tried 'to balance shared experience with reflection; opportunities for active exploration, with the presentation of considered conceptualization'. It was hoped to provide a lively participative forum which would stimulate a highly interactive exploration of good practice in the field. It was felt that the major need among those likely to attend the conference – face-to-face practitioners – would be to share and clarify what was good practice in experiential learning and its facilitation. There was also a substantial and rapidly growing interest in the assessment and accreditation of experiential learning and this provided a second conference theme. It was also the aim of the conference to promote theory and research in the field and this was adopted as the final theme although the potential contributors in this area were thought to be limited, but expanding.

It was clear to the organizing committee that the conference would be of great interest to many educators engaged in a variety of sectors in education, therapy and organizational change. The success of the 1987 International Conference on Experiential Learning indicated that the subject had great appeal and both the Human Potential Resource Group and the Learning from Experience Trust had excellent contacts with substantial numbers of educational practitioners committed to experience-based learning. Representatives on the committee from the School for Independent Study at the Polytechnic of East London, Goldsmiths' College of the University of London, Portsmouth Polytechnic, the Royal Society of Arts and the Open University, together with their extended networks, ensured that the conference would draw on varied and diverse interest and practice in the field.

Experiential learning, as an educational philosophy and method being somewhat adventitious (there is little reference to it in British educational literature before 1980), tended to attract those interested in innovation, those who were disaffected with traditional educational practice and those, particularly educators of adults, who felt that people's experience was not being given the recognition that it deserved as a rich resource for learning. 'Experiential learning, whether personal, in use in formal institutions or in the community, is usually concerned with swimming against the mainstream to bring about change' (Warner-Weil and McGill, 1989).

It was not surprising then to find that a common motivation among the conference organizers was that of empowering learners, the implication being, from members' different perspectives, that current educational practice was not helping learners to develop their full potential and at times it even prevented them from doing so. It was felt that a great many of those who might attend the conference would also share this motivation for their work. 'Empowerment Through Experiential Learning' was therefore adopted as the conference title. Contributors were specifically asked to ensure that their contributions addressed the conference title and also the subtitle 'Explorations of Good Practice'.

The problem was, however, that despite the likelihood of having such a major motivation in common there was likely to be considerably less agreement about what constituted 'good practice', not to mention empowerment. Warner-Weil and McGill (1989) had identified four distinct 'villages' within the field of experiential learning, each with its own values, assumptions and perspectives which were not necessarily shared by other villages:

• Village 1 is concerned particularly with assessing and accrediting learning from life and work experience as the basis for creating new routes into higher education, employment and training opportunities and professional bodies.

- Village 2 focuses on experiential learning as a basis for bringing about change in the structures, purposes and curricula of post-school education.
- Village 3 emphasizes experiential learning as a basis for group consciousness-raising, community action and social change.
- Village 4 is concerned with personal growth and development and experiential learning approaches that increase self-awareness and group effectiveness.

They pointed out that while much debate and discussion tended to take place about the issues within each village there was often little awareness, regard for or interaction with the other villages' perspectives and, at times even, the norms and assumptions of one were promoted at the expense of the others.

The challenge for the conference committee was to stage a conference which would promote dialogue between the villages, which was not only about empowerment and good practice in experiential learning but which also modelled empowerment, was experiential and demonstrated good practice. The challenge was all the greater because of the intention to bring together participants from as broad as possible a spectrum of those engaged in experiential learning, ranging from primary to higher education, from therapists to training managers, both practitioners and advocates.

It is not the intention here to go into detail about how the conference did or did not meet such diverse needs and expectations, other than to say that it was well-attended, over 160 people, and that a high level of satisfaction was acknowledged by the majority of participants. It does seem important, however, for the reader to have a sense of the conference from which this book has emerged so they can view the chapters within the context in which they were presented. All the more so, because these chapters represent only a small portion of the learning and good practice which was shared at the conference. Not only were there more papers submitted than we could include in a volume of limited size, but there were many workshops presented which, though of very high quality, were not accompanied by written papers and so receive little recognition in this volume.

There are clearly many more excellent practitioners in the field than there are advocates who are willing or feel that it is worthwhile to write up their work. Many experiential learners, at least initially, do not trust their experience or allow it to confound their beliefs and what they have read. So too, it seems, practitioners are not yet ready to publicly proclaim the validity of their experiential learning process and its outcomes. Brookfield (1991) has identified the 'impostor syndrome' among adult educators; perhaps there is a great deal of it about in experiential learning also. The mismatch between practitioners and advocates is not only reflected in the difference between the number of conference presenters and the number of papers offered for publication but seems sadly true for those engaged in experiential learning as a whole. Hopefully it will improve as experience-based learning gains more public credibility and institutional recognition.

The mismatch may also reflect a kind of anti-reflective, anti-theoretical attitude sometimes associated with experience-based learning and often attributed to a backlash against the overly theoretical, intellectual and abstract nature of traditional education, particularly at higher levels. However, it seems as likely that this stance is because of the inherent difficulty and complexity of the required reflective processes which enable experience to be transformed into learning. This view is borne out by the centrality attributed to reflective processes by several contributors to this volume as well as others writing in the field (cf. Brookfield, 1991 and Schön, 1983). Likewise it is anticipated that this complexity will be reduced as advances in institutional adoption of experience-based learning forces the pace of development in processes of experiential learning and facilitator practice.

Finally, while the conference was initially intended to be a national one it attracted significant attention from abroad through the Steering Committee for International Conference on Experiential Learning. As the list of contributors to this publication shows, there were contributors from four of the five continents which added greatly to the value of the conference and gives some idea of the international interest in the topic.

Organization of the book

To give some structure and coherence to the book, we have divided the chapters up into five different sections. Chapters are grouped within these sections based on their primary thrust, as we perceive it to be, and we have provided a brief overview of each chapter within this introduction for ease of access. It may help to keep in mind that the chapters were not prepared with these section headings in mind and that they have not been altered to suit them. Chapters clearly relate to more than one section and the introduction to the chapters in each section refers to chapters positioned in other sections which also have relevance to the section theme.

Section 1: Theories in practice
The chapters in this section all address wider conceptual issues arising

from experiential learning and its facilitation and locate it in philosophical, political, social and cultural contexts. Its relation to authority, knowledge, society, group dynamics and theory are all explored in diverse ways. Thus, the place of experience in different traditions of thought about human existence and human learning is brought into relation with different traditions of educational and social theory. Their primary concern is how theory can illuminate practice. Chapters presented here are, in their different ways, concerned with the role of experience, teaching and learning in human relations and social structures. They are mostly reflective in nature, and provide a basis for critical reflection on practice, a way of challenging our accepted beliefs, goals and methods and inviting us to re-examine our concepts and attempts to empower.

Colin Griffin's 'Absorbing experiential learning' offers a critical reflection on the concept of empowerment from a Deweyan perspective. While acknowledging the value of experiential learning, he suggests that Dewey would have considered it as symbolic politics which cannot be backed up by sociological or political data. He argues that personal growth cannot and should not be confused with empowerment.

Tony Saddington's chapter 'Learner experience: a rich resource for learning' looks comparatively at the significance of learners' experience in various theoretical traditions of adult education and provides an overview of five such traditions: liberal, progressive, humanistic, radical, and technological. Within each of these, the significance of learner experience varies dramatically and it is suggested that a critically reflective element is necessary to the experiential learning process unless the social and political structures are to be reproduced in education as much in the future as they have been in the past.

W M Mak's chapter 'Experiential learning: the Confucian model' offers a different cultural perspective on experiential learning. He draws some supportive parallels between the Confucian model and the ideas of Rogers and Dewey though one cannot help thinking that we are only scratching the surface of Confucian educational thinking as reflected in the seemingly obvious aphorisms.

Paul Barber's chapter 'An exploration of levels of awareness and change processes in group encounter' presents a framework for understanding and analysing the group dynamic in experiential learning groups. The framework identifies and illustrates four levels at which the group dynamic can be understood, analysed and facilitated: social, transferential, projective and primordial, which are derived from the author's research on groups aimed at personal growth and professional development.

Ranjan in his chapter 'Silent learning: experience as a way of knowledge' challenges us to allow our experience to confound our theories, to balance our knowledge of things with a knowledge of being and to develop wisdom through the process of experiential learning rather than simply knowledge.

John Heron's chapter 'The politics of facilitation' explores the ways in which power may be handled by the facilitator of experiential learning. He introduces three kinds of authority: cognitive, political and charismatic, and outlines the relevance of each to the facilitation process but selects political authority for in-depth attention. Four levels of decision-making are introduced and illustrated and their implications for practice discussed.

Section 2: Assessment and accreditation

Empowerment in the chapters forming this section is seen as a function of the public recognition of personal learning. In the last few years, accreditation and assessment of prior and other kinds of experiential learning have become a major aspect of the move to open up formal institutions of education to a wider population of learners. The policies and processes of access to higher education in particular have generated a body of practice and case study such as those represented here. This focus, in turn, has concentrated attention upon those areas of the curriculum which seem less accessible to 'non-traditional' students as well as upon the experiential learning of groups of people hitherto under-represented in the formal education system.

The process of assessment and accreditation has thrown up some highly significant issues about the ways in which knowledge and learning have been traditionally conceived in education. Whilst the system may have been opened up for variety of reasons, some no doubt political, a major challenge to conventional and stereotypical thinking about people's learning is implied by these understandings of science and technology or of learning in the community and the workshop. The ways in which assessment and accreditation of experiential learning should be conducted remain open to further debate and refinement, but there can be no doubt that they will find increasing prominence in all education and training systems.

Norman Evans in his chapter 'Linking personal learning and public recognition' raises the issue of what constitutes public (or corporate) recognition of learning. Assessment here provides the link between public and private learning, and the chapter describes the stages in the assessment of experiential learning necessary for the link to be made. The concept of empowerment is defined here both in terms of personal and institutional growth and development, and the stress on staff development reflects the major processes of institutional responses: adaptation, resistance and incorporation.

Anna Paczuska, in her chapter on 'APEL for access to science and technology' addresses a major concern of the conference in terms of assessment of experiential learning for purposes of access to higher education courses. In this case, the argument is that APEL is of special significance for women and the science curriculum, in that it may help to challenge stereotypical thinking and recognize the whole range of skills which are necessary to progress in science and technology, and which are not dissimilar from those necessary to progress in any discipline.

Sue Webb and Sharon Redhead's chapter on 'Women's informal learning in a neighbourhood setting' reviews the function of the Open College in empowering women through recognition of the experiential learning in work and community activities and the development of forms of accreditation. Such accreditation connects informal to formal learning, and takes account of the importance of the reflective process and of methods of facilitation which empower women.

Shane Blackman and Alan Brown, in their chapter on 'Constraints upon portfolio development in the accreditation of prior learning' describe a study of three colleges developing APL for work-related competencies, known as the Portfolio Project, the aim of which is to use portfolio preparation as a means of gaining NVQ competence accreditation. The chapter deals with institutional responses to work-based learning, and addresses the generational issues of young adults' experiences in relation to APL in an FE setting, together with its implications for staff development.

Cathy Hull's chapter 'Making experience count: facilitating the APEL process' offers an overview of portfolio construction with a view to the accreditation of prior experiential learning. While it is written with the facilitator's concerns in mind, it provides a useful insight into the subtleties of the process and evidence of its empowering effects, both in personal terms and as a method of access to further education. She suggests that APEL should be valued as an educational process in itself as well as a valuable tool for assessment.

Section 3: Integrating experiential learning
The chapters in this section all deal with different aspects of the institutional response to the experiential learning movement. This has been a complex mix of opportunism, rationalization, resistance and assimilation, and the experience of practitioners has consequently been very varied.

It could be argued that experiential learning was an idea whose time came at a point of demographic, social and economic changes which made 'rational' partnerships between learners, educators, employers and governments more inevitable than they would otherwise have been. This view might regard the experiential learning movement as the march through the institutions.

If such is the case, it has generated some interest in questions about the culture of formal institutions and organizations and the ways in which they change. The demand for more experiential modes of learning to be formally incorporated into education and training systems has come from many sources, and it has generally been the convergence of such sources that made its adoption inevitable. An understanding of educational and institutional culture helps us to understand why the most important source of resistance to the incorporation of experiential learning has come from academics themselves, whose social status is so tightly linked to abstract, theoretical knowledge. As these chapters convey, experiential learning continues to stimulate challenges for practitioners in their facilitation of learning but also demands a competence as an organization and policy change agent for which few recognize the need and even fewer are equipped.

In her chapter 'Empowerment through experiential learning' Pamela Tate describes the origins and development of CAEL in the United States, and the progressive institutionalization there of experiential learning in education and training. It charts the demographic, economic and social trends which have culminated in new partnerships between educators, employers, trade unions and governments to produce a more coherent system of education and training and a more 'empowered' vision of employment generally.

Judi Marshall's chapter 'Cooperative inquiry into organizational culture' describes recent research into processes of organizational change, with a view to better understanding the culture in which working practices are embedded. In the course of the inquiry (into local government organizations) major cycles of action and reflection were identified, and the concept of empowerment was located within the organizational culture of the workplace as an outcome of the reflective and research processes themselves, by which employees are introduced to new possibilities for personal and organizational change.

J. Bartrop's chapter 'Police probationer training: resistance to writing as an aid to reflection in experiential learning' describes the author's personal experience of using a journal as an aid to reflection. He also explores the constraints which have to be encountered by police probationers in training when using such journals and resistance to this on the part of trainees is analysed further. The chapter provides a good example of the ambiguity of institutional responses to such developments.

Section 4: Learning to learn
These chapters all deal with models and practices in relation to the

experiential learning process itself. They all, in different ways, offer insights into what actually happens, or needs to happen, in this kind of learning, with many implications for ways in which the process may be enhanced and facilitated. The stress upon empowerment through the realization of potential and fulfilment of purpose is a common theme. They effectively convey the core idea of independence in learning, but approach it in a way that stresses the potential which competence in such learning processes holds for empowerment through the personal generation of knowledge and meaning. Empowerment here can be seen as synonymous with greater discrimination and competence in the use of a wide variety of internal actions and strategies which are necessary to transform experience into learning.

In 'Adventure-based experiential learning', Anthony Richards offers some interesting insights into the philosophy and history of adventure-based education but his most valuable contribution is his use of key elements of the adventures of the Greek hero Ulysses as a model for structuring adventure-based learning. He identifies four elements of the learning journey: separation, encounter, return and re-incorporation to illuminate key phases necessary for effective learning.

David Boud and David Walker's 'In the midst of experience: developing a model to aid learners and facilitators' gives a useful summary of the authors' and their Australian colleagues' work in trying to identify processes which would be of benefit to learners and facilitators in the field of experience-based learning. They refer to pre- and post-experience practices as well as what occurs in the midst of the experience itself and identify areas where there is need for further research.

A further case study is offered by Susan Knights in 'Reflection and empowerment in the professional development of adult educators' in which she briefly examines some of the principles and assumptions underlying the practice of reflection. She then proceeds to give an account of her experience of introducing reflective processes into training programmes for adult educators, together with some responses from participating students which illustrate the empowering effects of such reflective processes in experiential learning.

John Mulligan's chapter 'Internal processors in experiential learning' explores what is going on internally within the learner during the process of learning from experience. A model of seven interrelated processors (ways of accessing and processing experience) is outlined together with some insights into the relevance of each processor to experiential learning.

Jane Henry's 'Creative capability and experiential learning' examines the development of creativity, in particular through the medium of problem-solving approaches. She also explores the relationship between these approaches and experiential learning processes.

Grethe Hooper-Hansen in her chapter 'Suggestopedia: a way of learning for the 21st century' presents us with a brief introduction to Suggestopedia, an accelerated learning technique developed by Lozanov of Bulgaria. Having outlined the key principles of the method she illustrates how they are operationalized in the course of a language learning class. She explains how music, peripheral stimulation, games and activities are all combined to achieve the desired effects. Finally she raises and answers some of the key criticisms which have been made against the method.

Section 5: Principles into practice
These chapters deal with ways of structuring and facilitating experiential learning by highlighting the principles distilled from practice or by demonstrating how key principles have been put into practice.

In their chapter 'Learning contracts: how they can be used in work-based learning' Iain Marshall and Margaret Mill describe some theoretical models of learning contracts involving learners, employers and HE institutions, and outline their use in a Higher Diploma course at Napier Polytechnic. The chapter explores issues around the culture of the workplace and that of HE institutions, especially with regard to student tutor and mentor roles in the facilitation process. It also stresses the centrality of the assessment element in work-based experiential learning and the empowering potential of learning contracts for students on these kinds of courses.

Betty Anderson and Margaret McMillan in their contribution, 'Learning experiences for professional reality and responsibility' outline the key principles in what they term 'practice-centred learning' and go on to describe how the learning and assessment processes combine to facilitate the desired professional competence. The remainder of the chapter focuses on evaluation of the method and its outcomes which support, among other principles, the focus on learning rather than teaching and reliance on the action context and the realities of practice to provide the stimulus and the organizing principle for learning rather than the traditional syllabus topics.

Joy Higgs in her chapter 'An experiential learning approach to developing clinical reasoning skills' delineates some key principles in the design and facilitation of good practice and then proceeds to illustrate how these are put into practice through a case-study approach to developing clinical reasoning skills with postgraduates. Besides being experiential, the methods used reflect a successful integration of collaborative design, experiential and theoretical knowledge and an appropriate balance of peer and expert authority which, it is claimed, lead to the empowerment of both the educators and their clients.

Bruce Anderson's chapter 'Task and reflection in learning to learn' likewise describes the author's philosophy and teaching practice in the area of technology education. He offers a structure for integrating group and problem-based approaches together with reflections on his experience of using it. It is particularly interesting for his handling of the individual in relation to the group and for the creativity and diversity in problem-solving which is facilitated by this approach.

Ian Taylor's chapter 'Encouraging experiential learning' describes some developments in the post-16 curriculum in the form of the enrichment programme organized by Liverpool University together with teachers and industrialists in the north-west. It explores some consequences for curriculum development in institutions which incorporate experiential learning projects. In stressing the value of group and project work, the chapter indicates a contrast with tendencies towards over-individualized learning which self-directed study may imply.

Experiential learning and empowerment

When papers from the First International Conference on Experiential Learning were published (Warner-Weil and McGill, 1989) the editors attempted to capture 'the sheer diversity and complexity of experiential learning'. This they did by identifying the four distinct 'villages' mentioned above, which made up the movement as a whole: assessment and accreditation for the purpose of access to education and employment; changing the post-school education system; changing structures of society itself; promoting growth and development.

This functional analysis still holds good, and diversity and complexity still characterize experiential learning. However, since then, the focus has sharpened here and there and some of the 'overlaps, nuances and differences' within the village metaphor have clarified. The titles chosen for the section headings in this volume give a clear representation of the broad issues to which contributors to the conference are giving sustained attention, though, it must be acknowledged, the conference was biased in favour of those who could afford it and this may have excluded some – particularly those working mainly in Village 3.

The primary emphases in the last few years concern not so much functions and conceptualizations of experiential learning as the processes of institutional incorporation and professional role developments. As Norman Evans in his chapter expresses it, experiential learning, especially in the varieties of assessment it entails, consists always of the link between personal learning and public recognition. As the chapters in this volume often suggest, these processes remain problematic.

In terms, for example, of the third functional village, represented as concerned with social change 'mainly outside educational institutions', it is difficult, or may be too early, to see what social changes could possibly be attributed to the experiential learning movement as such. However, there is more evidence to suggest that social changes (such as those in the demographic structure of education, or in organizational and corporate professional roles) result in the adoption of experiential learning approaches to education and training. There is little by the way of ideology represented in these chapters, but much instrumentalism and professional role development.

In the four years since the First International Conference the political climate in Britain for experiential learning has certainly developed, but in a rather paradoxical way. The political assault on the progressive or learner-centred philosophy of school education culminated in the public discrediting of the Plowden Report and the attempt to finally put to rest some of the egalitarian fantasies about education from the 1960s. The educational trends are nowadays in the direction of rote-learning and instruction.

On the other hand, in post-school education generally and professional continuing education in particular, the trend is towards experience-based and reflective learning and away from college-based theory, at least as far as teacher training is concerned. Whether these trends are contradictory or not cannot be pursued here, but experiential learning developments need to be located in this context. It may be the case that it is reflective experience and its uses that distinguish adult from childhood learning. Nevertheless it seems futile to try to fix the chronology of childhood, youth and adulthood too confidently, as some of the chapters here demonstrate.

So, as compared with the earlier conference, there is perhaps more development here in the direction of instrumental concerns arising from the process of institutionalization, and accreditation and facilitation are the themes of many chapters. The institutional base is broadening too, with further education, competency and NVQs much more to the fore than they were in 1987. However, such tendencies point firmly in the direction of curriculum development, assessment, institutional responses and the personal and professional development of the facilitator, and these are clearly concerns of the four 'villages' of experiential learning.

Where does this leave 'empowerment', and how does it find expression in the chapters in this book? The theme that runs through them all is that of the potential of experiential learning for developing a sense of autonomy and control on the part of the learner, through a process of reflection which brings him or her into direct contact with personal knowing, rather than with knowledge as some kind of educational construct. This is reflected not only in the concern of many facilitators, expressed so adroitly by John Heron, to balance 'facilitator authority with learner autonomy' but also in the clearly emerging shift of emphasis among leading-edge practitioners and theorists, from teaching process to learning process. Independence in learning through the development of extended learning process competencies is emerging as a cornerstone of personal empowerment.

The connections between experiential learning, personal development and social empowerment and change are highly complex, and they are not often directly addressed in this book or, indeed, elsewhere. But the sense of common values, educational philosophy and principles which underpin these diverse approaches to the common theme is very clear, and so are the implications for the empowering nature of the process of experiential learning itself. Although as a concept empowerment needs more refinement, it is quite sharply brought out by those chapters which, in various ways, address issues of personal recognition, facilitation, assessment and institutional accreditation of experiential learning. It seems clear that the incorporation of this kind of process into formal systems of education and training depends upon institutional and organizational cultures, as several chapters make abundantly clear: the experiential learning movement raises issues of organizational as much as personal growth and change.

Traditionally the system has relegated the significance of learners' experience to a subordinate role in relation to academic constructs of knowledge, the role of experiential learning being merely to illuminate or exemplify abstract knowledge, rather than to constitute a source of knowledge itself. But the educational discourse of 'knowledge' has also changed and broadened to take in such aspects of learning as attitudes, skills competencies and a whole range of applications. The post-school educational system is only just beginning to come to terms with the changing discourse of educational knowledge and with the often quite radical implications of the 'decoupling' of learning and education and the re-siting of learning away from the traditional institutions: these have in fact ceased already to be the 'seats of learning' in the old and exclusive sense. Partly this has happened as a consequence of changes in the division of knowledge itself; the generation of knowledge is often located in the production of material, social, cultural and personal life and learning must now move closer to the site of knowledge generation and thus away from its reproduction in educational institutions. Formal educational institutions are simply unnecessary for effective learning to be achieved in many instances.

This relocation of learning, especially into the workplace or community or personal life, is a theme of many of these chapters. On the institutional front, at the same time, we are witnessing an increasingly rationalized partnership between learners, educators, employers and governments, as Pamela Tate's chapter illustrates. Within this more rationalized provision the empowerment of the learner is increasingly contested. To talk of a more rational scheme implies a degree of harmonization of purposes, functions and interests. In some instances, as can be seen, harmonization has some way to go and bureaucratic institutions reflecting traditional divisions of knowledge often prove resistant or else will superficially incorporate experiential modes of learning, as long as hierarchies remain unaffected.

The development of new modes of learning from experience, facilitator practice and organizational change all contribute greatly to empowerment and it is clear that most if not all contributors to the conference and this volume feel they are contributing to this empowerment. Nonetheless, while there was considerable emphasis on reflection there was remarkably less by way of critical reflection on the 'good practice' presented. Perhaps it is not surprising given that most contributors were clearly practitioners rather than observers or academic advocates, but the lack of such critical reflection leaves the experiential learning movement vulnerable as regards empowerment. Is it possible that we practitioners may also be unwitting agents of the very oppression or limitations we seek to transcend by our good practice?

Critical perspectives are clearly necessary if we are to ensure that experiential learning continues to empower. No doubt, societal and educational changes will increasingly demand elements of the kinds of experiential approaches outlined in many chapters, and critical analysis of resistance and incorporation processes clearly need to be developed further from both personal and social perspectives.

However, while acknowledging this concern, we believe that, in different ways, all the chapters in this volume contribute to an understanding of how the empowering potential of the experiential learning process might be more fully realized in the wider contexts of people's lives, education, work and society.

References

Brookfield, S (1991), 'Grounding teaching in learning', in Galbraith, M (ed) *Facilitating Adult Learning*, Malabar, FL: Kreiger

Schön, D (1983) *The Reflective Practitioner*, New York: Basic Books

Warner-Weil, S and McGill, I (1989) *Making Sense of Experience: Diversity in Theory and Practice*, Milton Keynes: SHRE and Open University Press.

SECTION 1

Theories in Practice

This section is concerned with theoretical frameworks, philosophical and critical reflection related to experiential learning.

Taking the chapters in order of appearance, Griffin challenges the whole concept of empowerment through experiential learning from a Deweyan perspective. Saddington explores how different schools of educational thought utilize experience on learning. Mak draws comparisons between Confucius' views on learning and those underpinning experiential learning. Barber discusses the different levels of interpretation and facilitation of the group dynamic. Heron suggests that educational decision-making is a critical factor in non-oppressive use of authority by the facilitator. Ranjan delivers a potent call to balance our pursuit of knowledge with the pursuit of wisdom.

This section overlaps most with Section 4 where the reader will find worthwhile theoretical models and perspectives related to the learning process.

1 Absorbing Experiential Learning

Colin Griffin

As the title of this volume suggests, experiential learning is widely regarded as empowering learners, perhaps in ways that non-experiential learning does not. But in this chapter, I would like to raise some issues about empowerment as an object or outcome of the experiential process. In particular, I want to argue that we are witnessing the transformation of experiential learning from a progressive educational movement towards reconstruction as an object of institutional policy and professional good practice. As such, it is being incorporated or absorbed into the formal system of educational provision; I meant by the title of this chapter not only that experiential learning is of absorbing interest, but that it is being absorbed in the same way that other progressive movements have been in the past, so that they became more of a prevailing orthodoxy than a challenge to existing practice.

The concept of empowerment seems to me a useful and significant indicator of the process of incorporation which is under way. Assuming that empowerment is intended to convey a sense of politics, I want to suggest that whereas the capacity of experiential learning for personal empowerment is very real, as practitioners know full well, its capacity for social change or transformation is very limited indeed. In this sense, that is, the generally received sense of politics, we are looking at the symbolic politics of empowerment through experiential learning, rather than a substantive possibility for social change. The reason for this lies in the process of absorption or incorporation which I am concerned with here. The social structure of a free society is dynamic in its relations: it 'acts back' on developments such as the one we are concerned with, transforming them often whilst permitting them to survive in recognizable form. Nothing is more sociologically and politically ambiguous than the idea of empowerment, however clear about it we are in terms of learning and the learner. If we reflect upon it, it has no political base, no ideological roots. It is, for example, currently fashionable with the 'new right' of conservative politics and used to advocate the principle of 'active citizenship' or individual participation in society, with a minimum of state interference in the marketplace: individuals are empowered by being made independent of the welfare concept of the state. In this ideological usage, one way of empowering individuals is to free education from the control of local authorities, and, as we know, this constitutes a substantive rather than symbolic possibility for empowerment, in the present political climate.

As practitioners, I think we tend sometimes to use the word in an analogous sense, in that learners are empowered through experiential learning with a minimum of interference in their learning, which is recognized and perhaps accredited: in short, private learning is transformed into a form of public education. This, of course, is perfectly consistent with a 'new right' politics: people are said to 'own' their learning, which is thereby converted into a marketable commodity. Much of the discourse of experiential learning is individualistic, entrepreneurial, and reflects what the 'new right' tend to understand by 'empowerment'.

Experience and education

It is often said that experiential learning originates in the educational progressivism of Dewey. Is this what he meant by it? In my view, he would have consciously avoided the idea of empowerment, because he was against slogans and what he would regard as educational jargon in general. In fact, he was much closer to the thinking of our own 'new right' than might be supposed. The philosophical tradition out of which Dewey wrote was pragmatism (which, baldly stated, means 'if it works, it's true'). He was unlikely to be attracted to empowerment or liberation: the political tradition was liberal democratic, not social democratic, and it was all a long way from Freire.

The roots of experiential learning theory therefore invite the reflection as to whether by thinking of it as a kind of empowerment it is possible to avoid certain political consequences. If it comes to stand for a slogan or a symbolic politics then it is capable of being transformed from a movement to an institutionalized policy. In this way, the idea of empowerment is being incorporated into the discourse of professional educators, as in the case of its association with self-advocacy and citizen advocacy in relation to adults in basic or special needs provision. The received professional ideology of experiential learning is that it empowers individuals to gain control over their learning and hence their lives, and to take responsibility for themselves. This is a view perfectly consistent with the 'new right' doctrine of individualism: the 'nanny teacher' should go the same way as the 'nanny state'. Perhaps Dewey would have agreed, but not in the same terms.

Reflections on empowerment, however, might raise a different set of questions. For example, who is empowered – individuals or groups? Collective empowerment for political change is one of the original and historic sources of adult education in Britain, and, unsurprisingly according to this thesis, such movements were long ago effectively absorbed, transformed and incorporated into a state system which in fact selectively empowered a minority of individuals to achieve social and economic mobility. Traditional education systems, which Dewey was of course criticizing, always featured a substantive politics of empowerment: its symbolic representation was contained in the slogan of equality of opportunity. The state education system has always, in fact, empowered. It has also absorbed, selectively, Dewey' s progressivism, and forms of experiential learning have often featured in institutionalized education. In other words, the distinction between traditional and progressive education, or classroom and experiential learning, is by no means clear cut, and empowerment cannot be unambiguously attributed to one or the other. A distinction emerges, however, between radical and progressive education which reflects that between collective empowerment and the substantive politics of social change, and individual empowerment and the symbolic politics of social change as a sum of individual transformations. One attributes substantive reality to society, the other attributes a symbolic reality to it. The sociological view is that although society may consist of the sum of individual actions, it cannot be reduced to it. I think the analysis of experiential learning and empowerment reinforces such a view. Individual transformation is the substantive politics of empowerment, social change is its symbolic representation. To say the personal *is* the political reduces the whole thing to mere rhetoric.

The politics of experience

I am arguing that the concept of empowerment is highly problematic, and it can be used in many ways, as substantive, symbolic or rhetorical. From a sociological point of view, it could also be considered as an aspect of ideology, that is, as a concept which is at the same time both universally valid and expressing the interests of a particular group, namely us – professional educators. This is an important mechanism of the incorporation process, for in considering whose interests are served by experiential learning, or whom it empowers, the answer is, everyone's: learners, educationalists, employers, politicians. One characteristic of a substantive political programme is that it threatens someone's interests. The fact that empowerment poses no great threat to anyone's interests is a measure of its symbolic status. The early collective struggles for empowerment through learning did pose a substantive political challenge to vested interests and were either confronted or absorbed into statutory provision. In the current situation, however, there is much more of a coincidence of interests of all those concerned, so that learners' interests are served by more effective learning and respect for their individuality; teachers' interests are served by a more flexible response to policy and reformulations of professional practice; employers' interests are served by the stress upon workplace or 'real life' experience rather than abstract knowledge; politicians' interests are served through the symbolic possibilities of educational reform without the need for substantive change, and so on. If such an analysis is true, and there is an absence of focused resistance, empowerment by way of experiential learning represents the symbolic politics which I am describing, rather than a real threat to anyone's interests.

Empowerment and change

Whatever sociological perspective one adopts, the sum of individual empowerment does not entail social or political change. So it must be asked whether empowerment leads to individual or social change, and how these are related? Sociologically speaking, institutions react to, absorb and incorporate progressive ideas, particularly when they are of symbolic significance and find little resistance by powerful interests in society. The institutionalization of experiential learning by way of courses, roles, conferences and so on, suggests the ambiguity of 'empowerment'. In the past, progressive movements in society and education have often been 'dis-empowered' with respect to their capacity for substantive change: there are losses and gains in the long run and power itself should be seen as a reflection of dynamic social forces, rather than in the opposition of tradition and progress which characterizes ideology and symbolic politics.

It is for these kinds of reasons that Dewey himself would have rejected the idea of empowerment, as indeed he would have rejected that of progressivism itself and all the labels and slogans of symbolic politics that have since been attached to his work in education theory. Dewey believed in the *pragmatic effectiveness* of experiential learning, in terms of both educational and social principle. He did not claim that it empowers in any philosophical or political sense: indeed, he would not have wanted labels or slogans of any kind, progressive or not, to be attached to experiential learning. At the end of his book, Dewey (1963, pp 90–91) says:

> I have used frequently in what precedes the words 'progressive' and 'new' education.
> I do not wish to close, however, without recording my firm belief that the fundamental

issue is not of new versus old education nor of progressive against traditional education but a question of what anything whatever must be to be worthy of the name *education*. I am not, I hope and believe, in favour of any ends or any methods simply because the name progressive may be applied to them. The basic question concerns the nature of education with no qualifying adjectives prefixed. What we want and need is education pure and simple, and we shall make surer and faster progress when we devote ourselves to finding out just what education is and what conditions have to be satisfied in order that education may be a reality and not a name or a slogan. It is for this reason alone that I have emphasized the need for a sound philosophy of experience.

Empowerment, I suggest, is precisely the kind of name or slogan that Dewey would reject as a merely symbolic representation of progressivism. I propose a return to pragmatism where experiential learning is concerned, and the abandonment of claims that cannot be made out alongside the assertion of those that can. Dewey was operating within a philosophical perspective, but I think there are many sociological grounds for embracing pragmatism too, and have implied several: the track record of progressivism is not particularly good, since so much turns upon the way it is structurally absorbed and incorporated into social and economic institutions. The absorption of experiential learning into education and training systems is a transformative process in itself. What Deweyan pragmatism suggests is that when it is in the best interests of individuals and society that education should reflect experiential learning, then it will. A pragmatic approach also helps us to leave empowerment out of it, as Dewey suggests we should. It does indeed seem the case that, as a way of learning, the experiential method is in everyone's best interests, and this is why it is being absorbed into the education system.

When, however, we consider it in terms of the symbolic politics of empowerment, then we have lost the sense of pragmatism, and entered into a world where everyone's interests are identical: right-wing politicians, left-wing politicians, employers and employees, teachers and learners, we are all of us empowered and no-one dis-empowered. Confusing the possibilities for personal growth with those for social change seems to lie at the root of the symbolic politics of empowerment through experiential learning. The slogan of empowerment may imply that the great transforming capacity of experiential learning in individuals' lives will be reflected in substantive social change. But how could we ever have evidence of this? What the empowerment slogan really reflects may only be the fact that too much transformation theory of adult learning projects an entirely static view of society and economy, and neglects its flexible and dynamic structural relations and its infinite capacity to absorb and incorporate. In particular, the over-theorization of individual learning in adult education has tended to reduce the theorization of social and economic structures to the level of Dewey's names and slogans, and

I think this is where empowerment sometimes comes from. In an age when we rush to discredit Marx it may be salutary to reflect upon his observations concerning the adaptability of capitalist societies, as well as upon Dewey's passionate pragmatism as the true foundation of liberal democratic ones.

References

Dewey, J (1963) *Experience and Education*, New York: Collier Books.

2 Learner Experience: A Rich Resource for Learning

James Anthony Saddington

Introduction

> To an adult, his experience is him. He defines who he is, establishes his self-identity, in terms of a unique series of experiences . . . he has a deep investment in the value of his experience. And so, when he finds himself in a situation in which his experience is not being used, or its worth is minimized, it is not just his experience that is being rejected.[1]

The intrinsic tendency of people to draw upon their own experience for both knowledge and skills, and the vast accumulation of experience that an adult has compared to a child, makes learner experience an important concept in adult education theory and practice.[2,3,4]

This chapter will examine the various theoretical traditions of adult education and show how the experience of the learner is used within each of them.[5] This examination will reveal that whilst learner experience is valued within each of the traditions, the degree of emphasis and significance placed on this experience varies with each tradition. The examination will result in a 'map' of the traditions which will provide an overview from which to view learner experience and to explore which of the traditions makes use of experiential learning as the methodology by which this experience can become a rich resource for learning. I have used various theoretical writings to answer two questions:

i)   What role does learner experience play in adult education; and
ii) Which of the main traditions of adult education theory make use of the experiential learning methodology?

The theoretical traditions of adult education and learner experience

For the purpose of this chapter and following with some modification what has become an established classification, I have grouped the main traditions of adult education theory and practice into five areas: 'liberal', 'progressive', 'humanistic', 'radical' and 'technological'. This grouping follows the distinctions within adult education proposed by John Elias and Sharon Merriam except that I have relabelled 'behaviourist' as 'technological', a term used by some writers to describe this approach which is aimed at the development of a 'technology of teaching and behavioural management and control'.[6] I also omit 'analytical philosophy', as it is the only tradition which does not have a field of practice and is more an attempted philosophical basis for adult education in general than a distinctive tradition. I am aware that some writers see the progressive tradition as being one of two strands of the liberal tradition, the other strand being the 'cultivation of the intellect'. However, for the purposes of this chapter I have kept the two strands separate.

Any consideration of the theoretical traditions of adult education is a major piece of work. It is important, therefore, that I state at the outset what I will not be doing. Whilst each tradition has been greatly influenced by the particular problems, issues and challenges that existed in the context and culture in which it was developed I will not be dealing in any depth with the historical background or the social contexts within which the traditions arose. I will also not be attempting a comprehensive overview of each tradition. Rather, there will be a tentative 'stock-taking' of the role of learner experience in adult education theory and practice which will result in a simplified 'map' of the five traditions. This map will provide an overview from which to examine the use of learner experience within each of these five traditions.

The liberal tradition

The liberal tradition arose out of the 'great tradition' of liberal non-vocational adult education established in Britain in the early years of this century. It began with a deep commitment to social and political reform through education and a belief in the power of knowledge to bring about a better and more just society. Education was seen as a 'civilizing process – a way of 'developing good men'.[7] The roots of this tradition are to be found in the philosophical traditions of the classical Greek philosopher[8] and the central concern of the tradition is the cultivation of the intellect. Intellectual understanding by the individual is the goal with education being about initiation into established forms of knowledge (ie, mathematics, art, literature and history).

Liberal education is not, however, about mere transmission or absorption of factual knowledge. The development of wisdom, moral values, a spiritual or religious dimension and an aesthetic sense is gained through a dialectic conversation between the learner and teacher. Initially the learner is merely increasing her/his interest in a particular area of study; then s/he increases her/his knowledge and understanding; and only at a later stage when s/he has 'mastered' the area of study is s/he able to use the skills necessary for critical judgement and enter into full dialogue. The process is one of leading a person from information to knowledge to wisdom.

Liberal education stresses the training of the mind over the training for work and believes that there is a need to 'equip the individual to cope with a world whose future is unknown'.[9] The emphasis is on a teacher-centred approach where the teacher assumes the traditional role of constructing and delivering the curriculum. One of the most powerful components of the programme is voluntariness – the desire on the part of the learner to study. Some of the best known forms of liberal education are the 'great books programme', the Elderhostel programme and the wide range of liberal art programmes offered as non-credit courses by universities and colleges.

The experience of the learner has a place in this tradition only in so far as it allows her/him to participate in the process of learning. Liberal education requires of its learners a basic ability to engage in the dialectical process and thereby understand and grasp the concepts being taught. This ability is an academic ability which in turn requires a certain level of understanding and knowledge. Life experience therefore is useful inasmuch as it provides the capacity to engage in meaningful discussion. When life experience is recorded in books, then this encoding of experience gives it a validity which allows it to be seen as true knowledge.

The move towards vocational education and the strong thrust of a behavioural orientation in education has weakened the influence of liberal education. The sense that an educational programme can be value-free or that knowledge is neutral has led this tradition to be highly criticized and rejected. The approach with its teacher-centredness offends, for some, the freedom and autonomy of the learner. The major critique of this tradition lies however in its elitist focus on the individual rather than society.[10] Whilst the need to develop the capacity of the individual to be able to make informed opinions and autonomous judgements is important, this tradition essentially maintains the class divisions in society – 'a form of education that traditionally secures – or blocks – penetration into professional classes'.[11]

The progressive tradition
The progressive tradition in adult education grew out of a reaction to liberal education in an attempt to respond to the social and political changes in the early decades of the 20th century. The emphasis of education was changed from the intellectual development of the mind to a focus on individuals having a responsibility toward the society in which

they lived. Education was seen as an instrument of social and political reform, which had a major role to play in the maintenance and extension of democracy.

The progressive tradition sees education as life-long and therefore 'learning how to learn' is important for the learner, as s/he can then continue to use both the knowledge that s/he gains from her/his own experience and the knowledge that s/he gains from others and books in solving problems and bringing about social change. Because progressive education places human experience at its centre and is about developing methods for solving human problems, experimental or problem-solving methods are favoured. Leading progressive educator John Dewey argued for education to be both liberal and practical. Common forms of progressive adult education include community development, participatory planning, community education, group dynamics and experiential learning.

The centrality of human experience in the progressive tradition means that the learner's experience is highly valued and is at least equal to the experience of others stored away in the written word. Knowledge is seen as inseparable from life experience and finds its validity in the degree to which it can be linked to or integrated with the experience of the learner. This focus on what is useful to the learner changes the role of the teacher to one of a guide. Malcolm Knowles describes the educator as a 'helper, guide, encourager, consultant and resource' as contrasted with a 'transmitter, disciplinarian, judge and authority'.[12] The teacher is not the sole source of knowledge but can also learn from the knowledge and experience of the learner – s/he is a partner in the learning activities. 'The teacher is a learner, and the learner is, without knowing it, a teacher'.[13]

One of the critiques of the progressive tradition is that the focus on improving an individual's life in society can contradict and be in conflict with the creation a more desirable society. This promotion of individual growth sometimes at the expense of the promotion of the good of society causes this tradition, like liberal education, to be seen as élitist.

The humanistic tradition

The underlying approach of the humanistic tradition is based on the belief that human beings are inherently good and the tradition has its roots in the existentialist[14] and humanist[15] thought of the 20th century. Existentialists contend that a person is not ready-made but rather a 'designer of her/his own being and essence'.[16] The tradition is concerned with the development of the whole person. Learning is therefore a process of discovery and experimentation with the principle goal being individual 'self-actualisation'. Self-actualisation is described as 'helping the person become the best he is able to become', ie, a 'fully-functioning individual'.[17,18]

In this tradition the focus is on the learner, with the teacher acting as a facilitator and enabler of the learner's growth. Learning occurs through group interaction, participation, experimentation and discovery. The responsibility for learning is placed on the learner who is at the centre of the experience. Learner freedom and autonomy are linked to the concept of self-directed learning[19] in the drive towards personal liberation and enrichment. The focus is on personal integration and psychological development – 'it is education that has a lot in common with healing and it lives most comfortably in therapeutic contexts, encounter groups and counselling'.[20] Forms of humanistic education include growth groups, encounter groups, self-directed learning groups and experiential learning approaches.

Experience in humanistic education is the source of knowledge and the content of the curriculum. As the learner reflects on her/his own experience so s/he takes possession of it in a new way and gains for her/himself knowledge which is authentic because it is true for her/his life-world. This repossession of experience is a personal discovery of knowledge which enables the learner to become more whole. With the focus in humanistic education on personal discovery and experimentation, the use of the experience of others, actual or recorded, is limited and useful only as it supports the learner's own discoveries or poses questions which require further reflection upon her/his own experience.

The major critique of the humanistic tradition is its apparent ignoring of a less-than-perfect complex real world through its focus on personal development. There is also the issue of whether a learner-centred and/or a self-directed learning approach is possible or even desirable in every learning situation.

The technological tradition

This tradition with its roots in behavioural psychology is to be found especially in commercial, industrial, public service and military contexts. The drive towards greater efficiency and productivity in these settings makes it important to ensure that people are able to adapt and fit into both organizational and societal goals. The approach has three theoretical roots – change theory;[21] systems theory;[22] and behaviourism.[23] This model of teaching has a 'systems' concept of education in its design. Education is understood in 'assembly line terms – as the production of human skills and capacities'[24] which the learner needs in order to be able to successfully adapt to a changing environment and 'survive' in society.

Behavioural or performance objectives are used to specify the learning conditions, behaviour and evaluation criteria that will be used to measure the results of the educational intervention. Learning is based on the assessed needs of the learners. Key terms are 'training' and 'development'. Because the learning process is devised and controlled by the teacher, knowledge is therefore external to the learner. The learner's task is to go through a stepwise programme of learning efficiently, and thereby gain the new skill or desired behavioural change. The typical forms of practice include systems analysis, human resources development, organizational development training and workplace training programmes. Methodologies include learning through reinforcement and competency-based teaching.

The life experience of the learner is useful only in so far as it determines the entry point of the learner. The testing or measuring of the learner's experience, ie, her/his skills and knowledge, will determine where in this stepwise training process s/he will begin. A lack of experience merely starts the learning process at an earlier stage. The experience of the learner within the learning process is useful to the teacher, who, on observing it, can provide the learner with feedback which aims to either reinforce or modify the learner's behaviour or skills.

The major critiques focus on the sense that behavioural objectives set by the educator place skills and knowledge outside of the learner; that it is not possible to write objectives for all learning; that the emphasis is on the learner not society; and that not everything to be learnt can be reduced to small steps. The question of who should determine learning needs and the lack of flexibility has led many to reject this educational approach. However, the search for systematic approaches to education and a 'technology of teaching'[25] have also attracted many educators. This tradition with its 'extreme simplicity, close-fit with productivity ethics, its ability to appear to deliver the goods' has a powerful capacity for social control.

The radical tradition

The radical tradition has its historical roots in various movements: anarchism, Marxism, socialism and the Freudian left.[26] This tradition has two main strands – the deschooling movement[27] and Paulo Freire's theory of conscientization. Whilst it can be argued that the other traditions are all political through 'different forms of innocence'[28] it is the radical tradition that makes its central commitment explicitly political – education is part of social transformation. For this tradition education is not neutral and can only be understood by locating it in its structural and historical context.

With the exception of Freire, the main concern has been with schooling. Ivan Illich called for an elimination of schools because he felt that the mandatory nature of education oppresses and dehumanizes people. Schools were seen as part of society's shaping of a person's 'view of reality' and were therefore oppressive.[29] Illich's concern was for personal autonomy and the freedom to choose to learn. He proposed 'resource centres',[30] skill exchanges, peer matching and a system of independent educators as alternatives.

At the heart of Freire's work is the belief that societal and individual liberation are interdependent. The focus of education is on bringing about a new social order by changing the structures of society and liberating the individual from a false consciousness which is unaware of the structural and historical forces which have domesticated her/him. Reflective thought and action [praxis) are seen to be dialectically related. It is through dialogue and engagement in society that awareness and insight into the learner's world and social reality come about.[31] The teacher is a facilitator who guides and questions instead of providing answers and directions for the learner. Freire described the true function of education as radical conscientization and called for a problem-posing approach to education as opposed to the more traditional 'banking' form of education.

The life experience of the learner and a critical analysis of this are at the centre of this process of conscientization. As the learner interrogates her/his own experience so s/he is able to reinterpret this experience and understand the societal context within which s/he finds her/himself. This understanding leads the learner to action, which again becomes experience to be reflected upon. Life experience is therefore the source of the learner's knowledge which liberates her/him and provides her/him with the tools for changing the society in which s/he lives.

Both strands of radical adult education believe in the need to develop forms and practices within the context of revolutionary action but few examples of their practice are to be found, mainly because most educators, while challenged by Illich and Freire's writings, are working within 'stable' institutionalized education systems where reform and not revolution is the way change is effected. The major exception to this is Freire's work in Brazil, Chile and some other third world countries where the main thrust is literacy. Other examples of the radical tradition are to be found in A S Neill's Summerhill school in Britain and the work by D Reed on 'the empowering learning process'.[32]

While the radical tradition engages directly with the problems of political commitment, radical educators need to guard against the danger of education becoming solely a political arena and ignoring the pluralistic nature of most cultures. Emphasis on political revolution can lead to artificial polarization and actually create conflict. 'Coordinators' (teachers) need to avoid becoming the 'experts' and slipping back into a teacher-learner relationship of dependency. What the radical tradition has done most strongly for adult education is to challenge the other traditions. It has forced adult educators to examine their practice and has called them to commit themselves to the liberation of the oppressed.

Learner experience and the traditions

Figure 2.1 is a 'map' of the five traditions showing the important assumptions held by each and their use of the learner's experience. The map draws on the work presented in the preceding sections but is, however, necessarily simple and naïve in that whilst it represents the traditions fairly coherently it does so at the expense of the complexities of the real world of educational strategy.

Experiential learning and the traditions

Saul Alinsky in his work on training community organizers discusses the way in which people react to life as 'a series of happenings which pass through their systems undigested' and concludes that 'happenings become experiences when they are digested, when they are reflected on, related to general patterns, and synthesized'.[33] Thomas in his work on developing 'learning conversations' states that 'People do not necessarily learn from experience; it depends on the meaning they attribute to their experience and on their capacity to reflect and review it'.[34]

Clearly therefore for the learner to be able to learn from her/his own 'rich resource' of experience s/he needs to develop skills of inquiry which will enable her/him to reinterpret and appropriate this experience. The making sense of experience is a major task for adult educators, and was what Freire called 'critical reflection'. A methodology which encompasses this critical reflection and enables the learner to make sense of and learn from her/his own experience is 'experiential learning'.[35] Experiential learning is a process in which an experience is reflected upon and then translated into concepts which in turn become guidelines for new experiences.

In examining the use of experiential learning within the five traditions I have constructed another chart; see Figure 2.2. The chart displays for each tradition responses to five questions:

1. What is the role of the learner's life experience in this tradition? (taken from the 'map' in Figure 2.1)
2. Does the tradition place value upon learner experience as a source of knowledge?
3. Does the tradition make use of experiential learning as a teaching-learning methodology?
4. What types of learner experience are reflected upon?
5. In terms of the four villages of experiential learning proposed by Warner-Weil and McGill[36] which village fits this tradition best?

	LIBERAL	PROGRESSIVE	HUMANIST	TECHNOLOGICAL	RADICAL
What social problem is taken most seriously by this tradition?	Ignorance	Social change	Personal meaninglessness	Production and efficiency	Oppression
What theory of social development does this tradition rest on?	Incorporation through intellectual development	Reform	Self-actualization	Modernization	Social transformation
What metaphor best describes the nature of the educational process?	Initiation	Problem-solving	Growth	Moulding	Empowerment
What is the key value in this form of practice?	Reason	Democracy	Acceptance	Efficiency	Freedom
What really counts as 'knowledge' in this tradition?	Wisdom	Judgement and ability to act	Wholeness	Performance	Praxis (Reflective thought & action)
What is the educator's task?	Transmission	Guiding	Support	Instruction	Conscientization
How is an educated person described?	Knowledgeable	Responsible	Integrated	Competent	Liberated

Figure 2.1 *Theoretical traditions of adult education*

	LIBERAL	PROGRESSIVE	HUMANIST	TECHNOLOGICAL	RADICAL
What is the role of the learner's life experience in this tradition?	Determines ability to engage in the dialectic process	A source of learning and inseparable from knowledge	The source of knowledge and the content of curriculum	Determines entry point for learning process	Basic to understanding the societal context and therefore the source of knowledge
Does this tradition draw upon experience for knowledge?	Not directly - only as recorded in texts	Yes - knowledge & experience are inseparable	Yes - own experience is the source of knowledge	No - experience is tested	Yes - life experience within society as source of knowledge
Does this tradition make use of Experiential Learning?	No	Yes	Yes	No	Yes
What types of experience are used?	N/A	Structured	Personal focus	N/A	Self in society
Which village is at work here or could be used?	1	1 & 2	4	None	3

Figure 2.2 *Theoretical traditions and experiential learning in adult education*

From the chart it is clear that Experiential Learning as a methodology for utilizing the learner's experience finds strongest support and use in the humanist and radical traditions with the progressive tradition using it as a learning strategy. However it is important to note that there is a major difference between these traditions in the nature and purpose of the reflection. In the progressive tradition it is to tap experience as an additional source of knowledge. In the humanist tradition it is about learning towards personal wholeness, while in the radical tradition it is towards empowerment and social transformation. Radical educationalists argue that there is a need for learners to be able to reflect critically on their own process of socialization and to relate their personal learning to societal issues and structures. 'The celebration in experiential learning of the individual and of subjectivity has exacerbated the dominant focus on micro processes to the detriment of an assessment of macro or social structural processes and issues'.[37]

Conclusion

As has been shown, the place of experience within each of the theoretical traditions of adult education varies dramatically. In the liberal and technological traditions learner experience provides the capacity to engage and helps determine the level or entry point for the learner. In the progressive, humanistic and radical traditions learner experience is valued highly. Knowledge for the humanist and radical Freirian traditions has its source in the experience of the learners, and while their educational goals differ, the development of the learners' ability to reflect upon this experience is the key to their learning potential. The three traditions see experience as providing the learner with a 'rich resource' to learn from and a 'base' upon which to build new learning.

Finally, in charting the use made of experiential learning in the main traditions of adult education it has been shown that the humanist, radical and progressive approaches use it to varying degrees and purposes. However, there remains a challenge to the non-radical educationalists that unless experiential learning includes a reflection phase which is critical then learners will be avoiding the 'social structural processes and issues' of today's world.[38] *The danger of turning a 'blind eye'* to the social and political context in which learners live and which will therefore shape both the process and content of the curriculum is very real for an experiential learning approach which focuses solely on the individual in 'here and how' situations.

References and notes

1. Knowles, M S (1970) *The Modern Practice of Adult Education: Andragogy versus Pedagogy*, p 44, New York: Association Press.
2. Kilty, J (1982) *Experiential Learning*, Human Potential Research Project, Department of Educational Studies, University of Surrey, Guildford.
3. Knowles, M (1973) *The Adult Learner: A Neglected Species*, Houston: Gulf Publishing.
4. Smith, R M (1982) *Learning How to Learn: Applied Theory for Adults*, Milton Keynes: Open University Press.
5. Key references used in writing the sections on the theoretical traditions: Apps, J W (1979) *Problems in Continuing Education*, New York: McGraw-Hill; Darkenwald, G and Merriam, S (1982) *Adult Education. Foundations of Practice*, New York: Harper & Row; Elias, J L and Merriam, S (1980) *Philosophical Foundations of Adult Education*, Malabar, FL: Robert E Krieger; Tobias, R (1982) 'Adult education as a field of university study', pp 113–31, in Freer, D and Randall, P, (eds) *Educating the Educators*, Department of Education, University of Witwatersrand. Johannesburg.
6. Tobias, op cit. p 123.
7. Freda Goldman quoted in Apps, op cit. p 129.
8. Socrates, Plato and Aristotle.
9. Peter Siegle quoted in Apps, op cit. p 130.
10. 'The individual is born and raised within the framework of an established sociocultural system whose institutional foundations have developed in close accord with the logic and interests of the social classes which dominate the given society', Reed, quoted in Cunningham, P M (1983) 'Helping students extract meaning from experience', *New Directions for Continuing Education*, 19, September, pp 57–69.
11. Millar, C J (1991) 'Critical reflection for educators of adults: Getting a grip on the scripts for professional action', (unpublished), p 4.
12. Knowles 1970, op cit. p 34.
13. Dewey, quoted in Elias and Merriam, op cit. p 162.
14. Heidegger, Buber and Sartre.
15. Maslow and Rogers.
16. Elias and Merriam, op cit. p 111.
17. Rogers, C (1961) *On Becoming a Person*, Boston: Houghton Mifflin.
18. Maslow, A H (1970) *Motivation and Personality*, New York: Harper and Row.
19. Knowles, M (1975) *Self Directed Learning: A Guide for Learners and Teachers*, New York: Association Press.
20. Millar, op cit. p 4.
21. Forced field analysis developed by Kurt Lewin.
22. Also called 'scientific management' and developed by Frederich Taylor.
23. John Watson (the founder of behaviourism) and behaviourist B F Skinner (with his theory that all forms of action and knowledge are reducible to observable behaviours).
24. Millar, op cit. p 4.
25. Tobias, op cit. p 123.
26. Key person in the Freudian left is Wilhelm Reich.
27. Key person is Ivan Illich.
28. Millar, op cit. p 4.
29. Illich, quoted in Darkenwald and Merriam, op cit. p 59.
30. Resource centres were described as places where learners could freely choose to pursue their own learning goals.
31. This was described by Freire as a process of 'conscientization' which he said was particularly important for those living in what he called a 'culture of silence', Freire, P (1978) *Pedagogy in Process: The Letters to Guinea-Bissau*, London: Writers and Readers Publishing Cooperative.

32. Amongst Reed's principles for the 'empowering learning process' are the 'use of the social experience of the learners as the basic content, the raw material of the learning process' and the need to 'link learner's practice to the historical development of society', Cunningham, op cit. p 63.

33. Alinsky, S D (1972) *Rules for Radicals*, pp 68–9, New York: Random House.

34. Thomas, L F (1983) 'Learning conversations: the skill of managing learning', pp 267–81, in Singleton, W T (ed) *Social Skills: The Study of Real Skills*, Vol. 4, Lancaster: MTP Press.

35. Key references to experiential learning are: Boot, R and Reynolds, M (eds) (1983) *Learning and Experience in Formal Education*, Manchester: Manchester Monographs, University of Manchester; Boydell, T (1976) *Experiential Learning*, Manchester: Manchester Monographs No.S, University of Manchester; Boud, D, Keogh, R and Walker, D (eds) (1985) *Reflection: Turning Experience into Learning*, London: Kogan Page; Kolb, D, Rubin, I and McIntyre, J (1971) *Organizational Psychology: an Experiential Approach*, New Jersey: Prentice-Hall; Warner-Weil, S and McGill, I (1989) *Making Sense of Experiential Learning: Diversity in Theory and Practice*, Milton Keynes: SRHE and Open University Press. (Note: in discussing experiential learning I am not referring to the term as used to describe the assessing and accrediting of life and work experience.)

36. Warner-Weil and McGill, op cit. (Weil and McGill provide a framework to describe the various practices of experiential learning – they describe them as four 'villages' where: village 1 – experiential learning as the assessing and accrediting of prior learning from both life and work; village 2 – experiential learning as a 'basis for bringing about change' in the structure of education; village 3 – experiential learning as the 'basis for group consciousness raising, community action and social change'; village 4 – is 'concerned with personal growth and development – and increased 'self-awareness and group effectiveness'.)

37. Hudson, A (1983) 'The policies of experiential learning', pp 81–92, in Boot, R and Reynolds, M (eds) *Learning and Experience in Formal Education*, Manchester: Manchester Monographs, University of Manchester.

38. Hudson, op cit. p 81.

3 Experiential Learning: The Confucian Model

W. M. Mak

Confucius and Confucianism

Confucius means 'Kung the Master'. It is the name given by the Jesuit missionaries for they misunderstood that Confucianism was a religion. In fact, it is a way of life, and it has deeply influenced the behaviour of Chinese people.

Confucius (551–479 BC) was the greatest teacher in China. His real name was 'Kung Tzu'. However, the Chinese people respect him and call him 'Master Kung', or 'Master'. He taught six arts, ie, archery, charioteering, history, mathematics, music and rituals to his students. He promoted the idea of providing education to all people. 'In teaching there should be no distinction of class' (*Analects* 15.38, Lau, 1979). Throughout his life he taught over 3000 students, a huge number for that time.

After his death, his ideas spread all over China; they have become known as 'Confucianism' and have had a great impact on the political and economic life of China. Since the Han Dynasty (206 BC–AD 220) Confucianism has been chosen as the mainstream of the Chinese philosophy. The Confucian publications, the four books and the five classics, were adopted as textbooks in the national curriculum. The five classics are: *The Book of Song, The Book of History, The Book of Propriety, The Book of Changes* and *The Book of Spring and Autumn*. The four books are: *The Great Learning, The Doctrine of the Mean, The Analects,* and *The Mencius*. Between 1313 and 1905, they were used as standard textbooks for civil service examinations in China. As a result, all government officials were expert in Confucianism.

As time went by, the influence of Confucianism spread all over southeast Asia. Some people attributed the economic success of Japan and the four little dragons, ie, Hong Kong, Taiwan, South Korea and Singapore, to the influence of Confucian ideas. In 1990, Professor Hofstede presented a paper on 'Confucianism and economic success' at the Hong Kong Polytechnic.

The Great Learning and *The Doctrine of the Mean*

There are numerous publications on Confucianism. If we want to have a glimpse of it, we can start with *The Great Learning* and *The Doctrine of the Mean*. They are very short books and present the essence of the Confucian ideas. From a learning perspective, *The Great Learning* is more on the path of self-development (Mak, 1988), while *The Doctrine of the Mean* is more on learning how to learn. *The Great Learning* points out that the first step in self-development is to 'Investigate things' or learning; *The Doctrine of the Mean* describes the process of investigation, or the learning process.

The Confucian model of experiential learning

Kolb (1984) defined experiential learning thus: 'Learning is the process whereby knowledge is created through the transformation of experience'. The Master said, 'By nature, men are nearly alike; by practice, they get to be wide apart' (*Analects* 17.2, Lau, 1979).

If we want to enrich our knowledge, we must study extensively; if we want to confirm our knowledge, we must inquire accurately; if we want to examine our knowledge, we must reflect carefully; if we want to judge our knowledge, we must discriminate clearly; and if we want to apply our knowledge, we must practise earnestly.

Dewey (1933) described the five phases of reflective thought: suggestion, intellectualization, hypothesis, reasoning and testing. Confucius and Dewey shared similar ideas on learning and thinking. Chan (1963) commented, 'The five steps of study, inquiry, thinking, sifting and practice could have come from John Dewey'.

Extensive study

It is a large scale collection of the body of knowledge. It is similar to a reservoir which needs a large network of catchwater to fill it up. We can achieve it by reflecting our own experience and observing the experience of other people. In fact, the more one learns, the more one realizes one's inadequacies; and the deeper and higher one's knowledge, the more one realizes one's shallowness. It is the right attitude to learning. One who regards one's knowledge as extensive is merely exposing one's shallowness.

'There may be those who act without knowing why. I do not do so. Hearing much and selecting what is good and following it; seeing much and keeping it in memory' (*Analects* 7.27, Lau, 1979).

Accurate inquiry

Investigation of the body of knowledge will perfect the knowledge we possess. The catchwater will collect not only water but also litter. We must filter the litter and let water flow into the reservoir. Our task is to find out what is unknown, dispel queries of what is known but not true and complete knowledge already known.

'When he (Confucius) entered the grand temple of the state, he asked about everything' (*Analects* 10.14, Lau, 1979). Asking is the best way to learn something new. There is no shame about it.

Careful reflection

Thinking about the body of knowledge will allow us to understand it completely. When the water flows into the reservoir, it will store for a while before it is used. We should think, where do we come from? Where are we now? Where are we going? It is time for reflection.

'When we see men of worth, we should think of equalling them; when we see men of contrary character, we should turn inwards and examine ourselves' (*Analects* 4.17, Lau, 1979).

Clear discrimination

Classification of the body of knowledge permits us to know what is right or wrong, good or bad, true or false. We have to establish our value standard. How should we use the water: as drinking water, or as a playing pool for water sports? Which would serve the public better? Hence, clear discrimination must come only after much observation, analysis, measurement and comparison. Only from these exercises can correct conclusions be drawn. It involves painstaking effort.

'Learn broadly yet be determined in your own dispositions; enquire with urgency yet reflect closely on the question at hand – becoming an authoritative person lies in this' (*Analects* 19.16, Lau, 1979).

Earnest practice

It is the practical application of the body of knowledge which makes it perfect and effective. After due consideration, the water is either sent to the household users as drinking water or remains in the reservoir for water sports, according to its own value. Sometimes, it can serve both purposes.

The Master said, 'Though a man may be able to recite the three hundred songs, yet if, when entrusted with a governmental charge, he knows not how to act, or, if , when sent to any quarter on a mission, he cannot give his replies unassisted, notwithstanding the extent of his learning, of what practical use is it?' (*Analects* 13.15, Lau, 1979). This explains how the value of learning lies in its application and not in the quantity of knowledge acquired. Even if the reservoir is full of water, it is useless if it cannot be used.

Thought and action

Although the process of learning has been divided into five stages, these do not necessarily follow one after another. In fact, it requires simultaneous action. We can say that study, inquiry, reflection and discrimination belong to the field of knowledge, or our thought, and practice is a form of action. Thought and action are not opposed to each other and do not differ in importance. Although there are many facets in human life, we can sum it up as the intermingling of knowledge and practice, or the unity of thought and action.

Learning by doing is essential. 'Is it not pleasant to learn with a constant perseverance and application?' (*Analects* 1.1, Lau, 1979). Also, there is a close relationship between learning and thinking: 'Learning without thought is labour lost, thought without learning is perilous' (*Analects* 2.15, Lau, 1979). Moreover, what one says and what one does are also closely related: 'The gentleman wishes to be slow in his speech and earnest in his conduct' (*Analects* 4.24, Lau, 1979).

In summary, action is the true evidence of thought. Without going down the path of action, thought cannot be proved correct. Action is the last stage in the quest for knowledge, following study, inquiry, reflection and discrimination.

Facilitator in a learning process

Without a facilitator, one can still complete one's learning cycle. However, it takes a long time and sometimes it may end up at the wrong destination.

The task of the facilitator is to speed up the learning process of the learner, guide him or her in the right direction and make sure he or she will end up in the right place. Rogers (1983) pointed out the differences between a teacher and a facilitator.

Confucius as a facilitator

'The Master taught four things: literature, conduct, loyalty and good faith' (*Analects* 7.24, Lau, 1979). For Confucius, there is no formal class or examinations. He used tutorial methods to guide his students. *The Analects* is a book written by the students of Confucius about the teachings of the Master. From a few pieces of dialogue, we can see how Confucius facilitates the learning of his students.

The Master said, 'When I walk along with two others, they may serve me as my teachers. I will select their good qualities and follow them, their bad qualities, and avoid them' (*Analects* 7.21, Lau, 1979). It is whom we can learn from.

The Master said, 'If a man keeps cherishing his old knowledge, so as continually to be acquiring new, he may be a teacher of others' (*Analects* 2.11, Lau, 1979). And so, you can be your own teacher or teacher of others.

Chi Lu asked about serving the spirits of the dead. The Master said, 'While you are not able to serve men, how can you serve their spirits?' Chi Lu added, 'I venture to ask about death?' He was answered, 'While you do not know life, how can you know about death?' (*Analects* 11.11, Lau, 1979). Confucius encouraged his student to be more practical.

'Yu', the Master said to Tzu-lu, 'shall I instruct you what knowledge is? When you know a thing, to hold that you know it; and when you do not know a thing, to allow that you do not know it – this is knowledge'.

The Master, when he entered the grand temple, asked about everything. Someone said, 'Who will say that the son of the man of Tsau knows the rules of propriety! He has entered the grand temple and asks about everything'. The Master heard the remarks and said, 'This is a rule of propriety' (*Analects* 3.15, Lau, 1979).

He sometimes gave different students entirely different answers to the same question. On one occasion Tzu-lu asked him whether, when he was taught anything, he should at once put it into practice. Confucius told him no, that he should consult his father and elder brothers. A little later, Jan-chiu asked the same question, and the Master told him yes, he should practise what he was taught immediately. The disciple Kung-hsi-hua, knowing of the two answers, was puzzled and asked the reason for the difference. Confucius told him, 'Jan-chiu is lacking zeal, so I urged him on; Tzu-lu has more than his own share of energy, so I held him back' (*Analects* 11.21, Lau, 1979). This did in fact correspond to the characters of the two students.

To a group of students the Master once said, 'My children, why do you not study *The Book of Song*? It will stimulate your emotions, help you to be more observant, enlarge your sympathies, and moderate your resentment of injustice. It is useful at home in the service of one's father, abroad in the service of one's prince. Furthermore, it will widen your acquaintance with the names of birds, beasts, plants and trees' (*Analects* 17.9, Lau, 1979).

In the Confucian school, inquiries were made into many things, among them 'benevolence', 'filial piety', 'government' and 'scholars'. Confucius answered these searching questions according to differences in an individual's personality and environment, with the result that the inquirers reaped the tremendous benefit of rectifying their thought and action while increasing their body of knowledge. It is the idea of learner-centred teaching. Creel (1951) said, 'This was the only method that Confucius could have used successfully. For he was not merely teaching scholars, but producing gentlemen capable of playing decisive roles in the world. He was not teaching certain subjects, but certain students. Therefore, his methods were intensely individual, different for each student since each student presented a different problem'. In short, the way Confucius taught fulfilled all the requirements of facilitator of learning defined by Rogers (1983).

The Doctrine of the Mean (Chapter 20)

19. 'To this attainment there are requisite the extensive study of what is good, accurate inquiry about it, careful reflection on it, the clear discrimination of it and the earnest practice of it.

20. 'The superior man may not engage in studying, but once he does, he does not give up until he can understand all that he studies. He may not make an inquiry, but once he does, he does not give up until he knows everything about which he inquires. He may not reflect, but once he does, he does not give up until he apprehends everything on which he reflects. He may not discriminate, but once he does, he does not give up until he is clear in his discrimination. He may not practise, but once he does, he does not give up until he is earnest in his practice. If another man succeeds by one effort, he will use a hundred efforts. If another man succeeds by ten efforts, he will use a thousand.

21. 'Let a man proceed in this way, and, though dull, he will surely become intelligent; though weak, he will surely become strong.'

References

Chan, W T (1963) *A Source Book in Chinese Philosophy*, New Jersey: Princeton University Press.

Creel, H G (1951) *Confucius: The Man and the Myth*, London: Routledge & Kegan Paul.

Dewey, J (1933) *How We Think*, revised ed, New York: Heath.

Kolb, D A (1984) *Experiential Learning: Experience as the Source of Learning and Development*, Englewood Cliffs, NJ: Prentice Hall.

Lau, D C (ed) (1979) *Confucius: The Analects*, Harmondsworth: Penguin.

Legge, J (1973) *The Four Books*, Hong Kong: Wei Tung Books Company.

Mak, W M (1988) 'The great learning: the Confucian way of self-cultivation', unpublished seminar paper, CSML, Lancaster University.

Rogers, C (1983), *Freedom to Learn for the 80s*, Columbus, OH: Charles E Merrill Publishing Company.

4 An Exploration of Levels of Awareness and Change Processes in Group Encounter

Paul Barber

Introduction

We are born into, educated and work in groups. In the family group we receive nurture, enact our first relationships and form our earliest sense of self. In school and work groups we widen our career as social beings, negotiate our social position and learn to relate to society at large. Because self-image and social behaviour originate from group experience, groups present a most potent agent for intrapersonal exploration.

The potential of the group to act as an 'agent of change' has for long been recognized by clinicians in social psychiatry, especially within therapeutic community practice where social roles are let slip – within secure boundaries – to enable renegotiation of 'the self' and the working through of emotional agendas otherwise masked by conventional role engagement.

Though I deem it desirable in formal academic settings for the hidden emotional agenda to be raised to awareness rather than colluded with or tutorially repressed, in programmes where personal development exists as a stated aim I believe exploration into the same is essential. In this chapter I will attempt to provide a rough map to help you inquire into, and begin to make sense of, the various hidden agendas that arise from experiential groups.

What is described below has arisen out of collaborative inquiry into experiential educational groups where therapeutic community (Jones, 1953) principles (after Rapoport, 1960 – Figure 4.1) were used to set the climate for group inquiry and to construct an operational contract for exploration of 'the self' (Figure 4.2).

This study, involving some 23 experiential learning groups with life-spans varying between three months and two years, conducted over a six-

Permissiveness: Tolerance, acceptance of others, and cultivation of the ability to witness a wide degree of behavioural response without undue distress or the acting out of punishment, victimization or compulsive rescuing.

Communalism: Allowing intimate relations to flower, encouraging sharing, informality and free communication to knit the community together at a pace and time appropriate to those involved.

Democratization: Encouraging all members to equally share in the exercise of power and decision-making via regular community meetings and face-to-face discussion.

Reality-confrontation: Presenting individuals with the consequences of their actions while emphasizing that they are responsible to their peer community.

Figure 4.1 *Therapeutic community principles* (after Rapoport, 1960)

1. Risk experimenting with the philosophy that an individual's problems are mostly in relation to other individuals and are capable of resolution through face-to-face discussion.
2. Risk sharing your thoughts, feelings, sensory awareness and fantasies with others so as to better understand the hidden agenda and motives of social interaction.
3. Work to flatten the prevailing authority pyramid of the group and to open up for examination your own authoritative responses when these occur.
4. Engage in on-going analysis of those social events that unfold and their effect upon yourself and others.
5. Persevere to constantly put to examination roles and behaviour with a view to increasing understanding and current awareness of the community's progress to date.
6. Listen to all of yourself and endeavour to hear the whole of another's communication.
7. Honour your own process, open yourself to others and respect the messages of stuckness and confusion when these arise.
8. Accept emotions as energies rather than problems or symptoms to be resolved, and be alert to the child-like part of yourself within.
9. Experiment with owning and exploring different ways of being.
10. Engage with the unfolding moment.

Figure 4.2 *Rules of engagement for exploration into self*
(Adapted from Clark, 1965)

C **SOCIAL - Reality as intellectually constructed**
O
N Current level where group is experienced as representing the
S community and/or public opinion
C
I Here the facilitator is experienced as playing out a
O conventional leadership role
U -
S

TRANSFERENCE - Reality as felt

S Where the group is experienced as a family
E
M Here the facilitator may be viewed as a parent figure or other
I family member

C Four common areas of transference:
O – a super-being, infallible, all knowing and understanding
N – personifying authority and control
S – resembling a particular family member
C – an emotional presence influencing the group
I -
O
U **PROJECTIVE - Reality as imagined**
S

Where unrecognized and/or unowned parts of self are reflected onto others
or the group.

U Here the facilitator may be experienced as an idealized or
N persecutory figure
C -
O
N **PRIMORDIAL - Reality as intuitively created**
S
C Where the group represents the collective unconscious and
I symbolic rituals, magical rebirths, rites of passage and
O initiation may be enacted
U
S Here the facilitator may become associated with and/or incorporated into
the unconscious symbolism of the group

Figure 4.3 *Levels of experiential group reality*

year period (Barber, 1990), causes me to suggest that four levels of psychological function co-exist within groups, (Figure 4.3).

As the levels and their corresponding 'experiential realities' (Figure 4.3) profoundly affect the performance of facilitation and fuel its hidden agendas, they merit further discussion as to their effects.

Influences of the social level within group facilitation

When I facilitate, the social level of the group is present for me when I intrude upon, or venture into the conventional social world of participants; this I see happening when I initiate a group, set the scene for work to commence or negotiate the facilitative contract to which I am to work. In this, the orientation phase of a group, participants are apt to resist and test out my leadership function, to strive to hold onto the social roles they enact in their everyday life and to demand of me that I do the same. Teacher-student roles and managerial concerns I perceive as acted-out and supported within this level of groupwork.

The social level I perceive as attached to – and in turn stimulated by – the objective 'task' or social purpose of the group. Dynamics of the social level which attend successful task performance are described in Tuckman's (1965) model of grouplife: forming; storming; norming; performing; ending.

From a transactional perspective, it appears to me that the initiation of a group – its forming stage – solicits a social regression, in that participants remain watchful, waiting for the 'authoritative role' of the facilitator to emerge so that they may be told – in a parent to child way – what to expect and/or do. When, as in the case of an experiential teacher, the traditional teacher-student – or parent-child – role fails to emerge, participants begin to feel at sea. This sense of deprivation may contribute to 'Critical parent-rebellious child' teacher-student dynamics at the storming stage of the group. Having catharted disruptive energies the stage of norming can then occur as the 'adult' of participants resurfaces to question 'What can be done with the world as it is?' The stage of performing I view as demonstrating a successful social system in action, and the stage of ending a reluctance to let go of social bonds once created.

Interestingly, it appears that the social level re-enacts the psycho-dynamics of socialization – and the infant's commitment to the conventional social world – all over again.

My facilitation informed by therapeutic community principles I see as confronting and questioning traditional social engagement. I believe that when conventional ways of behaving and structuring time are suspended we have the potential to live beyond mere role play and conquer a greater part of ourselves. But, unstructured time, and the values suggested in

Figures 4.1 and 4.2, although potentially therapeutic and educationally good for us, represent everything in conventional living we try to avoid.

Transactional literature cites reasons why we cling to socially structured time so firmly, namely, it satisfies major psycho-social hungers. First of these is 'stimulus hunger', the most favoured form of which is physical intimacy, but this tends to become the more infrequent as we develop beyond infancy and mothering sublimation occurs, and it is transformed into 'recognition hunger'. Social intercourse now fills the hole left by our need for intimacy. Coupled with this is the drive of 'structure hunger' itself:

> The perennial problem of adolescents is: 'What do I say to her (him) then?' And to many people besides adolescents, nothing is more uncomfortable than a social hiatus, a period of silent, unstructured time when no one can think of anything more interesting to say than: 'Don't you think the walls are perpendicular tonight?' (Berne 1977, p 15).

'Stimulus hunger', 'recognition hunger' and 'structure hunger' are to the fore at the social level of a group, especially in the beginning, when all those programmed ways we have learnt to feed the above hungers are put up for question.

Withdrawal, ritual, pastimes and the playing of social games are integral to our social scripts. We use them to satiate fears of non-stimuli, non-recognition and non-structure. These interruptions to real intimacy permeate educational workshops and need to be made the more conscious and in part worked through if experiential education is to bear its fullest fruit.

In Figure 4.4 the fears an individual brings to an experiential group/workshop, the expectations they have of the facilitator and the resistances they act out, are seen to fuel the hidden agenda of education.

Social contrivances cannot be allowed to shield us from the world of shadows and surprises, nor may we live forever in the unattached world they support. Any educator worth his or her salt must address resistance at this level in order to enhance communication with their subjects and to move them on. Facilitators have such power because at the social level they are perceived as a group leader and the representative of authority.

Influences of the transference level within group facilitation

The transference level of groupwork is present for me whenever a participant's past is rekindled by current group events or when earlier life scripts are restimulated. Here learners may view me, as a facilitator, in the archaic way they saw their parents and teachers during infancy or

COMMON FEARS ON ENTRY	COMMON EXPECTATIONS OF FACILITATOR	COMMON RESISTANCES
Fears of others; breaches of confidentiality; being punished or trapped.	That facilitator will lead and initiate happenings.	Group conspires to be jocular and cynical (cocktail party).
Fears of losing self control; being made worse by exposure to others' distress or demands of intimacy; concerns about hurting others.	That facilitator will adopt the role of expert and impart information. That facilitator will act as an authority to be blamed if things go wrong.	Participants retreat into conspiratorial whispers or silence (subgroups/ pairings). Waiting to be led and/or lost silence (dependency).
Fears of being rejected; anticipation of ridicule and criticism or of offending facilitator.	That facilitator will assume responsibility for the group and its learning process. That the facilitator will acknowledge status barriers and stay emotionally remote.	Retreat into self: daydreaming (flight into fantasy). Criticism and blame of persons or authority outside the group (scapegoating/ stereotyping). Facilitator's worth and/ or personal contributions attacked (counterdependency). Angry silence (passive aggression).

Figure 4.4 *Hidden agendas in experiential groupwork (fears, expectations and resistances)*

adolescence, colouring their present vision of me with their past. Seduction may also be enacted at this level, possibly as a remnant of restimulated Oedipal themes?

Where the social level solicits role play, the transference level strikes a deeper layer more akin to psychodrama. As a facilitator I must guard against those counter-transferences that emerge in myself at this level of groupwork. For instance, if a group relates to me as 'all knowing' and from a regressive position I must be on my guard to buying my own bullshit and deluding myself that I am tinged with sagehood. I have found supervision enabling of facilitative clarity and useful in checking-out budding transferences such as these.

My observations of group life lead me to believe that the idiosyncratic style a facilitator brings into a group may hook into or invite a particular transference. The work of Randall and Southgate (1980) is indicative, I believe, of the kind of 'transferential parent' a group perceives its leader to be. A facilitator perceived as empathetic and nurturing is, I believe, more likely to effect positive transference and to solicit a creative group; conversely, a facilitator perceived as remote and critical invites negative parental transference and reaps a destructive group. Indefinite facilitation and parenting, falling between these two, I see as soliciting an intermediate group.

Influences of the projective level within group facilitation

Phenomena of the projective level I perceive as the meat of therapeutic groupwork, where a facilitator attempts to enable the 'unconscious-withheld' to become the 'conscious-withheld, and eventually the 'conscious-disclosed' (Cox, 1978). This is a slow client-directed process. It is also intensely personal. Because phenomena of the projective level lie at a deeper stratum of group life than those of the social and transference levels, they are less affected by – or amenable to – intellectual rationalization. A facilitator cannot hurry along insight at this level of work; they must wait for their group's 'readiness'.

My facilitation is at its most gentle at the projective level. I watch very carefully for a group's own self-regulating mechanisms to emerge, gauging my approach and matching the timing of my interventions to the group's own pace and tolerance. This is a tentative process, which requires me to tolerate a multiplicity of purpose, to stay with my own confusion while responding in an intuitive rather than intellectual way.

At this level the facilitator functions as an opaque screen on which 'projective group meanings' play; a fantasy figure created out of reality. In the 'projective eye' of the client the facilitator is a powerful magical figure. How I as a facilitator tolerate such projected idealization determines how well a group may work these through. I need a full store of well-being and self-containment when working at this level. My own experience suggests that facilitative work at this level stimulates material needing therapeutic address in the facilitators themselves.

Influences of the primordial level within group facilitation

The primordial level relates closely to the projective level; indeed I believe it fuels the same. What is first sensed without – in the subconscious 'primordial' fabric of the group – solicits projections from within the psyche of participants. Activity generated at the primordial level and the group's store of unconscious emotionality is in part described under Bion's (1961) concept of the basic assumption group where unconscious drives are seen to channel group behaviour towards:

- Dependency: where the group adopts dependent behaviour and seeks to entice the leader into making decisions for them.
- Fight/flight: when the group attempts to seduce the leader to rally them against external forces, or pursue vehicles for flight from the here-and-now.
- Pairing: when two members are nominated as a chosen couple, nurtured and invested with the power to 'give birth' to a magical panacea that will solve all the group's problems.

There is a deeper strand of the primordial level than this, a place where the 'now' feels so vibrant and potent as to heighten our senses and still the intellect. A level which, I suggest, equates with an experience of Zen:

Now, at the beginning, I ask you to remember that the world you are entering is odd to almost everyone, even to those who have lived in it for a long time. It multiplies paradoxes; and yet its oddness, like the paradoxical oddness of a dream, verges upon the familiar. Odd and familiar as a dream, Zen is meant, however, to occupy the daylight, by means of an irrational reversal of the quality of our lives. For Zen says we are self-deceived, split, and unhappy. Its disciples are trained to arrive at least at equanimity. This aim is, no doubt, subject to practical limitations. Maybe, it too, is a dream of sorts; but, if you are open minded, you may prefer to consider it tentatively before deciding whether or not to shrug it off.

Even if Zen is not what it takes itself to be, it is an unusually interesting human and cultural phenomenon (Hoffman, 1977).

So much of the above passage resonates for me the oddness of group encounter at this level:

- the multiplication of paradox;
- the vague familiarity of content;
- the irrational reversal of what we have learnt earlier in our lives;
- the dawning assumption that we may have led our lives steeped in self-deception split-off from our true self;
- the awareness that openness of mind is necessary for fruitful inquiry and that growth is more like a letting go;
- the energy we feel within a deafening group silence;
- the fertile void that threatens to break out all that we hold within.

Indeed, communal silence plays an important part in the primordial life of a group. It allows us to journey inward, to escape from our flight into over-activity. Whether dependent, waiting, reflective, meditative or spiritual, a group's silence acts as a qualitative thermometer of where we are at now.

At the primordial level of experiential group work thinking is secondary to feeling and reflection is secondary to impulse. When working at the primordial level I have found intuitive, subtle, non-directed interventions most fitting. The use of metaphor may here reach where cold reason and logic fail. But such poetic vision needs an anchor and the facilitator has to demonstrate – within themselves – a link with social reality and the world beyond in order to provide a route along which intuitive insights may enter into every-day reality.

Summary

The experiential realities described are far less distinct than they diagrammatically appear. In practice they are rather more akin to tides that ebb and flow and merge one with the other, and come round again as the emotional seasons of the group change. This said, exploration of the various levels requires a like medium. The social level I find is best explored via observational inquiry, peer review and sociogram; the transferential level approached via biographical review of familial patterns; the projective level suited to such as psychodrama; while the primordial level I experience as approachable through free imagery and guided fantasy.

I believe I must at this stage declare a bias, namely: 'If in your facilitation you don't reach the primordial level of your group, or meaningfully shape the same, the fruits of your facilitation will not last'.

As facilitator, although I aim to work through the material of each level as I deemed appropriate to the developmental phase of a group and/or its emerging needs, I have found that spurts of high quality sharing and real ownership of new learning appear to follow from periods of reflective silence when influence of the primordial level has been high. During these periods individuals report experiencing an objective witnessing state where they stop their internal chatter, cease splitting experience into 'rights' and 'wrongs' and projecting judgements onto themselves and others. At such times, they seemingly experience themselves as sensitive and open to the stream of their moment-to-moment experience. When a group of individuals reaches an experiential place such as this, an experience akin to transpersonal awakening seems to occur. This awakening comes quietly. It is a time when the continuum of our experience begins to speak for itself:

Until a person confronts himself in the eyes and hearts of others, he is running. Until he shows his secrets he has no safety from them. Afraid to be known, he can know neither himself nor any other – he will be alone (Phoenix House internal report, 1974).

Where else than in the experiential group, the climate which originally formed us, may we undo our past and truly learn to be? And where else than here, where the interpersonal joins with the intrapersonal, may experiential learning be said to truly occur?

References

Barber, P (1990) 'The facilitation of personal and professional growth through experiential groupwork and therapeutic community practice', unpublished PhD thesis, Department of Education, University of Surrey.

Berne, E (1977) *Games People Play*, New York: Grove Press.

Bion, W R (1961) *Experience in Groups*, London: Tavistock.

Clark, D (1965) 'The therapeutic community concept, practice and future', *British Journal of Psychiatry*, 111, 974.

Cox, M (1978) *Coding the Therapeutic Process*, Oxford: Permagon.

Hoffman, Y (1977) *The Sound of One Hand*, London: Paladin.

Jones, M (1953) *The Therapeutic Community: A New Treatment in Psychiatry*, New York: Basic Books.

Randall, R and Southgate, J (1980) *Cooperative and Community Group Dynamics: or your meetings needn't be so appalling*, London: Barefoot Books.

Rapoport, R (1960) *Community as Doctor*, London: Tavistock.

Tuckman, B W (1965) 'Developmental sequence in small groups', *Psychological Bulletin*, 63.

Yalom, I D (1975) *The Theory and Practice of Group Psychotherapy*, New York: Basic Books.

5 The Politics of Facilitation: Balancing Facilitator Authority and Learner Autonomy

John Heron

Three kinds of facilitator authority

The challenge of all teaching is to integrate the authority of the facilitator and the autonomy of the learner. The facilitator has three kinds of authority – cognitive, political and charismatic. Cognitive authority means that the facilitator has mastered some body of knowledge and skill, and can communicate effectively to learners through the written and spoken word and other presentations. Political authority means that the facilitator takes decisions that affect the whole content and process of learning. Charismatic authority means that the facilitator models an educated person in his or her presence, style and manner, that is, in how he or she exercises the previous two kinds of authority.

Authority and authoritarianism

We need here to distinguish a benign, luminous and truly educative authority from a punitive, indoctrinating and intimidating authority. The latter is oppressive authoritarianism and has been the bane of education at all levels. Traditional teaching, still strongly with us, is beset by authoritarianism because it runs the different kinds of authority into each other.

Traditional confusion of three kinds of authority

Traditional, old-style teaching confuses the three kinds of authority in the crudest possible way. It assumes that because teachers have cognitive authority – as repositories of knowledge – they should therefore exercise total political authority in a *directive* way, making all educational decisions *for* their students. Then it assumes that because they have to direct everything that students do, they should exercise their charismatic authority as disciplinarians and judges, meting out punishments to the disobedient and judging the learners' conformity by acts of unilateral assessment.

Thus the traditional teacher decides what students shall learn, when and how they shall learn it and whether they have learned it; and presides over this regime with a forbidding authoritarian charisma. Student autonomy is relegated to in-the-head following of large numbers of long lectures, to answering questions or asking them, and to doing home-work on prescribed reading, writing or practical tasks.

Need for authority

Why have any kind of educational authority, however benign? The obvious answer is so that knowledge and skills can be passed on. Otherwise, everyone has to learn everything from experiential scratch – which would be the *reductio ad absurdum* of experiential learning theory. But herein lies the tension, between the passing-on on the one hand and the primacy of personal learning on the other.

For learning itself is necessarily autonomous, that is, self-directed: it is constituted by interest, commitment, understanding and practice. Each of these is self-generated – they are negated or distorted by any attempt to instil or impose them.

Learning is also necessarily holistic, that is, it involves – either by inclusion, or by denial and alienation – the whole person, a being that is physical, perceptual, affective, cognitive (intellectual, imaginative, intuitive), conative (exercising the will), social and political, psychic and spiritual. Again, the unfolding and integration of these different aspects of the learner is a matter of self-development. A person blooms out of their own entelechy or formative potential, in accordance with their own choices. The idea of a person who lives out an externally imposed, other-directed, programme of development is a contradiction in terms.

Paradox of facilitator authority

So the facilitator has to pass on some body of knowledge and skill – the content of learning – by a process of learning that affirms both the autonomy and wholeness of the learner. We thus get the paradox of facilitator authority exercised to generate free and rounded learning. This paradox is exacerbated in this era because it is a watershed time between two educational cultures. An authoritarian educational system, using oppressive forms of teacher authority, is still widespread; hence learners who emerge from it are conditioned to learn in ways that are relatively short on autonomy and holism. In a special sense they need leading into freedom and integration, when they enter the other culture where these values are affirmed.

The concept of *initiation* is, I think, the best one to illuminate this paradox. The facilitator's authority – cognitive, political, charismatic – is used to launch people into freedom and integration, to provide *rituals of entry* into the heritage of personhood. This does mean a careful rethinking of what these three kinds of authority mean, especially the political kind. What happens to the facilitator's authority – cognitive, political and charismatic – in the model of teaching as initiation into autonomous and whole personhood?

Cognitive authority as initiation

Cognitive authority remains basic: the facilitator is still a person who has mastered some body of knowledge and skill and can pass this on. But both what is passed on and the 'passing on' become much more complex and varied. (1) 'Cognitive' is construed in wider terms, including not only intellectual competence, but emotional, interpersonal, political, spiritual and other competencies as well. (2) There is a great emphasis on the provision of open learning materials: systems and packages of information and exercises – words and graphics – which are presented in a way that takes account of the self-pacing, self-monitoring learner. (3) Much importance is given to the design and facilitation of holistic, participative methods – games, simulations, role plays, and a whole range of structured activities – which will involve the learner in self-directing action and reflection, in affective and interpersonal transactions, in perceptual and imaginal processes. (4) Projects, field-work, placements and inquiry in the real world, case studies, problem-oriented learning, all these become vital aspects of the learning process. (5) The amount of stand-up teaching becomes greatly reduced compared to the old approach: the facilitator becomes much more a resource and consultant, available to be called in when needed by the self-directing, active learner – to clarify, guide, discuss and support. (6) The student is supported and helped to plan their own programme of learning and assessment of learning, by the use of collaborative contracts with the facilitator. This last item overlaps with the facilitator's exercise of political authority.

Political authority as initiation

The three decision-modes
A crucial shift is taking place in the use of political authority, the concept of which thereby undergoes a complete redefinition. I am not sure that the

full implications of this shift have as yet been fully articulated and grasped, hence it is the principal point I want to make here. The shift is from deciding in terms of just one decision-mode to *deciding which decision-mode to use*. The result is a vast increase in facilitator flexibility and facilitative power. Let me explain.

By a 'decision-mode' I mean one of three basic ways of making educational decisions in relation to learners: you can make decisions for them, you can make decisions with them, or you can give them space to make decisions on their own, by themselves. These three decision-modes I will for convenience call, respectively, direction, negotiation and delegation. I have also called these hierarchy, cooperation and autonomy (Heron, 1989).

What the decisions are being taken about, centrally, are the basic elements of the learning process: learning objectives, the topics to be learned, the pacing and progression of learning, the teaching and learning methods, the human and physical resources to be used, the criteria and methods of assessment. If we combine topics with pacing and progression in the one item of the course programme or timetable then we have five main areas for educational decision-making: the objectives of learning, the programme of learning, the methods of learning, the resources (human and physical) for learning, and the assessment of learning (see Figure 5.1).

Direction means that you exercise educational power unilaterally: you decide everything in these five areas for your students. Student self-direction is with respect to all these aspects of learning entirely subordinate to your commands. Full-blown *negotiation* means that you exercise educational power bilaterally: you decide everything with your students. Your decision-mode is cooperative. You take into account student self-direction and seek to reach agreement in setting up mutually acceptable contracts about objectives, the programme, methods, resources and assessment. *Delegation* means that you give space for the unilateral exercise of educational power by students themselves. In full-blown delegation, you have declared your own redundancy, and students are entirely self-determining with respect to their objectives, programme, methods, resources and assessment. Normally, of course, the decision-modes of direction, negotiation and delegation will be used in differing serial and concurrent ways on any progressive course as it unfolds.

The old-style political authority of the teacher lacks any sophistication. It just identifies unawarely with the decision-mode of direction – and applies this across the board of all educational decisions. The new facilitative political authority is altogether more subtle and challenging: it means *exercising liberating power by choosing the appropriate decision-mode*, whether direction, negotiation or delegation, for these learners, at this stage of their learning, in respect of this or that aspect of the educational process. It means that you can control the degree and the pacing of empowerment.

The four decision-mode levels

Now I want to refine this notion of political authority further, for there are three different levels at which these decision-modes can be applied. There is the main level, already mentioned, of planning the learning process in all its five aspects: learning objectives, the programme, the teaching and learning methods, the human and physical resources to be used, the criteria and methods of assessment. As I have said, I can plan all this, or I can negotiate it with the learners, or the learners can put it together on their own. Below this, there is the ground-floor level of the immediate learning activity: here too, I can manage it for the learners, or I can manage it cooperatively with the learners, or the learners can manage it on their own.

It is important to note that these two levels are quite distinct in the sense that different decision-modes can be used on them, and a lot of educational wisdom is involved in using these differences. Thus I can *directively* plan and devise a whole series of learning activities which in themselves involve a lot of autonomous management by the learners. This is a relevant combination for initiating people into deeply holistic forms of learning. There is also a more abstruse third level, the level of deciding which decision-mode to use when planning. Again, I can decide this on my own, I can negotiate it with the learners, or the learners can decide this on their own. I am not sure that many facilitators are aware of level 3; that

Table 5.1 *Decision-mode levels*

Level 4: Choosing a decision-mode to use in choosing a decision-mode in planning	Direction		
Level 3: Decision-mode to use in choosing a decision-mode for planning	Direction	Negotiation	Delegation
Level 2: Decision-mode used in planning learning activities	Direction	Negotiation	Delegation
Level 1: Decision-mode used in learning activity	Direction	Negotiation	Delegation

is, they are unawarely directive at this level without realizing there is a choice to be made between direction, negotiation and delegation.

Now there is a fourth level, but it is *necessarily and exclusively directive*, the final resting place of the facilitator's political authority. It is the level at which I decide which decision-mode to use at level 3, that is, which decision-mode to use in choosing a decision-mode for planning. It is at level 4 that I say to myself that I am going to ask my learners, for example, to negotiate with me (at level 3) in deciding whether (at level 2) I do the planning, or I do it cooperatively with them, or they do it. If you say, well wait a minute, I could negotiate or delegate at level 4, this is true, but then the decision to do either of those will have been taken directively at level 5. In other words there is an infinite regress of delayed decision-making, unless the series is closed by unilateral direction at some level and level 4 is the highest possible level for rational closure.

Level 4 is a very abstruse level and many facilitators will not use it intentionally at all. Without noticing what they are doing, they will in effect decide directively at level 4 to decide directively at level 3 to use this, that or the other decision-mode in planning at level 2. If they are *very* unaware they will decide everything directively even at level 2, the level of planning, without realizing they have other choices at that level.

Empowerment through mastery of decision-mode levels

Facilitators tend to wilt rather when I go on about levels 3 and 4; it does require something like an altered or at any rate an extended state of consciousness to keep effectively alert at those levels. But I take the rather stringent view that until we have mastered those levels and know that we are using them and how we are using them – which usually means being directive at 3 as well as 4 so that we unilaterally choose decision-modes for level 2 – then we have not really taken charge of our power to empower our learners.

In other words, facilitators are, at crucial points in the process of learning, exercising a subtle kind of unilateral directive authority. No facilitator can abdicate from it at level 4, and will usually use it at level 3. Unless they are exercising it intentionally, and really know what they are up to, there is the ever-present issue of unaware overcontrol or undercontrol of the empowering process.

Unilateral direction on principle at level 3

Many progressive facilitators are, even if they have not made this fully conscious to themselves, entirely directive at level 3 *on principle*. For example, they may believe strongly in a significant measure of student autonomy, such as student participation in programming their own learning and in assessing their own learning in collaboration with staff. They are committed to learning contracts as a matter of principle, and this principle is non-negotiable: they are not open to their learners negotiating them back into unilateral programming and assessment. So at level 2 there is to be negotiated programming and negotiated assessment, but this use of negotiation at level 2 is itself non-negotiable at level 3.

Again, progressive facilitators may be committed to holism on principle, to educating the many different dimensions of the human person, so that both course content and learning methods are multi-dimensional. So they are non-negotiably directive at level 3 about being directive at level 2 regarding holistic elements in programme design and in learning methods. Incidentally, facilitators who are committed at level 3 to both autonomy and holism face the challenge, at level 2, of using *negotiation* to affirm the autonomy and *direction* to establish the holism. I am not sure that this creative tension has yet been adequately faced.

This business of being directive at level 3 on principle is, I think, entirely right and proper – so long, that is, as it is fully conscious and intentional. Authentic educators stand for certain inalienable and non-negotiable values to which they are deeply committed. If they do not stand for anything and can be negotiated into any position, then they are not really educated and have no charismatic authority. It is, ultimately, our non-negotiable values that empower people – or disempower them, depending on the values.

The importance of advertising non-negotiable values
This means that facilitators' non-negotiable educational values – whether about autonomy or holism or both – which make them directive at level 3, should be consciously held, and above all clearly identified and made explicit in the course prospectus and again at interview, so that the prospective learner can make a free and informed choice about joining this particular community of value. This is vital in principle and especially in practice in a watershed culture where old and new models of education exist side by side and people are moving between them. It is clearly immoral and not at all empowering to spring the new educational values on students when everything they have so far read or heard about the institution has led them to expect that it would deliver the old values.

It may be that facilitators tend to be entirely directive at level 3 precisely because we live in this watershed culture. If learners are heavily conditioned by the old values, to negotiate with them or delegate to them at level 3 may simply mean that they unawarely press the claims of these old values. So it is better to decide directively at this level, make it clear in all the course publicity what your values are and invite learners to join you if these values appeal to them and to recommend that they do not join you if they do not.

A full-blown level 3 course

There may come an era when the values of autonomy and holism are the norm in the educational culture. Then we have the prospect of a full-blown level 3 course which is advertised as one in which the learners will be asked on arrival to cooperate with the staff, say, in deciding whether the five main elements of the learning process will be planned by the staff, by staff and learners, or by the learners, or in different respects by each of these groups. Such a course does indeed sound empowering and full of potential learning.

Even now it can be realistic and grounded. I used something like it with a course to train experienced GPs to become trainers of young hospital doctors entering general practice for the first time. To get a relevant course going we needed to agree on who should plan what: I certain things, I and they other things, they certain things.

The numerous options within level 2 courses

Let us now focus on level 2 and assume facilitators are directive at levels 4 and 3, that is, they exercise their political authority unilaterally to decide who shall determine the many different aspects of the learning process: the facilitator alone, the facilitator in negotiation with the students, or self-directing students on their own. The facilitator as political authority in the new approach makes a selection from the level 2 options (see Figure 5.1).

The column on the left in Figure 5.1 shows the three basic decision-modes of direction, negotiation and delegation; the top row shows the five main areas of educational decision-making. The facilitator in setting up

Objectives	Programme	Methods	Resources	Assessment
Direction: Facilitator alone				
Negotiation: Facilitator/Learners				
Delegation: Learners alone				

Figure 5.1 *Decision-modes for planning learning at level 2*

and running any course has enormous scope for making innumerable different combinations of the decision-modes and the five areas. Different decision-modes can be used within one area – which can be broken up into several components – as well as between different areas. The combination used at the start will depend on the purposes of the course and the level of the learners and may change as the course proceeds. There is also the possibility of opening up level 3 to learners at later stages of the course and inviting genuine negotiation or delegation at that level.

It is important to remember, as I have already mentioned, that the decision-mode used in planning learning is quite distinct from the decision-modes used in managing the learning activities that are planned. For example, I can plan directively a lot of autonomous learning activities, or I can plan directively collaborative assessment, or we can plan cooperatively learning methods that include directive ones such as stand-up teaching.

The modern revolution in education and training has as yet scarcely got to grips with the flexible and imaginative use of this table, and the many subtle and changing ways of distributing power between facilitator and learners throughout level 2, not to mention the different ways of distributing power as between levels 2 and 1 and within the learning activities on level 1 itself. The typical progressive course is unilaterally directive at level 3, may use any of the decision-modes at level 2, with much delegation – autonomous practice – at level 1.

Examples of level 2 courses

Let me show this table at work in terms of two examples. First, consider a typical five-day management training course used by a major UK company today. The trainers specify the objectives of the course, design the programme, choose the methods and resources – all in the directive mode, but the assessment is to be in part collaborative, based on negotiation between trainers and trainees and in part delegated to trainees to work out their own form of self- and peer-assessment. So on level 2 all the basic educational decision-making is done in the directive mode with the exception of assessment.

The main method is the use of a business simulation with role play, which runs throughout the five days. The trainees manage the defined business themselves. So on level 1 the learning activity involves a great deal of self-directed initiative and problem-solving among trainees, together with significant collaborative prompting from the trainers, and all within the parameters of the given business simulation.

The trainers were functioning with some awareness on level 2, but by no means with full awareness, since they simply had not considered the full array of options open to them at level 2. They chose to be mostly directive in planning the learning and though this was probably appropriate, it was by default not by conscious selection.

Second, consider a day-release professional development course for experienced professional helpers, run over several weeks at a UK postgraduate centre. Participants first determine their own personal learning objectives and these are shared with other participants. In the light of this, facilitator and participants negotiate a final set of objectives, a provisional course programme, learning methods and resources to be used. The design of assessment procedures is entirely delegated and is to be executed by self- and peer-assessment among the participants. So here at level 2, objectives are dealt with by delegation and negotiation, assessment by delegation and the programme, methods and resources by negotiation.

At level 1, the actual training activities involved a lot of structured interpersonal skills exercises, the management of which combined direction, negotiation and delegation, that is, practice in small groups, the last of these occupying the most time.

These two examples only scratch the surface of the inexhaustible store of models made possible by the modern learning revolution. Access to this store depends above all, in my view, on facilitators realising that their political authority has now shifted to the subtle business of working awarely and flexibly with different decision-modes at different levels. This enables them very precisely to define the degree to which they can empower their students and the rate at which they empower them.

Charismatic authority as initiation

Earlier, I defined charismatic authority as the facilitator modelling an educated person in his or her presence, style and manner, that is, in how he or she exercises the previous two kinds of authority. I think this means emanating respect for the autonomy and wholeness of learners through a tone of voice, timing, behavioural manner, as well as choice of ideas and language, so that these things also *elicit the emergence* of such autonomy and wholeness – at all times, whatever decision-mode one is in or whatever decision-mode level one is on. It is this expressive presence that charismatically initiates empowerment. It generates *self-confidence* in learners.

Reference

Heron, J (1989) *The Facilitators' Handbook*, London: Kogan Page.

6 Silent Learning: Experience as a Way of Knowledge

Ranjan

Introduction

The basic thesis of this chapter is that our future need is the balance that comes from a science of life (knowledge of being) as sophisticated as our science of matter (knowledge of things).

Within this perspective education is perceived as life-long in terms of self-awareness and wisdom. It is intrinsic to our most ancient heritage that self-awareness through inner attention (meditation) and outer attention (experience) are seen as the twin pillars of a balanced core education. Everything else is mere training, specialization of adornment.

For the school timetable, that means a model similar to that of ancient Ayurvedic medical education: half the time for academic, examination-oriented pursuits concerned with the knowledge of things; half the time for character-building pursuits where the focus is on refining perception itself.

Have we the courage to let experience confound our theories? That is the question posed for me, working as a healer, teacher, researcher and a life-long learner. So my intention is to explore a new framework for learning, arising from these experiences.

Consider a Mr. Wright, hospitalized terminally ill. Initially turned down for a new wonder drug, Krebiozen, as being too close to death to meet experimental criteria, he contrived to get accepted, believing it his last hope. Recovery was dramatic. Then the American Medical Association announced that nationwide tests showed Krebiozen to be useless against cancer, and Wright died!

Wright, a perfectly healthy man, died because he believed in our medical paradigm, the bio-medical model, rather than in his own experience. Our faith in the dominant paradigm of reality can lead us into denying the evidence of our senses. For example, dismissing it as 'psychological' when in fact the evidence points to our *dismissal* as being 'psychological'.

The origin of this paradigm can be traced to Roger Bacon (1928):

> There are two modes of knowledge, through argument and experience. Argument brings conclusions and compels us to concede them but it does not bring certainty nor remove doubts in order that the mind may remain at rest in truth, unless this is provided by experience.

The cultural element that was introduced in the creation of our knowledge system was that the notion of 'experience' (as the mode of empirical verification) was interpreted as 'experiment'. This was the first step in excluding human being from our knowledge-system. The second step was taken by Galileo. In his letter (Stilman Drake, 1957) to the Grand Duchess Christina he bifurcates knowledge, separating knowledge of things from knowledge of human being (what he calls 'salvation'). In this historic separation of facts from perception, data from interpretation, knowledge from values and in the end, power from responsibility, lies the core problem of our education system.

From philosophy of science to psychotherapy, the fruits of modern learning are that such a separation is not possible; and it is physics that gives us the confirmation: 'Natural law is not simply the observation and explanation of nature, it is the interplay between nature and ourselves' (Heisenberg, 1959). Within the conventional knowledge-system the implications are unintelligible. How do you take into account the quality of the self that participates in the experiment? But this should not surprise us. Our knowledge of things may be sophisticated enough to get us to the moon, but it is not subtle enough to definitively distinguish love-making from rape.

The need for a knowledge of being

In health, what Galileo excludes from our knowledge-system can be a matter of life and death. That it is as critical in education is the implication of the connection psychologist Rudolf Dreikurs (1971) makes between knowledge and behaviour via 'expectations':

> We all act in accordance with our expectations. . . . They form the secret plan that guides all our actions. It makes little difference if we anticipate events with pleasure or horror; as long as we expect them we move towards them. Only when our goals are constructive do we admit them to ourselves, but distressing expectations have the same motivating effect, even though we may not be aware of our direction. . . .
>
> Expectations . . . are our strongest – and strangest – motivating forces. Anyone who can alter the expectations of people can change their behaviour.

In 'Song of a man who has come through', D. H. Lawrence (1920) suggests that it is by sculpting the human ego into finer form that expectations change. He uses metaphors of wind, chisel and three angels for the sculptor(s):

Not I, not I but the wind that blows through me
A fine wind is blowing the new direction of time.
If only I let it bear me, carry me
If only it carry me.
If only I am sensitive, subtle, oh delicate, a winged gift;

If only most lovely of all, I yield myself and am borrowed
By the fine, fine wind that takes its course through the chaos of the world

Like a fine, an exquisite chisel, a wedge-blade inserted.
If only I am keen and hard like the sheer tip of a wedge
Driven by invisible blows
The rock will split,
We shall come at the wonder,
We shall find the Hesperides.

O, for the wonder that bubbles into my soul
I would be a good fountain, a good wellhead,
Would blur no whisper, spoil no expression.

What is the knocking? What is the knocking at the door in the night?
Is it somebody wants to do us harm!
No, no. It is the three strange angels.
Admit them, admit them.

The work is to free the wonder deep within our souls, so it can be a verdant spring in the lives of those around us. It is like Michelangelo 'freeing' the form he perceives deep within a rough-hewn marble block. It can be a hard sweat, and frightening, even. (What is the knocking, what is the knocking in the night we are buried in, deep in the uncut marble of our unsculpted egos?) Letting go of some of the basic assumptions of reality as depicted by the dominant paradigm of our culture can be a terrifying experience. We risk everything, even our sense of belonging. Can this be undertaken in an institutional context? It is work where atmosphere is more relevant than content. It needs deep, secure, pure, unconditional empathy; the kind of love that is to do with the spiritual rather than the merely human.

While it may come as a shock (to the westernized mind) that justice is part of the *biological* equipment of the human being, it is nevertheless true (Bronowski, 1973). Could the same be true of real love? Cornhill (1980) reports: 'Tender loving care ... dramatically reduced arteriosclerosis'. His experimental results showed the amount of disease reduced by 50%.

Describing this sculpting as of 'higher state of consciousness', Professor Glen Schaefer (1981), a physicist and Fellow of two Royal Societies says:

Future education will teach a higher state of consciousness, achievable through love
. . . and a deep study of nature. It will teach . . . that's where the power comes from. Not
by willing . . . but by expecting. . . .

What he is suggesting is that such expectation grows as we cultivate our
capacity to love. Could it be that it is love, not mental capacity, that is the
crucible of wisdom?

Towards nurturing wisdom

Our knowledge-system has been concerned with getting reliable data.
When we ask a question we want a valid answer. We are only just
beginning to learn that it is more important to learn to ask the right
question! Our experience with cigarettes illustrates the difference. When
some decades ago the question was asked, did they help with stress, we
relied sufficiently on the scientific method's answer for doctors to go on
television commercials urging the general public to smoke them. Forty
years later when we asked the question, can cigarette smoking kill, equally
objectively it answered, 'Yes'. It would seem our scientific method is no
more use to us than the three witches were to Macbeth, until we can select
the right question to ask. For me, this is where experiential learning comes
into its own. Consider my experience with a case-study on 'Infectious
diseases and human welfare' in the Polytechnic of East London's
department of physical sciences.

When we started to work together I explained to the students that the
data necessary for controlling many of the diseases that still plague the
third world villager have been available for at least 20 years, suggesting
that the real problems might relate to implementation and so to human
beings rather than to knowledge. What about some first-hand experience,
through attempting to bring either their diet or exercise into line with
modern research? They were not amused. In the end, however, they were
persuaded to have a go.

Then one student met with a motor accident and couldn't get over the
trauma. That was until he did that day's exercise, a long swim. 'I left the
accident in the pool', he reported to the group. The experience changed
his 'mindset' (it hadn't occurred to him before that exercise could affect
emotional states); changed his idea of the role of human experience in
respect of knowledge. In contrast, his academic work had shown no power
to modify his behaviour. As the Arab poet Rumi put it, 'He who tastes
not, knows not'. Experiential learning engages not just the head but the
whole person, so it touches not just minds but entire lives. My experience
is that it has the power to transform a student (who learns at school from
books) into a life-long learner (whose openness is to learning from life

itself). The quest shifts from data and skills acquisition to attaining wisdom.

The pre-requisite for that is humility: *acceptance* that what we call reality is a construct of our paradigm, *openness* to trusting our experience even if it contradicts the paradigm. Until we are aware of the way our paradigm affects our perception and behaviour we are its prisoners.

Secondly, we need to learn balanced functioning of our minds. Our tendency to divide the perceived world into individual and separate things and to experience ourselves as isolated egos in this world is seen as an illusion created by an 'unquieted' mind, our intellect when it is not balanced by an equal degree of intuitive functioning. This is what is called 'avidya' (ignorance) in Buddhist philosophy. It is seen as a state of imbalance in the mind:

When the mind is disturbed, the multiplicity of things appears
When the mind is quieted, the multiplicity of things disappears
Buddhist text cited by Capra (1976).

Visualization and auralization (hearing in one's mind's ear) are part of the ABC of this learning: a disciplining of the imagination that is understood to be able to harness a whole new range of powers for the human. It begins when the mind can move into inner silence. Then we can experience the interconnectedness and interdependence of all things that the experiments of the physicist now confirm. Far from being unique, Capra's (1976) experience is what lies at the heart of our spiritual heritage.

Silent learning. It is the knowing that cannot be taught, the listening for what cannot be heard. It is letting in the divine light that heals and makes whole. It is going beyond the senses of the body to the light of the heart and letting Being be our teacher. It is relevant to young, middle-aged and old alike. It is overcoming our fear of Lawrence's three strange angels and admitting the power that sculpts our egos into harmony with the cosmic dance that integrates all.

Such a change in our 'educational' syllabus is only achieved by a shift in our perception. On All-India Radio I was once questioned by a bright young Kashmiri interviewer, in relation to children and meditation: 'You mean we should incarcerate our children for hours to teach them to be quiet?' He seemed nonplussed by my rejoinder: 'No, I mean *when* we incarcerate our children to develop their intuitive faculties!'

For the life-long learner, this perspective means seeing in each circumstance, crisis or relationship an opportunity and a challenge to access deeper and richer resources within ourselves. When life itself is perceived as the syllabus for the learning, then we can begin to ask the 'right' questions: move from the lust for power over others to the love of empowering others, move from fragmented knowledge to wisdom, begin to learn how we may manifest a finer quality of loving.

References

Bacon, R (1928) *Opus Maius*, 1268, trans. R B Burke, Philadelphia, PA: University of Philadelphia Press.

Bronowski, J (1973) *The Ascent of Man*, London: BBC Books.

Capra, F (1976) *The Tao of Physics*, London: Fontana/Collins

Capra, F (1982) *The Turning Point*, London: Flamingo, Fontana Paperbacks

Cornhill (1980)

Drake, S (1957)

Dreikurs, R (1971)

Heisenberg, W (1959) *Physics and Philosophy*, London: Allen & Unwin.

Lawrence, D H (1920)

Schaefer, C E (1981)

SECTION 2

Assessment and Accreditation

This section contains various chapters dealing with the accreditation of prior experiential learning (APEL).

Evans provides an overview of APEL exploring rationale, process, applications and its potential for empowerment. Paczuska's chapter on science and technology access courses and Webb and Redhead's chapter on informal learning both highlight the substantial benefits which APEL affords women learners. Blackman and Brown's evaluation of an APEL portfolio development project suggests that the main constraints are institutional in nature. Hull's chapter suggests that the APEL process should be viewed as a learning process in itself and not just as a means to an end-product.

Related chapters in other sections are Tate (Chapter 12) in Section 3 and Marshall and Mill (Chapter 21) in Section 5.

7 Linking Personal Learning and Public Recognition

Norman Evans

The title of this volume, *Empowerment through Experiential Learning*, is problematic. Empowerment means different things to different people and certainly means different things in different decades. But for these purposes it will do, because the fundamental rationale for the assessment of experiential learning is that it is personal, commands recognition and therefore speaks of the empowerment of individuals. Empowerment, however, implies development, or at least the opportunity for development, so the learning which is experiential, being personal, is rooted in the idea of human growth and development, hence the interest in the connections between personal learning and public recognition in relation to empowerment.

It is almost impossible to think of any learning which is not personal. Some of it is a rather second-hand kind of learning, filling empty minds. We all have a happy knack of learning what we choose to learn whoever is trying to fill our allegedly empty minds – see how students manage to subvert the intentions of their tutors with consummate ease and pursue genuine personal learning. Experiential learning may be unintentional, accidental, often unwitting, but it is first-hand learning because the personal is integral. As personal learning, it is concerned essentially with personal development and so with empowerment.

Experiential learning and public recognition

At one level empowerment through the public recognition of personal learning which is experiential is straightforward. Assessment of experiential learning can lead to qualifications, credentials, occupational and career development, all of which have public standing and status. But what kind of public recognition is that? It is a borrowed status from credentials and the institutions which award qualifications. That may be connected with personal development, but everyone knows highly qualified people who do not seem to have developed much beyond the cradle. Equally some public recognition is only skin deep. Some people do not seem to attach much importance to it. The point is that the most significant form of public recognition is when it is internalized, when the individual somewhere deep down believes it, cherishes it, is strengthened by it. The significance of public recognition, then, is to do with the psychological stance of the individual. This may come through the kind of public recognition which comes from qualifications and the like. It most certainly can and does come through the assessment of experiential learning.

That is the vital importance of the kind of public recognition which comes from the personal learning which is experiential. Non-campus, non-formal, in life, work and leisure, experiential learning is owned by the individual. No one else has anything to do with generating it, directly. There may have been some help in acquiring it, but essentially experiential learning is a personal achievement. Hence the assessment of experiential learning can produce a personal inner recognition which is priceless and of great psychological significance. It can lead to a sense of public recognition in one of two ways or a combination of the two. When the assessment of experiential learning leads to accreditation for formal purposes the public recognition which follows is informed by, infused with, an inner sense of recognition which in its turn results in a marked degree of personal development. At the highest level this can be rehabilitating. When people who believe themselves to be hopeless as learners prove to themselves that they are rather good at learning, something of the deepest significance has taken place. That is the public recognition connected with the personal experiential learning which is so richly significant.

APEL does not by any means imply taking that sort of route towards public recognition. Going back to the personal recognition the evidence is clear. The assessment of experiential learning can lead to enhanced employment possibilities and promotion as a result of the greater self-confidence which flows from a better understanding of self and comes implicitly through the systematic reflection on experience as the source of experiential learning. Equally, that enhanced self-confidence can mean that people like themselves better, become better partners, better parents, better friends, contribute more generally. Motivation for attempting new things is stronger because of that sense of greater confidence. People can and do change through the assessment of experiential learning and for one cardinal reason. The self-assessment which by definition must precede any other assessment of experiential learning results in a self-recognition, a revaluing and enhanced valuing of self which can show itself in a variety of public ways.

Some characteristics of experiential learning

What then is this experiential learning? How can it be evaluated? What are its applications? What issues does it raise? The rest of this chapter tries to answer those questions relating them to the notion of empowerment through links between personal learning and public recognition.

The experiential learning under discussion is really no more than a common sense statement of the obvious. It is based on the assertions that people learn without being taught, that they learn eclectically in a variety of different ways from a variety of different sources, that often they have little idea of what it is that they have learnt. Hence experiential learning remains invisible until it comes to be revealed for some purpose or another. The manner of revealing it can be different, but throughout the vital principle is that since experience is the source of this learning, systematic reflection on experience is the means of articulating it and so making the invisible manifest.

For the credential category of public recognition there are requirements which must be met. Experiential learning cannot be accredited before it has been assessed. It cannot be assessed unless there is evidence on which assessment can be based. Any evidence must relate directly to what has been learned. But since what has been learned is invisible the first step is to get at it, and that is the point about systematic reflection on experience.

There are two kinds of experiential learning to differentiate. There is prior experiential learning which is what people have acquired without recourse to any formal education institution. If they do apply to a formal institution it is all the un-certificated learning which they bring with them. Then there is what the Americans call sponsored experiential learning, referring to the experiential learning which is derived from work experience periods arranged as part of a course under the direct authority of college or university. In Great Britain the two are becoming blurred through the rapidly developing variety of schemes for collaboration between higher education and business, commerce and industry. Where work-based experiential learning acquired through current employment leads to academic credit towards an award then technically it can be either prior or sponsored.

A sequence

Whatever its label, there is a four-stage sequence which has to be completed by an individual before experiential learning can be assessed and therefore accredited. These can be expressed as:

- systematic reflection on experience to identify significant learning;

- identification of significant learning, expressed in precise statements, constituting claims to the possession of knowledge and skills;
- synthesis of evidence to support the claims made to knowledge and skills; and
- assessment for accreditation.

For prior learning there may well be a fifth stage which comes at the beginning for some people who have little confidence in themselves as learners. It is the psychological jump of believing in the possibility of experiential learning at all.

There are important riders to the four- or five-stage sequence. It is not a mechanical progression. The items can and do overlap, but the first three (or four) have to be worked out in a person's head so that things can be articulated clearly. Then everything up to the last stage, assessment and accreditation, is the responsibility of the individual; hence the emphasis on personal ownership of experiential learning. However, assessment and accreditation is the sole responsibility of those with the authority to act for an examining and awarding body.

As far as individuals are concerned, everything begins with the self-assessment which is involved in reflecting on experience. That is where the empowerment lies. It is solely up to an individual to choose what to do with the experiential learning which has been revealed. And it is personal all the way. No empty minds have been filled up. Minds have filled themselves – or not, as the case maybe. It is likely to lead to a personal sense of public recognition.

Some implications for institutions

It is obvious that this view of experiential learning raises some searching questions for higher education which can turn into fundamental considerations of policy. Assessment of experiential learning brings to the forefront questions about the nature of evidence which is acceptable, the means of making judgements about its quality and quantity, their validity and reliability, and ultimately the vexed questions of objective and subjective elements in all forms of assessment. Almost by definition the kinds of evidence offered to support claims for experiential learning are initially unfamiliar to academic staff. Tackling those issues generally leads to recognizing the value of expressing learning programmes in terms of learning intentions, and outcomes as a complement to syllabus descriptions so they can be used as an assessment tool. Very quickly the grading of work comes into the reckoning when it is to be incorporated in classified honours degree results. So motivation, pedagogy, curriculum design, assessment schemes as well as financial and political matters are involved when institutions undertake the assessment of experiential learning.

Some applications of APEL

Experiential learning with its assessment, whether for formal purposes or not, has an almost limitless range of applications. For education it is obvious, especially for part-time students at all different levels. It relates not only to access to learning programmes but to academic credit towards awards and qualifications. Hence, it raises questions of time and money for individual students, and so of motivation. For institutions it can be a way of increasing participation rates through bringing into the network of recruitment possibilities other categories of potential students, among whom there are the thousands of men and women who work in voluntary and community organizations and who often consider themselves to be ineligible for formal study. In employment experiential learning and its assessment is seen increasingly as a vital ingredient for training, improving or acquiring skills and redeployment. For employment and youth training programmes it has long been seen as a necessary part, though so far its possibilities have not been exploited, largely as a result of unhelpful conditions attached to those programmes by government departments. In professions such as social work and nursing, experiential learning has now a firm place in the regulations issued by the Central Council for the Education and Training of Social Work and by the United Kingdom Central Council for Nursing Midwifery and Health Visiting. Similarly engineering, the police and architecture have incorporated experiential learning in some of their training programmes.

In every case those activities relate directly to the theme of this volume: empowerment through experiential learning, and to the theme of this chapter: the connections between experiential learning as personal learning and public recognition. This becomes explicit as some of those examples are explored.

APEL and higher education

In higher education the Learning from Experience Trust (LET) is currently doing a project with Liverpool University, Liverpool Polytechnic and Chester College on work-based learning for academic credit within three-year non-sandwich degrees and on a non-vocational basis. Students spend a term in employment on a learning agreement basis and they will receive the same amount of academic recognition as if they were spending that term in lectures, classrooms or laboratories. It is optional. Students are volunteers. They are being empowered to make their own choices, become responsible for their own learning which becomes essentially personal and they will be recognized for it, academically. Four universities, Goldsmiths' College, University of London, the University of Kent, the University of Nottingham and the University of Warwick are involved in another LET project: the Potential of APEL in Universities. This is to try and work out what it means for universities to incorporate APEL in their regular provision. They are interested in APEL as a means of widening access and as a route to greater collaboration with employment. The credit rating of companies' in-house education and training schemes for academic credit, an earlier pioneering project of LET, means that employees who grasp the idea that what they have had to do for their company may ease their route towards some qualification or other, quickly begin to ask questions about possible credit for their on-the-job learning and immediately it is APEL all over again. Employees are being empowered to take decisions about their own educational and possibly career development which experiential learning has made possible.

APEL and further education

It is quite obvious that the National Council for Vocational Qualifications cannot deliver without APEL. Competencies cannot be disaggregated from learning programmes and related directly to assessment without that being the case. Access to assessment for determining whether someone has or has not a particular competence means just that. This poses the most daunting range of issues for further education but essentially it is to do with finding ways of enabling individuals to make the best of the knowledge and skills they have acquired however they may have come by them, and like other examples that is to do with opening possibilities to people – and that is empowerment. It does not feature prominently in public pronouncements about NCVQ but the implication is there.

APEL and employment

APEL and employment relates to the societal problem of skill shortages and deficiencies in the workforce generally and so it goes beyond the connections already mentioned. If the great need is for more people to learn more at all levels of the workforce then the personal motivation for learning which comes from APEL can be the best starting point for any training programme. Generally this is just what is not done, and it is a quite unnecessary waste of human potential. That waste is greater than skills required for the particular job an individual is employed to do. Most employers know comparatively little about their employees outside their particular occupational roles. They may have acquired a whole range of knowledge and skills from voluntary and community work for example which could be used for advantage at work, if only employers knew about it. This is the kind of learning with no specific connection with day-to-day work which lies at the centre of the Ford UK's employee development and assistance programme and in similar programmes at Lucas' continuing education scheme and Peugot's assisted development programme. In the first case APEL has led to access to a degree programme for workers at the Halewood plant. So at many different levels APEL has much to offer employers and hence to the nation generally because of the contribution it can make to a company's profitability and so to the national economy.

There is another application of APEL within employment which is almost largely neglected. That relates to the role of line managers and supervisors. It is quite obvious that one of the most effective ways of employees becoming more skilled is if their line supervisors encourage them to learn more through their jobs on a day-to-day basis. That implies supervisors becoming coaches or mentors, and one of the best ways of helping them adopt that different role is to use APEL so that they too, the supervisors, can realize how much they have learned from their own jobs without adequately being aware of it. The LET has a project on exactly that, working with four GEC companies and a food-processing plant. Line managers and supervisors were asked to reflect on their experience of supervising and supplement it with their ideas on what would be helpful to include in a guidance handbook designed to help other colleagues develop into mentors and coaches for those for whom they were responsible. Very quickly it became obvious that the work was becoming speculative about the possibility that APEL could make a contribution to a cultural change within employment.

The work-based learning for academic credit project raises the same possibility from a different direction. Work-based learning has to be distinguished from work experience. It is intentional and planned if it is to happen. Necessarily that involves employers in ways which are utterly different from their being asked to provide work-experience places. They become co-negotiators with students and academics in planning what is to be learned. They undertake a significant role as co-assessors. They become essential partners in the provision and assessment of experiential learning. As such, their commitment is evident, especially to themselves. Collaboration between employers and higher education takes on different meanings, and perhaps the most important additional meaning is this. The request to them to become intimately involved in students' learning can, for some, touch the latent teacher in so many adults who relish, even cherish, the notion of helping the next generation to find its way in the world. Induction, in a word. In terms of increasing the skills of the workforce generally it is hard to think of anything which could make a more profound impact on notions of training and re-training. As with the connection between supervisors and APEL, this is talking about cultural changes within employment.

It emerges, therefore, that where the possibilities of APEL are taken seriously, there is a range of staff development issues which are every bit as significant in employment as in education. This suggests the possibility that employment and education are converging as places where learning can be promoted, which has always been the case to some extent. The difference now is that the point is becoming explicit; increasingly it is being recognized that this is so. Every time a company's in-house provision for its own employees is awarded formal academic recognition, every time an employee receives academic credit for APEL derived from work, every time a National Vocational Qualification is awarded to an employee on the basis of skill and knowledge acquired through work, the point is being made. The workplace can be a learning place. As such, APEL takes on a significance which expands notions of empowerment and stands as a matter with far-reaching implications for public and financial policy.

The simple ideas on which APEL rests can apply not only to assessment and accreditation and to experiential learning as empowerment for individuals but carry implications for national and local institutions of all kinds as well. For those who undertake the development of APEL schemes there can be a richly satisfying sense of achievement in the slip-stream of others' growth and development. They can become witnesses as links between personal learning and public recognition lead to a sense of empowerment through experiential learning.

Both for individuals and institutions those are the central purposes of the Learning from Experience Trust. Every project undertaken so far is literally a first initiative. Every time the hope is that in demonstrating that APEL works well in yet another context, the likelihood of it becoming a mainstream activity increases. In attempting to encourage the widest possible application of the assessment of experiential learning in employment, education and training, the assumption is that people who go on learning are valuable wherever they are and that since the assessment of experiential learning is such a powerful motivation for further learning, it is too valuable to be neglected. It is empowering.

References

Boydell, T (1976) *Experiential Learning*; Manchester: University of Manchester, Manchester Monograph.

Evans, N (1981) *The Knowledge Revolution*, London: Grant McIntyre.

Evans, N (1985) *Post Education Society; Recognizing Adults as Learners*, Beckenham: Croom Helm.

Evans, N (1992) *Experiential Learning: Accreditation and Assessment*, London: Routledge.

Griffin, C (in press) *Experiential Learning: An Introduction to the Theory*, London: Routledge.

LET Publications for handbooks and project reports.

Marsick, V (ed) (1987) *Learning in the Workplace*, Beckenham: Croom Helm.

Warner-Weil, S and McGill, I (eds) (1989) *Making Sense of Experiential Learning*, Milton Keynes: Open University Press.

Winter, R (1989) *Learning from Experience, Principles and Practice in Action Research*, London: Falmer Press.

8 APEL for Access to Science and Technology

Anna Paczuska

> The APEL course has enabled me to identify skills in areas I knew I had but found hard to identify. *Suzanne.*

> The APEL course has been very helpful. I realized I had more skills than I would normally put on a CV. It made me think about what I had achieved and about things that I had not considered important before. *Marie.*

> APEL will help me in interviews. Portfolios will make it much easier for the interviewer to find things to talk about. *Franklyn.*

Students find APEL useful in a number of ways. Even students on science courses, however, rarely mention science when they talk about their work in compiling a portfolio. Yet APEL has a specific relevance for access to science. It can provide a focus for good practice on Access to Science courses, has particular relevance for the entry of women to science and broadens the prior learning students can present as a basis for progression in science.

Access to science courses

Overall progression rates to higher education in Britain are poor. Progression rates to science, and in particular to chemistry and engineering, are worse. The reasons lie both with the entry criteria to science courses and in the nature of the science courses themselves. Science admissions tutors put a great deal of stress on formal entry qualifications, especially in maths. They see the problem of small numbers of applicants as based in schools and with the image of science, rather than trying to make science more accessible by changing admissions procedure.[1] The courses themselves are also formal. Even Access courses are formal, as a recent report noted: 'Science Access courses, unlike those in other disciplines are not yet distinguishable by the innovatory aspects of their curriculum'.[2]

Many Access to Science courses are heavily content-laden. Attempts to design courses which concentrate on providing students with the 'basic skills and competencies to enable them to assimilate scientific knowledge' are resisted by tutors who insist on factual content.[3] HE science admissions tutors show little awareness of the needs of non-traditional students. Learning support and study skills are rarely built into science courses. Tutors expect that students will achieve confidence, competence and skills awareness but equally expect that these will be achieved through the standard course offer.[4]

Despite the overall formality of science curricula, however, there are exciting innovations. Most of these come from women's technology courses. Attempts to establish courses which take account of the particular educational experiences, attitudes and skills of women returners have resulted in courses which cater for a variety of learning styles, value informal learning and give students the opportunity to negotiate individual learning paths.[5] Women-only courses usually include:

- encouraging confidence-building;
- learning support;
- different modes of delivery;
- flexible work programmes which encourage students to work at their own pace;
- course programmes which stress student self-assessment;
- education guidance and career planning;
- use of staff as role models; and
- catering for a variety of teaching and learning styles.

These initiatives form many of the attempts to make technology courses more attractive to women. But what is good practice for women is not good practice for women only. The inclusion of such initiatives in science and technology courses as a whole makes science and technology accessible not just to women but to a range of non-traditional students.

APEL represents a development of the best of what already exists. It structures and brings together elements of the good practice that exists on science and technology courses and provides a framework for:

- confidence building;
- self-assessment;
- skills identification;
- career planning; and
- CV preparation.

Women, science and the curriculum

The recognition that women are systematically excluded from science and technology has led to a series of initiatives to redress the balance. These are of three main types. First, there are 'numbers' initiatives, where quotas and positive discrimination in admissions are used to increase the number of women accepted onto courses. The approach is accompanied by other positive discrimination techniques such as aiming advertising at women, providing nurseries and child care, shorter teaching days, etc. Second, there is a radical feminist or separatist response, where 'women-only' courses are set up and women are taught by women in a separate environment. Third, there is a curriculum response, which attempts to change curriculum practice.

Many initiatives include elements of each. The curriculum approach is particularly relevant to APEL. It involves looking at the divide between women and science and identifying the ways in which the division is forced and maintained.[6] This includes examining how science teaching and science practice exclude women and how the culture of science excludes femineity, and how women are socialized into being 'feminine' and how femineity excludes science.

APEL practice is relevant. By reflecting on their experiences both students and teachers can examine how:

- teaching styles in science exclude women;
- the sociology of science teachers excludes women;
- teaching and learning styles could be changed; and
- informally learned science skills can be recognized and acknowledged.

Many students have little awareness of the influences and pressures which shape attitudes and cultures. Reflection can help both students and tutors to gain a greater awareness of the learning process. Awareness of the various factors which shape attitudes and cultures does not necessarily lead to better learning, but it can help students to understand the situations in which they find themselves.

Skills for science

Widening access to science entails asking 'what is a science skill?' The identification of skills deemed appropriate for progression in science lies embedded in a number of other procedures: admissions, syllabuses and culture. The three are inter-related – the 'hidden agenda' of a science admissions tutor is based not only on their idea about what makes a good student, but also on their idea about what kind of person a scientist is. It's the reason one mature woman applicant for HE in science was greeted with the comment: 'You look more the "arty" type to me'.[7]

The exclusive culture of science influences our ability to identify skills on which progression in science can be based. It's difficult to resist the idea that because science is different and somehow special, the skills required for learning it are different and somehow special too.[8] Where attempts have been made to identify appropriate skills for progression into science these have turned out to be similar to skills necessary for continuing study and progression in *any* discipline. Recent development work suggests that progression and continuity in education, as well as selection for employment or higher education, would be made easier by basing all assessment on such 'core skills'.[9]

Like any skills, core skills for science can be learned formally, informally through experiences outside the classroom, or through courses which are not overtly science oriented. Science skills can be learned in unexpected ways. Meg McDonald's work with women attending adult education classes in dressmaking and textiles showed students had acquired competencies similar to those required for entry to BTEC courses in science and computing.[10] Students on other 'non-scientific' courses doubtless acquire skills appropriate for science too.

Science Access courses must take into account the fact that students may have acquired science knowledge or skills informally. Curricula on such courses must acknowledge this and enable both students and tutors to recognize and assess these skills. APEL as an integral part of an Access course enables students to recover and represent their learning so that it becomes visible. At present, many skills go unrecognized and students have to relearn skills they already have. This is because the prior learning students have is not recognized by admissions tutors:

> the prior learning women students bring with them is located in a discourse of domestic, local and specific science which is unfamiliar (or perhaps all too familiar) to admissions tutors and therefore dismissed.[11]

APEL enables students to present their skills in a recognizable form for admissions and can lay the basis for a 'conversion curriculum' through which students can progress to higher education.

The relevance of APEL

APEL is relevant to current educational developments in:

- bringing together academic and vocational modes of assessment post-16;

- acknowledging and building on the development of Records of Achievement (ROAs) in schools;[12]
- encouraging reflection, student self-assessment and portfolio production as a basis for professional development;
- providing foundations for portfolio production for post-professional assessment in practice-based professions such as nursing, midwifery, social work, etc;
- enabling the recognition of work-based learning as a basis for progression; and
- providing a framework for existing good practice in tutorial work on Access courses.

APEL and learning styles

Every student comes to a course with a preferred learning style, which may differ from the predominant style of the course. Students may even reject contemporary workshop methods in favour of more didactic methods which are familiar to them, and staff have had to revert to traditional teaching to cater for this.

APEL can provide a means of transfer between preferred or familiar learning styles by enabling students to recognize learning and how it occurred and enabling them to present it in the style of the course. APEL provides a 'bridge' between past learning experiences and current ones.[13]

References and notes

1. *Women's Attitudes to Science and Technology Courses* – report of a project between Division of Continuing Education, South Bank Polytechnic and Hillcroft College, 1991.
2. *Aspects of Assessing Experiential Learning* – Case Studies, FEU, 1988.
3. *Angles and Attitudes to Access to Science and Technology*, Brunel University, 1991.
4. *Women's Attitudes to Science and Technology Courses*, op cit.
5. See for example, *Technology Foundation Course for Women*, application to the West and North Yorkshire Access Validation Consortium, Huddersfield Polytechnic, April 1991.
6. This entails looking not only at questions of access to 'taken for granted' areas of technology but also involves challenging definitions of technology. See Pam Linn, 'Gender stereotypes, technology stereotypes', *Gender and Expertise*, ed Maureen McNeil, Free Association Books, 1987.
7. *Women's Attitudes to Science and Technology Courses*, op cit.
8. Some workers argue that science skills cannot be learned through everyday experiences. Lewis Wolpert of University College, London emphasizes that the ability to think 'scientifically' cannot be acquired informally because scientific thinking is 'counter-intuitive'. His views are summarized in 'Uncle Albert's guide to the mysteries of the Universe', *Independent on Sunday*, 5 May 1991.
9. *The Core Skills Initiative*, FEU, 1990.

10. *Where There's a Skill There's a Way*, the Progression of Women into Technical Training, Meg McDonald and Ramona Stirling, ILEA, 1988.
11. *Women's Attitudes to Science and Technology Courses*, op cit.
12. *The London Record of Achievement* – Putting Students First, ILEA, 1991.
13. *Making Experience Count*, John Storan, LET, 1990.

9 Women's Informal Learning in a Neighbourhood Setting

Sue Webb and Sharon Redhead

Patterns of Disadvantage

In the last decade, many women in Britain have been employed in a limited range of occupations which are typically defined as low skill and involve low pay and poor career prospects and large numbers have worked part-time, (Dex, 1985; Hakim, 1979; Martin and Roberts, 1984). Nevertheless, a growing proportion of women have demonstrated a permanent attachment to this paid work, even though they may have had periods of not working, (Dex, 1984; Webb, 1991). Work history data (Dex, 1984) suggest that in particular, women responsible for young children or elderly relatives are disadvantaged in career terms. Women's occupational 'choice' is more likely to be influenced by factors such as the hours of work and locality, than consideration of the nature of the job, its pay status and prospects. Consequently, women frequently experience downward occupational mobility and routes of upward progression in education or career become more difficult.

When such women become involved in activities outside the home, other than part-time work, these are frequently shaped by their caring responsibilities. Involvement in local community centres, running play-groups or voluntary and advice work, are some areas where women with dependants find it possible to become involved. These are usually local activities which can be fitted around other responsibilities.

In any of these areas, women may develop their skills and have experience of education and training but it is unlikely that they will have received any formal recognition for this learning. Butler (1991) suggests that when such women do seek paid employment, there is a cultural devaluation of these experiences both by women and men, in so far as they relate competencies acquired in unpaid work to formal qualifications and paid work. Not surprisingly, so-called women 'returners' are often reported to be lacking in confidence and ambition and progression is difficult and haphazard.

An Open College Federation

Against this background, what have Open College Federations done to reduce these barriers to progression? Open Colleges began in 1976. The idea was introduced by David Moore, then Principal of Nelson and Colne college, with the foundation of the Open College (Federation) of the North West (OCNW). The original aim was to provide alternatives to GCE 'O' and 'A' level courses and certificates, for adults. This activity was soon recognized by a growing number of universities, polytechnics and employers and OCNW certificates gained widespread currency.

Within a few years, these ideas were taken up and developed in other parts of the country. In 1981, Manchester Open College Federation (MOCF) was created, to offer a distinctive accreditation service and thereby wider recognition for adult learning which had never been formally acknowledged. This new system of credentialling adult learning was designed to value achievement in a variety of contexts and at a range of levels spanning basic education through to admissions to higher education.

By 1991, and enhanced by a UDACE-DES national project, Open Colleges were within reach of most adult learners in England and Wales (UDACE, 1989; National Open College Network AGM, 1991). These Open College Networks are all locally based and locally controlled organizations that bring together institutions of adult, continuing, further and higher education, together with a range of other organizations such as public and private employers, voluntary and community groups with an interest in education or training. The learning opportunities recognized by Open College Federations, cover a wide range:

- community-based activities;
- access courses to further and higher education;
- training courses provided by voluntary organizations, public and private employers and colleges.

Frequently, Open College Federations recognize courses and programmes that may previously have led to no certificate. By awarding credits to learners on these programmes opportunities are opened up. In making credit awards available throughout a variety of settings and curriculum areas, by placing learning in a framework of learning time and learning level, Open College Federations are creating alternative pathways through the systems of qualifications (UDACE/NCVQ, 1990; ACRG Advice and Progress Reports, 1989–90). Adults have been enabled to choose pathways that reflect the way that they learn rather than follow educational routes involving barriers which they must surmount if they wish to gain recognition for their learning. It is in this context that Open College Federation activities have been described as providing 'Credit where it's due' (Browning 1989; Sanders, 1987).

The accreditation of adult learning

Unlike most other accreditation systems, the syllabi, modes of delivery and methods of assessment are developed wholly by practitioners who will operate the programmes. Courses are submitted to the Federation and presented to accreditation panels consisting of tutors and trainers who have experience in that particular area of learning; for example, these may be curriculum-specific panels (such as humanities, social studies, art, craft and design, languages, science and technology, information technology, numeracy/maths, business studies, language and communication, English language support) or 'thematic' panels (such as access to higher education, women's education or community activities). Discussion at a panel will focus on the course design to establish the coherence of the learning programme and its appropriateness for the people for whom it is planned so that agreements may be reached on credits and levels.

The concept of peer-group appraisal and review is central to Open College Federations and is reflected through the process of accrediting courses in panels and in recognizing the achievements of people on those courses via the award of credits following external cross-moderation. Moderators are experienced tutors and specialists in their field who ensure that the learning programme operates effectively and that there is consistency in the award of credits and levels. Furthermore, the moderation process enables a regular pattern of review to be built into the accreditation structure.

This system of accreditation gives value to people's learning in a variety of ways, so that they can use it as a personal record of achievement, as a basis for further study or to apply for jobs. In bringing a coherent system of accreditation into hitherto unrecognized learning, real possibilities for progression are enabled and it is this which is the concern of the rest of this chapter. The developments which are described are underpinned by two assumptions: first, that much systematic learning can and does take place far from formal institutions, and second, that the experience, skills and strengths built up in community settings can and should form the foundation for further learning.

Recognition of learning in a neighbourhood centre

Much excellent work takes place with local neighbourhood centres and although the style of delivery may be informal, this should not imply any lesser degree of commitment on the part of either tutor or learner than that found among students and teachers in more formal or mainstream educational provision. Indeed, it is precisely because of the high level of commitment and the eagerness to work hard on the part of such adults that the recognition of achievement, made possible by accreditation with an Open College Federation, is so important.

There have to date been several examples of MOCF-accredited neighbourhood-based courses (Harford and Redhead 1989). One such example is to be found at Royle Green, a small neighbourhood centre once part of a community college and now part of Manchester Adult Education Service. It is located in Northenden, a suburb adjoining Wythenshawe, with a population of approximately 6000. Housed in what was a purpose-built infant school of the mid-1960s, the facilities are good and the buildings conveniently placed for use by many drawn from the community, which is predominantly white, working/lower middle class, with a high proportion of elderly people. The centre's programme includes traditional non-vocational classes, adult basic education, elderly people's activities, a women's group and parental/play training. Support is also given to groups meeting outside the centre in, for example, the local library, primary school and health centre. It was the excellent work being done by parents in the various toddler groups in these venues that prompted the centre's first course submission to MOCF.

The parents, all women at this time, though running the groups very well, expressed a lack of confidence in their own numeracy and literacy skills and their knowledge of any child development theory. It seemed important that the practical skills and achievements of these parents should be recognized and valued, while at the same time their confidence should be increased by offering them a chance to return to further study within their local community rather than at a more formal, distant and intimidating institution. From the five different parent/toddler groups, 15 women came together to discuss what they wanted the course to cover and how and when they wanted it to run. It was decided to involve other agencies so that the group would gain experience and confidence from having several tutors. Sessions were therefore run by colleagues from community development, adult basic education and the Manchester City Council's 'Books and Stories' project. The final arrangement was for a day-time course of 10 two-hour contact sessions within school hours and with adequate, free child-care. The facilities at the centre were made available for quiet study for those women who had difficulty working at home. The standard of all aspects of the work (group discussion, written work and practical application) was high, and the group members were very supportive of each other, so that the 'formal' course structure and accreditation did nothing to undermine the 'neighbourhood' or 'informal' nature of this work; the starting point was still the student and her needs and expectations. Drop-out was almost non-existent. Of the original group of 15, one left when she moved house, and the remaining 14 all successfully finished and were awarded MOCF Credits.

Success and empowerment

The completion of the course and the gaining of credits is a criterion by which the success or otherwise of the course can be judged. Using this criterion, it is clear that for the vast majority the course was extremely successful. There are, of course, other criteria that could be applied, the most telling being whether the gaining of MOCF accreditation enabled participants to run their groups more effectively and encouraged them to consider further study. Although it is not appropriate here to detail each student's progress, for over half the group this first attempt at returning to education has led to their involvement in other provision offered by the nearby further education college.

It was particularly satisfying that eight women from the group went on to help to devise a second 10-week course on health-care of the under-5s, which the whole group felt would be an excellent extension of the work they had so far done. This participation in itself indicates the increase in confidence that can be gained by people who see their work being valued and rewarded by the educational establishment. It is at this level of building confidence and enhancing self-esteem that MOCF is of most value to a neighbourhood community education programme. It can provide a starting point on a journey whose length and direction is determined by each individual learner, but which is essentially grounded in her particular experience and the skills she has built up within the community of which she is a member.

Valuing experiential learning

By becoming part of a system of accreditation at a local level, many adults feel more able to proceed into more 'formal' educational establishments. In making what previously might have been an unthinkable step into college, frequently they have revalued their previous experiences as they find that these have a relevance to formal qualifications' frameworks.

Within the Royle Green community centre a number of women have had experience of working unpaid on holiday play-schemes or with the parents and toddlers group. These women were finding that they had much to contribute in the 'formal' courses they participated in and began to discuss with the tutor the extent to which they could draw on their previous experience to demonstrate their understanding of, for example, the key issues in organizing play. Although not articulated in this form, the women were seeking assessment of their prior learning and achievement. The learning programmes at Royle Green were already acknowledging these women's experiences, but in an informal way. The next step was to formalize the recognition of this life-long learning and to give a credit certificate for this or to enable exemption from parts of a course of study.

Discussions with MOCF led to a submission of a programme for the 'Recognition, assessment and accreditation of skills gained working with young children'. It was assumed that it would be relevant to those adults, in the main women, who were seeking external validation of the knowledge and skills they had acquired as part-time or informal voluntary or paid workers in any of the following situations: crèches, parent-toddler groups, playgroups, classrooms or play-schemes.

Initial consultations with such a group of women from Royle Green and other neighbourhood centres in Wythenshawe, Newall Green and Baguley, led to the identification of the range of experiential learning for which accreditation might be sought. Further activities involved designing a process for supporting the women in the identification and assessment of their experiential learning and clarifying how such learning would be recognized and evaluated. Since the aim of the assessment of prior learning was to enhance students' progression within wider qualifications' frameworks, the tutors developed a profile of the likely skills and knowledge for which learners would be claiming credit or exemption. In addition they identified the assessment criteria and types of evidence which might be provided to authenticate such learning. The following is an extract from the submission document, summarizing the process.

Introduction

Many people learn throughout their lives without being formally taught. That learning is of value and can be recognized through MOCF accreditation.

Basic principles

APEL should not be seen as merely an inventory of skills or knowledge measured at a particular moment in time.

APEL is a dynamic process which requires appropriate levels of support and guidance from tutors and trainers who can identify positive qualities, promote the development of self-confidence and elicit skills and knowledge.

It is intended that the process will include the following elements:

1. an introduction to the concept of the accreditation of prior learning;
2. an assessment using, wherever possible, a negotiated methodology of an individual's prior experiential learning;
3. an attempt to match experientially gained knowledge and skills against a set of competencies in particular areas of work with young children;
4. to develop a method of accrediting this process using MOCF, so that individuals

can gain accreditation for those competencies for which evidence of competence can be provided.

The complete process would need to be in modular form so that individuals could claim assessment and or accreditation in those areas in which they felt competent. Modules might possibly cover these areas:

- programme and session planning;
- use of equipment and safe and effective play;
- child development and child observation;
- liaising with other community agencies;
- administration.

The following is an example of how a module might be structured in terms of units and elements. Each element is a competency for which evidence of ability to perform that competence can be provided. The tutor will support and guide the learner in the review of the prior experience in order to identify possible learning and sources of evidence to authenticate this. Guidance will be provided about the nature of evidence – indirect and direct – and on how this evidence will be assessed by the tutor and externally moderated.

MODULE 1. PROGRAMME/SESSION PLANNING

UNIT 1. TIMETABLING

ELEMENTS 1. Able to produce various timetables for six sessions that show ability to make use of various physical environs.
2. Able to produce six session timetables that show ability to cater for different age groups.
3. Able to produce six session timetables that show ability to cater for differing social and emotional needs.
4. Ability to work as part of a small group.

UNIT 2. RUNNING A SESSION

ELEMENTS 1. Able to select activities suited to a particular group of children.
2. Able to choose appropriate materials and equipment.
3. Able to prepare and organize the activity.
4. Able to involve other adults.

UNIT 3. PLANNING AN OUTING

ELEMENTS 1. Able to seek any information necessary.
2. Able to make and confirm arrangements.
3. Able to organize insurance, guardian consent, health and safety and worker/children ratio.
4. Able to communicate with and gain confidence of parents.

UNIT 4. EVALUATION

ELEMENTS 1. Can identify children's responses.
2. Can evaluate own performance.
3. Can present evaluation outcomes for discussion with other workers.
4. Can encourage and support other workers.

Empowerment through experiential learning

At the time of writing a number of women are engaged in collecting evidence for portfolios of their experiential learning in work with young children. It seems very likely that some of these women will be able to demonstrate learning equivalent to the entry requirements for a range of vocational and professional courses (for example, the Initial Play Training Certificate; NNEB; BTEC National; Diploma in Youth and Community Work) and in some cases gain exemption from elements of these further courses of study. Accreditation of this experiential learning has provided access routes into a range of qualifications in work with young children but also in areas including National Vocational Qualifications in the area of Business Administration (UDACE/NCVQ, 1990).

The achievement of such qualifications and, with this, often pay or higher pay for work which had previously been undervalued, is not insignificant for people who have not received recognition for their informal learning in the past. Confidence-building is essential for anyone, and particularly women, if they are seeking to take more control over their lives, their careers and their education. That these women have gained confidence from such activities may be seen in the events of the Summer of 1991 at Royle Green.

Financial difficulties within the local government and in particular the education service, resulted in a proposal to close the Royle Green centre from September 1991. The women who had used the centre both as volunteer play-workers and as learners on MOCF courses mounted a protest campaign and lobby of the local councillors. It culminated in the organization of a meeting between the women and the chair of the education committee for the city and to date, as a result of such activities, the decision to close the Royle centre has been rescinded. What provisionally for these women might have seemed an unthinkable step into local politics can become a natural progression once one has a better understanding of one's skills and abilities and one knows that others have recognized these.

Conclusion

Open College Federations exist to widen access to education and training opportunities for those who have benefited least from existing provision. For such 'students', particularly those whose learning takes place in informal settings, the flexible yet rigorous accreditation system means recognition by the educational establishments and employers of their achievements. This can act as a spur to further study, as a boost to self-confidence, as an aid to gaining employment or can stimulate more organized activity in the community for those that want that. It also presents a challenge to those developing national accreditation and qualifications' frameworks to ensure that such systems are more responsive and more comprehensive.

References

Access Courses Recognition Group (ACRG) *Advice and Progress Reports 1989–90*, CNAA-CVCP.

Browning, D (1989) 'Open colleges', in Rumney, A (ed) *New Directions in Vocational Education*, London: Routledge.

Butler, L (1991) *Unpaid Work: the developing potential for accreditation*, London: Learning from Experience Trust.

Dex, S (1984) *Women's Work Histories: An Analysis of the Women and Employment Survey*, Research Paper 46, London: Department of Employment.

Dex, S (1985) *The Sexual Division of Work*, Brighton: Wheatsheaf Books.

Hakim, C (1979) *Occupational Segregation*, Research Paper 9, London: Department of Employment.

Harford, L and Redhead, S (1989) *The Credentialling of Neighbourhood-based Adult Education*, Manchester: Manchester Open College.

Martin, J and Roberts, C (1984) 'Women's employment in the 1980s', *Employment Gazette*, 92.

National Open College Network AGM (1991) 21 June 1991 NOCN launched as a national organization with national officers and supported by development worker funded by UDACE.

Sanders, J (1987) *Credit Where it's Due*, ALBSU Basic Skills Special Development Project Report 1982–83, Manchester Open College Federation.

UDACE (1989) *Open College Networks: Current Developments*, Leicester: Practice Unit for the Development of Continuing Education.

UDACE/NCVQ (1990) *Open College Networks and Qualifications*, Leicester: Unit for the Development of Continuing Education.

Webb, S (1991) 'Shop work: an ethnography of a large department store', unpublished Ph.D thesis, University of Manchester.

10 Constraints upon Portfolio Development in the Accreditation of Prior Learning

Shane J. Blackman and Alan Brown

The Portfolio Project

This chapter is based upon research carried out by the authors as evaluators of an attempt by an LEA in the Midlands to develop APL for work-related competences, known as the Portfolio Project. This project set out to provide trainees with a competency 'banking system' of previous experience: that is, a portfolio from which individuals can make accreditation challenges upon NVQ units of competence. A central aim of the project is to provide the basis through portfolio preparation for accelerated assessment of prior competences, in order to determine rapidly a trainee's appropriate entry point upon an incremental scheme. Within the LEA three colleges are making progress towards embedding the new NVQ vocational system of accreditation in the areas of care, clerical administration, heating and ventilation, carpentry and joinery, painting and decorating, plumbing and brickwork.

Preoccupation with initial assessment

The project teams found, as others had (eg Gregson, 1990), that if the only measure of success of APL processes, including the use of portfolios, were in the number of people who made immediate claims for APL then the process was a failure. That is, the amount of staff time and effort seemed wholly disproportionate to the few claims which resulted. However, if APL processes, including the use of portfolios, are judged in accordance with what they contribute to learning and assessment as a whole, then the equation changes. APL processes can have relevance for the management of learning, work-based assessment and can lead to accelerated assessment throughout a learning programme. The switch of concern from initial accreditation also removes the source of disappointment which staff often expressed when learners had experience which staff believed they could use for APL, only for the learners to express no wish to have that experience accredited. In some cases, especially for returners to learning who also hoped to become returners to work, the learners wanted to get into a learning programme more fully *before* making judgements about whether their prior experience meant they did not wish to take parts of the learning programmes. Even in such cases, they often welcomed an initial 'taste' and then opted for accelerated assessment (Evans, 1987). The attitudinal problem for many learners is that unless they are very confident and knowledgeable about the contents of learning and assessment programmes they may consider an initial decision to opt for APL as premature. They may even feel it could disadvantage them in the rest of their learning programme. In some areas, learners are often already in work and have a fair degree of confidence in their own abilities (their reason for wanting accreditation often being directly related to legislative requirements for qualified staff). In such circumstances, evidence collection processes could relate to achievements in previous or current work, as well as in college or on placement. That is, a full range of performances is considered if appropriate in relation to each competence.

In contrast to exclusive use in initial guidance, the use of portfolios, guidance, periodic reviews, bringing prior experience to bear whenever appropriate in the evidence collection could be seen as valuable throughout the learning and assessment process (Storan, 1988). These could then lead to more effective learning, not least because tutors have a more complete picture both of learners' past experience and their future aspirations and accelerated assessment.

Another advantage of spreading use of prior learning in the evidence collection process throughout the year is that it becomes very much less time-intensive, because it is then much more likely to be used in a corroborative way rather than as the prime source of evidence. An example from construction may illustrate this. If a learner wants to claim APL for certain competences before embarking upon a learning programme, then a tutor is likely to want a considerable body of evidence (for example, letters from employers, possible site visits, skill demonstrations and so on) before it is allowed. However, if evidence from prior experience is used as part of the evidence collecting process (in the course of the learning programme), then a tutor will have a whole range of other evidence to corroborate the claim and should not feel the need to investigate the prior experience claim with the same rigour as if it were the only evidence.

Differentiation within APL

The shift from undifferentiated experience to experiential learning derived from that experience has no parallel in APL; as yet APL is still largely seen in an undifferentiated way. Usher (1989) argues that there exists a clear contradiction:

> Experience has always been 'recognised' as a useful indicator of maturity, positive motivation and serious study intentions [yet] very often experience was ignored on the grounds that it was a poor indicator of intellectual and academic aptitude (p 65).

In this case study we found that initial guidance needs to take the format of a curriculum entitlement for all learners on any learning programme. This can assist in the process of 'matching' learners to learning programmes and 'tailoring' learning programmes to learners as appropriate, even if there is little scope for formal APL in a particular programme. However, subsequent use of APL processes may need to differ between programmes and according to individual requirements. That is, in some occupational areas it is very much easier and quicker to get corroboration of learner claims, for example by use of skills test and oral questioning, than in other areas. As already argued, if it was particularly difficult to corroborate stand-alone APL claims (as is sometimes the case in some areas in the care and construction sectors), then attempts should be made to spend less time on initial APL, but rather to integrate the use of prior learning as one form of evidence collection throughout the whole learning programme.

Perhaps a crucial factor in determining the success of APL is whether FE or HE identifies it as 'bolt on' or integrated. It is on this distinction that an understanding is formulated concerning the range of APL opportunities. The importance of APL is in the way in which it affects college requirements and programme development; if a college is full (in terms of student numbers) it may perceive little need of APL, or at best may see it as a longer 'getting to know you' interview; whereas APL can be a real opportunity to evaluate existing practices in college. Furthermore, we have been informed in relation to HE admissions that certain universities and polytechnics are not even interviewing candidates due to oversubscription; alternative entry candidates 'did not even get the slightest chance of entry', while certain colleges see APL as merely a form-filling exercise. Often where this occurs, it is further supported by the assumption that an interviewer possesses the skills to elicit full information from an applicant. This type of attitude was more prevalent within the traditional male craft area. Feminist studies and theory have given us the insight that men experience and express unfamiliarity as a weakness; rather than admit to ignorance, the masculine stereotype is to bluff yourself through by an inflation of confidence (Roberts, 1981). Here it is possible to suggest that within certain occupational sectors male tutors were reluctant to reveal they did not possess the interactive and communication skills necessary to accomplish APL.

Youth and adult APL

Although there exists a clear need for differentiation of adult experience within the APL process, perhaps the greatest need for differentiation that remains to be explored is that for young people between the ages of 16 and 30 [Jesson and Gray, 1989]. For example, some young people may have spent considerable time on schemes or in unemployment. That is, they may not have a clear fund of experiences at work upon which to make an APL claim.

Tutors may also encounter a set of hostile expectations when dealing with some young people who may still bear substantial resentment towards authority figures within formal education. In handling adults the primary issue for the tutor will be reassurance and ability to sustain motivation. In contrast we found that tutors are sometimes not able to motivate successfully young people until the negative side of resentment is resolved. Furthermore, from data supplied by the LEA on the Youth Training Programme, it was discovered that employers and YT managing agents possessed very limited understanding of young people's culture and their aspirations (Blackman, 1988). Taken together these factors may make young people the most difficult APL client group to deal with because they may have most recently failed to achieve their full potential at school: 'daily meeting with underestimations of their worth and ability'.

At the colleges we found that young students can experience taking responsibility for their own learning as too demanding, where the onus is on the learner to make informed decisions about the timing of assessment and also the security of their record system (Brown et al, 1992). Without full staff support non-standard students may encounter learning difficulties and this may lead them to question the value of this autonomy and indeed ownership of learning itself. Therefore, the issue of counselling for adults and youths on individual programmes of learning was seen as an area in which both learner and facilitator required support.

Problems in the accumulation of evidence

In all colleges we found problems concerning the practical accumulation of evidence from past employers: in catering, labour mobility was seen as a major obstacle to trying to gain verification of performance from supervisors in previous employment. The variable nature and quality of building work in small construction firms was seen as a problem by some staff in construction departments; unless the firm had an established reputation and/or was personally known to departmental staff they would be reluctant to accept a letter from an employer as sufficient to substantiate an APL claim. Students sometimes had difficulties providing full and accurate details of employers; with larger employers there were sometimes difficulties as to whom should be contacted. Furthermore, there is the issue of practicability: how easy it is to produce evidence of past achievement. Both employers and college staff agreed it may be impracticable to set up simple simulated tests. All these difficulties could be compounded by non cooperation and/or uncertainty about the process even if the 'correct' individual is identified.

Constraints
APL is a very practical opportunity allowing an individual to receive certification for prior learning, most often that which had been developed at work. However, this opportunity can be severely restricted in the case of unemployed people. Cost is always a fundamental constraint, and here we found problems concerning funding and location of any visits or practical demonstrations that were required to corroborate APL claims, that is, being able to find employers who would permit work-place assessment to be conducted on their premises or on site. Even where limited financial incentives were available from the local TEC, large numbers of employers still identified allowing evidence collection processes linked to APL processes on site as a potential hindrance.

In certain occupational sectors this was a major problem, for example construction. Here employers raised questions concerning health and safety and insurance, and the whole issue of allowing visiting FE staff on site. Timing was seen as absolutely fundamental as work locations changed rapidly and work performed may in fact be covered on site before completion of the assessment. The conclusion is that work-related assessment of competences in the workplace may not always be possible in certain occupational sectors (Blackman et al, 1990).

Furthermore, in the case of the care sector, a major issue raised was confidentiality of the client-professional relationship. The stipulation of using natural observation wherever possible with respect to evidence collection has to be viewed with caution. Observational methods have been subject to critical scrutiny within the social sciences for almost a hundred years, especially in relation to problems of reliability (Bulmer, 1984). It is not so much that observation is itself a problem (although it can be) but the context in which this occurs. Social carers may be required to perform differently according to the needs of each client. Therefore the carer may need to be able to respond in an almost infinite number of ways according to marginal changes in clients. The qualitative nature of these types of interaction means that the role of assessment as object can be seen as reductionist, divorced from the process in practice (Holmes, 1990). Assessment should be seen not as object but as subject, to the social carers' practical and moral reality, especially if carers are trying to promote intimate forms of expression, awareness and identity (Ashworth and Saxton, 1990).

Under circumstances such as these, occupational sectors in some colleges have developed new introductory courses or customized skill-testing to enable individuals to demonstrate their prior achievement in their own time rather than be forced to demonstrate their skill in a rigid test environment. However, it still remains unclear quite what are the credits and exemptions gained from APL.

Current wisdom considers APL as vital in the development of a more responsive and flexible means of curriculum delivery, but a number of colleges have established that it is impossible to implement in full without considerable staff development. Evidence also shows the process as labour- and resource-intensive and that institutions will be reluctant to carry the additional costs themselves. Again, without much thought and commitment to implementation the whole thrust of the exercise will be compromised. Resource allocation is proving an effective brake on implementation of innovation in a number of areas of education. More specifically it has been reported that new modes of operation, indications for quality and formulae for resourcing will be required if flexible systems of assessment are to be introduced effectively. How college policies on assessment of prior learning and accreditation of prior achievement are administered can condition opportunities for learning and assessment of a number of possible client groups. We found evidence that in regions where the local labour market is in decline, certain colleges have highlighted difficulties in accommodating APL facilities for the unemployed. The action of one local TEC in withholding 15 per cent of funding until certain NVQ targets are reached has acted as a spur to some colleges to pay particular attention to processes of initial assessment.

Some colleges saw portfolio development as one way of addressing problems both of initial and continuing assessment. Within such a development, the processes underpinning APL can be given full rein. In the portfolio preparation colleges firstly generate a CV for each individual along with a programme of learning. The second part of this is the accelerated assessment profile. Here competences are turned into something more readily understandable by candidates, that is tasks and activities which enable each person to identify those which she or he has covered in his or her work role. The college then turns these back into the NVQ format. In combination with the strategy of portfolio preparation, there now exists the possibility to find out what level and type of training is required.

Achievements: ways forward for APL

Training in support of embedding NVQs will need to address a number of issues which go across colleges as a whole; APL is one of these. Such training (for example, funded under GEST) could draw upon exemplary and supportive materials; these could include examples of APL processes in practice drawn from the three colleges. Thus models of the use of portfolios in two occupational areas could be included as part of an APL pack.

The whole approach to training could relate to notions of curriculum entitlement. That is, rather than the 'lead' being training for APL, the focus is upon the development of processes to support effective learning. It would then be a matter of judgement of trainers whether to disclose the whole model. The obvious advantage would be that it could give staff a clear vision of what they are moving towards in the medium term. The disadvantage could be that it may be seen as rather daunting, if the skills required are very different from those currently owned by staff. If the latter is the case, trainers may prefer to develop staff skills on a step-by-step basis; this is by starting from the approaches and skills currently used by staff and signalling training as trying to help them improve their effectiveness.

Another point to stress in any future training would be the way the project teams built up their skills in support of processes of APL development partly by coordinating resources, materials and skills already available in different parts of the college. This is important in that experience, both in the Midlands and elsewhere, shows that if departments or sections try to develop and implement APL procedures on their own they are likely to find the task beyond them. This is because both development and implementation of APL is likely to be very time-consuming, particularly if the common mistake is made of concentrating enormous effort upon initial assessment, rather than seeing evidence of prior achievement being one of a number of sources of evidence which could be drawn upon *throughout* a learning programme (Broadfoot, 1988).

The skills required, the requisite college/departmental structures and the support to make APL effective are complementary to those required for the effective implementation of NVQs. For example, developing skills in action planning, guidance and review, supporting evidence collection and processes of assessment underpin both. Similarly college and departmental/divisional management have to recognize the need both to develop cross-college support and to facilitate programme teams such that they have sufficient time and support to carry out the activities mentioned above. The GEST priorities through to 1994 mean that it is feasible to plan a medium-term programme of staff development along these lines.

There is a danger that colleges will feel that one immediate effect of a successful project outcome is that they now have a body of people (that is, those that constituted the project team) with expertise in APL processes and that is sufficient. In practice, they could represent 'innovation enclaves', which have little effect upon the processes and practices of the rest of the college, unless there is an explicit attempt to pass on what has been learned. Indeed without this there could be even some reversion to former practices as it is almost impossible to support APL processes without a fuller framework of college support.

Conclusion

In conclusion, one key point is that portfolio construction is in itself a fairly minor activity, but it assumes a wider significance in that to be effective so many other elements have to be in place and related to one another in a coherent way. These elements underpin many of the key processes which will be required of colleges in the future. These elements (guidance support, processes of evidence collection and the like) are already in colleges at least in part, but they are not structured in such a way as to provide a coherent and comprehensive system of learner support. The portfolio should be seen as an 'ongoing document' which is capable of being added to in a developmental way. It should facilitate the assembly of evidence towards accreditation. Further, the portfolio itself could be seen as a tool to be used in induction, guidance, action planning, review assessment and evidence collection processes leading to accreditation.

References

Ashworth, P D and Saxton, J (1990) 'On competence', *Journal of Further and Higher Education*, 14, 2, pp 3–25.

Blackman, S J (1988) 'Youth training and the Manpower Services Commission: possibilities and limitations', pp 221–43, in Lauder, H and Brown, P (eds) *Education: in search of a future*, London: Falmer Press.

Blackman, S J (1991) 'The Politics of pedagogy: problems of access in higher education', pp 135–44, in Chitty, C (ed) *Post-16 Education: studies in access and achievement*, London: Kogan Page.

Blackman, S J, Brown, A and Haffenden, I (1990) 'Resource allocation: the brake on innovation, National Vocational Qualifications in England and Wales', paper given at International Association for Educational Assessment, Maastricht, The Netherlands, June.

Broadfoot, P (1988) 'The national assessment framework and Records of Achievement', pp 3–14, in Torrance, H (ed) *National Assessment and Testing: a research response*, British Educational Research Association.

Brown, A, Haffenden, I and Blackman, S J (1992) *The Implications of the Implementation of Competence-led Curricula*, London: FEU.

Bulmer, M (1984) *The Chicago School of Sociology*, Chicago: University of Chicago Press.

Evans, N (1987) *Assessing Experiential Learning*, London: FEU/Longman.

Gregson, M (1990) *Credit Accumulation Project: final report*, London: Haringey Education Service.

Holmes, L (1990) *Soft Heads, Brick Walls? Open learning, competences and occupational closure*, London: The Business School, Polytechnic of North London.

Jesson, D and Gray, J (1989) *Access, Entry and Potential Demand for Higher Education*, Sheffield: Sheffield University Educational Research Centre, Youth Cohort Study of England and Wales.

Roberts, H (ed) (1981) *Doing Feminist Research*, London: Routledge and Kegan Paul.

Storan, J (1988) *Making Experience Count*, London: Learning from Experience Trust.

Usher, R (1989) 'Qualifications, paradigms and experiential learning in higher education', in Fulton, O (ed) *Access and Institutional Change*, Milton Keynes: The Society for Research into Higher Education and Open University Press.

11 Making Experience Count: Facilitating the APEL Process

Cathy Hull

The most commonly used means of documenting prior experiential learning in order that it can be formally assessed is the construction of a portfolio. If undertaken correctly the process is extremely rigorous and demanding. It is time-consuming and requires that learners not only develop their powers of self-assessment but also their written and communication skills. It is certainly no 'soft option'. Rather, the development of a portfolio should be seen and valued as a complete educational process in itself as well as an effective and reliable means of assessment. More particularly, it is a genuinely student-centred approach placing the responsibility for demonstrating prior learning firmly with the student. Those who have successfully completed their portfolios have a much clearer idea of what they do know, what they do not know and what they want to know. The portfolio process is therefore a most effective way of developing responsible and self-motivated learners with the skills and confidence to begin to chart their own progress through the educational system or employment market. In this way it can most definitely be an empowering process. In this chapter I begin by describing the portfolio approach as developed at Goldsmiths' College, then move on to look at the key issues for educators seeking to facilitate such a process.

Although Goldsmiths' College has been involved with very many initiatives concerned with recognizing, assessing and validating experiential learning, its approach is rooted specifically in establishing taught courses to assist adults to construct a portfolio based on their personal learning objectives. These 'Making experience count' courses are advertised in the College's short course programme and attract adults from a wide range of backgrounds who want to construct a portfolio for a variety of purposes. An analysis of the students on one such course shows that some came purely for personal development, whilst others were more concerned to access education or to enhance employment opportunities. There was, for example;

- A woman with a PhD from Oxford University who said, 'I have been right through the educational system and yet I still have no idea what I have learned from this – what my education means to me. I hope this course can help me'.
- A woman, currently bringing up two young children, who wanted to try and document what she was learning from this experience and then hand her portfolio back to her children when they had reached maturity.
- Two people who were seeking to return to paid work or to educational study and wanted to use their prior experiential learning when applying for jobs or to access further and higher education.
- Another who had been working for many years as a designer. In order to gain promotion he needed to get a first degree in design. He was seeking exemptions from part of the degree course so as to complete his degree by the fastest possible route.

The course was seen by all of the group as a valuable means of developing confidence. As one woman said at the beginning, 'If I can find out what I have learned from bringing up the children I don't think I will feel so inadequate when I do eventually return to work'.

Our courses typically run for two hours per week for 20 weeks. The aim is to help adults to analyse their past experience and present this valuable learning in a way that makes sense to others. In this way, the course enables others to recognize learning through life as an alternative to formal qualifications. An outline of the different stages in facilitating this process has been documented elsewhere.[1] Briefly, it involves the learner in:

- reflecting upon experience;
- identifying where significant learning has occurred;
- giving evidence for that learning; and
- submitting the portfolio of learning for assessment

Initially the students are simply encouraged to take stock of their past experiences. This is achieved in a variety of ways – including structured exercises, group discussion and the keeping of personal diaries. The benefits to the learner at this stage are enormous and should not be underestimated. For many students it is the first time they have been encouraged to talk about themselves in this way. That it is a recognized educational activity taking place in a formal institution suggests that the learning experiences articulated are taken seriously by group, tutor and institution alike. One woman said, 'My secret dream is that one day I shall go to college. I told my husband this once and he laughed. He thinks college is for brainboxes. This is the first time I have begun to think it might become more than a dream'.

Educational guidance is fundamental to the portfolio process and it is particularly important in the early stages of work. People often enrol on the course with a clear outcome in mind. However, through careful reflection the intended outcome might change. Many women, for example, enrol because they want a career in nursery nursing or primary school teaching. This decision is based upon the fact that they have been bringing up children for a long time and feel that they might be able to get credits for some of the learning they have acquired from this experience and thereby return to the job market swiftly. Through rigorous self-assessment students come to realize that they are good at very many different activities and that they have been in the business of learning for a long time and have learned a great deal. So, they are able to identify many skills, qualities and knowledge that will enable them to seek access to a range of other job or educational possibilities. In this way participants on the course are much more likely to identify future education and employment based upon informed knowledge of what they already know and can do.

Having identified the purpose in constructing a portfolio the next stage is to clarify what the portfolio will need to contain in order to achieve that purpose. As APEL becomes increasingly part of mainstream educational thinking, particularly through recent national developments in accreditation, more and more organizations should be able to describe clearly the kinds of knowledge, skills and qualities required in a portfolio. However, where this is not the case appropriate assessment criteria have to be negotiated with the receiving organization. Having decided upon the criteria the onus is then on the participant to identify where they have acquired appropriate learning. Again this is where the group approach is useful. Many learning experiences are not recognized by the learner until s/he has been encouraged to reflect upon the experience in the group. The very act of making public what had, until that moment, been an essentially private experience can be crucial in eliciting and evaluating significant prior learning.

In due course the students begin work on constructing the portfolio by looking for learning experiences that match the criteria that have been identified in accordance with their aspirations. So, for example, students may be able to identify good communication and interpersonal skills as a result of informal learning acquired through running a voluntary organization, taking part in an adult education class, or through other social situations. Reflecting upon learning acquired informally in this way can quickly develop confidence as students begin to recognize the extent of their own learning. In this respect facilitators will often encourage the learners to reflect on their informal learning as a first step. It is often at this point in the process that participants feel themselves to be weak in the area of study skills.[2] This is invariably as common a feeling amongst those who are well qualified as those with no qualifications at all. Through the approach developed at Goldsmiths' it is possible to provide study skills and a considerable element of educational guidance. One woman, for example, wanted to be a primary school teacher and was seeking access to a B.Ed course at another college. We asked the admissions tutor, therefore, to set an essay question for her to tackle. After several attempts she said, 'I'm not worried about my ability to write essays at this level any more. But I found the subject unexciting – and educational theory does not appeal to me'. She then had to decide whether it was this particular course which did not appeal or studying for a B.Ed generally. In the end she decided she would prefer a career in training and was able to change the focus of her portfolio accordingly.

Whilst students need to work on their own and away from the course in order to construct their personal portfolios they still value the opportunity to meet as a group. They continue to come into the college once a week, to talk informally with other members of the group and the tutor about how their portfolio is progressing as well as to work in the library. Within one group session therefore, one student might be writing a computer package, another writing a music score and a third writing away for references from former employers or tutors, a fourth listening to how another participant is progressing and so on.

When the portfolio is completed it is shared with other members of the group before being submitted for its assessment purpose. The members of the group have become a support to one another rather than competitors as is so often the case in other courses. Individuals have, however, developed their own aspirations and prior learning rather than those of the course or the institution.

The role of the facilitator

Clearly, many skills are required of the facilitator if s/he is to facilitate the process effectively. A key skill is the ability to encourage students to move through the various stages in the process swiftly in order that they really do complete their portfolio by the end of the course. Adults often find the opportunity of talking and, more importantly, being listened to in this way a novelty, and one they do not give up readily. So, in the early stages as they describe past experiences they can be reluctant to move from simply describing their experience to the more difficult task of analysing where significant learning has occurred. The facilitator therefore has to constantly remind individuals and the group as a whole of the purpose of engaging in this dialogue. S/he has to be a progress chaser.

We have found that the disposition to reflect and self-disclose is invariably influenced by class, gender and culture. For example, often the facilitator may have a hard job in encouraging members of the group to reflect on learning originating in familial or social settings. More often than not students find it much more comfortable reflecting on employment-oriented skills and past qualifications. Because the APEL process is keen to recognize the affective as well as the cognitive side of learning it is important to encourage reflection on all learning. The facilitator has to be skilled and sensitive in handling issues of a personal or intimate nature.

This of course raises the issue around the privacy and ownership of learning. As one man said, 'You say my experiences are valid – I've talked about them, in my own language and for the first time I'm beginning to understand things about myself. But they are still private experiences and I don't want every Tom, Dick and Harry judging them'. It is important to recognize, therefore, that the onus is always on the learner to disclose and make decisions about what will go into the portfolio. Often the facilitator will see the student demonstrate good quality pieces of learning which readily match up to the criteria. However, the participant always owns his or her own learning and must make decisions on what can or cannot be included in the portfolio.

The APEL process also recognizes that we often learn as much from negative experiences as from positive ones. Accordingly, students reflecting on their past frequently disclose deeply emotional experiences which have also been major learning experiences. Bereavement and divorce, for example, are frequently cited. Occasionally, however, the portfolio process will lead a student to confront an experience that has not been confronted before. In this respect, it is important to define what should *not* be expected of the facilitator. S/he should not take on the role of personal counsellor. This is a specialized and immensely complex task and, if it becomes appropriate, the facilitator must direct the student towards specialist personal counselling. Clearly this will be a matter of judgement. Suffice to say that the portfolio facilitator is concerned with educational support and guidance arising from the central task. Nevertheless, it is reasonable to say that any institution which is developing portfolio-based courses to any significant extent should give the most serious consideration to what other support, guidance and counselling is available either within or proximate to that institution.

Finally, the facilitator has a key liaison and information brokerage role. S/he will need to work closely with receiving institutions and know what they are expecting. So, for example, will the admissions tutor or employer expect the student to present themselves for interview in addition to submitting a portfolio? This will, in part, determine what should or should not go into the portfolio. More importantly, the receiving institutions themselves must have some understanding of the APEL process and how to assess the portfolio. Here again the facilitator may well have a key role. For the time being, while many institutions will not accept portfolio evidence, careful attention must be paid to making sure that the student understands this and is not made to feel that they have somehow failed as a consequence.

If APEL is no soft option for the participant, then it is even more the case that it is no soft option for the facilitator. As one of my colleagues observed when taking her first APEL course, 'I've never felt so alone and responsible as I did at that first meeting. No amount of training could prepare me for that!' Asking people to reflect in depth on their prior experiences and share these with others is challenging for all concerned. From the facilitator's point of view it is important to know the limits of the exercise as well as its potential. In particular, the key point to stress is that the focus is on the nature and quality of prior learning and its applicability in terms of appropriate assessment criteria.

From the students' point of view, working towards this objective can and should be a liberating and empowering educational process. As one student commented graphically, 'It was like fireworks going off in my head. It is the first time I've felt like a real person in my life'. Here is education at its best – valuing rather than devaluing what the student brings to the learning process; having control over that process rather than being just its subject; and taking responsibility for learning rather than the much softer option of allowing others to make decisions about what constitutes real learning.

Notes

1. For example, one useful publication is *Assessing Experiential Learning*, Norman Evans, Further Education Unit Publications, 1987.
2. This is equally true of people seeking entry to employment as it is to education.

Integrating Experiential Learning

This section deals with issues related to the institutional assimilation of experiential learning.

Tate demonstrates how experiential learning can be supported at individual, organizational and public policy levels through 'Joint venture' programmes. Marshall, through case study on organizational culture, shows how organizations too might proceed to learn from their own experience. Bartrop's chapter shows that some cultures, in his case an action-centred police culture, may not be sympathetic to learning processes (reflective writing) which run counter to the dominant culture.

Chapters in Section 2 and also Marshall and Mill (Chapter 21) in Section 5 are relevant to this theme.

12 Empowerment through Experiential Learning

Pamela Tate

Experience of learning to me means that the learner is directly in touch with the realities that are being studied. It involves a direct encounter with the phenomenon being studied, not talking about it, not reading about it, not simply considering it or thinking about it but instead a direct encounter with the realities being studied.

CAEL (Council for Adult and Experiential Learning) was founded in the USA in 1974, with a mission 'to expand lifelong learning opportunities for adults and to advance both experiential learning and its assessment'. In the last two years there has been a change which demonstrates some important changes in our philosophy about empowerment. We have added a sentence to the mission emphasizing that, 'This learning should positively affect individuals, institutions and ultimately the society'. We are suggesting then that experience of learning is not the end in itself nor is the growth and development of the individual which results. Rather the learning should be a means to a larger social goal. To achieve our mission, we are trying to work with a whole network nationwide in colleges, in universities and vocational and technical institutions to overcome the many barriers that have kept adults from furthering their learning.

Although CAEL began in the early 1970s with a focus on tertiary education, we now find that to achieve the mission we have to begin wherever the adult is. That means whether they are in need of basic reading, writing and maths skills or whether they are ready for battle with study. This means that we have to reach adults at all levels of their work. We find ourselves having to work to create a continuum of learning opportunities for them and this has made it necessary to bring together institutions from the high-school level, community colleges and four-year institutions and universities to create a continuum of possibilities for adults so that they are not dead-ended along the way.

This has, in other words, forced us to take the fragmentation of the

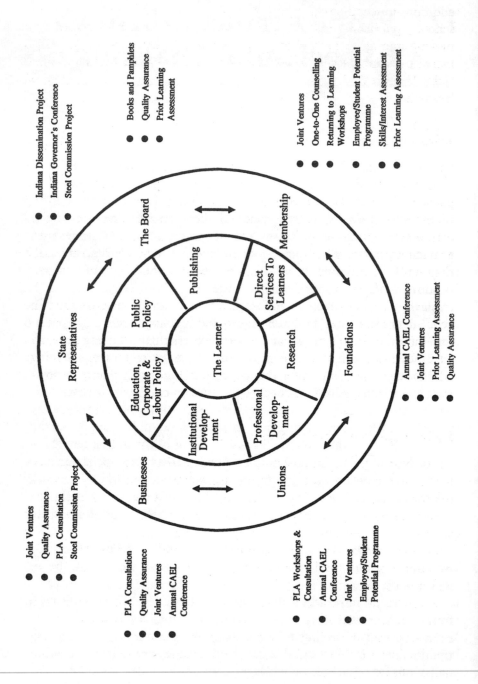

Figure 12.1 *CAEL's efforts of behalf of adult learners, 1991*

educational system in the USA and to try to do something about it. In addition to conducting training in colleges, universities, vocational schools, publishing and doing research and conferences, we are now moving into an arena of managing very large programmes that aim to increase learning access to all employees. These programmes are called 'Joint Ventures', designed to empower adults and to foster experiential learning.

Joint ventures

One of the things that we have found in recent years is that because of the work force crisis in the USA, labour unions for the first time, and particularly since 1984, are moving with some encouragement to invest funds in 'employee growth and development programmes' rather than corporate training programmes. These programmes are designed to provide access for all employees at all levels, a very different approach than has been apparent in corporate training in the USA. We see joint ventures as an active partnership between the educational institution, the employer, a labour union, if there is a union in this industry, and the government to enable adults to acquire the skills and knowledge needed for employability through that partnership, which I will describe briefly later. We believe that these joint ventures are working now to encourage adults. We think that they have some unique elements to them, which are making them happen; some of those elements are described below.

Influencing corporate and public policies

In addition to the direct services we provide, we have also begun to work to change the policies of corporations and labour unions in ways that will foster experiential learning in the work place. We are convinced that simply changing the colleges to access learning from experience is not sufficient to remove the barriers at the work place and the only way to get out of the problem is to change corporate and public policies. That is why we have begun to tackle the public policy problem of how training and education is funded in the USA.

An indication of the challenge can be seen from some statistical data from the American Society for Training and Development. They have estimated that 30 billion dollars a year are spent by corporations on training; what is not pointed out is that 27 billion dollars is spent by one half of one percent of all US employers. Of what is spent, 70 per cent goes on management training and only 8 per cent of the front-line work force in the US receive any training at all. Most of the training offered is not the type that lends itself to building general capabilities; it is orientation training, safety or team training, very narrow job skill training, useful for immediate performance and conducted in a very formal way. It is rarely experiential and has little utility for future employment security. It does not involve the mixture of theory and practice that we think leads to empowerment.

These corporate practices and the problems in higher education are causing a growing gap between the knowledge and skills of the work force and the knowledge and skills that are needed for work in the future. Most of the pressures in the USA are caused by increasing global competition, losing our share of the world market, deregulation, the pressures of new technology, yet in most work places opportunities for the front line work force to gain these necessary skills and knowledge have not been developed. We believe that a major effort must be mounted to change, so that learning for all employees may be enhanced and supported, not just learning for executives and managers. We have to demonstrate to people in both companies and unions that a combination of learning strategies is critical. It is critical both for the success of the organization and for the success of the individuals in it.

Criteria for empowerment in the workplace

Experiential learning in the workplace, formal training at work and a range of educational opportunities that one can choose to do in one's own time, are three things we believe are necessary for empowerment of people. It might be useful to think for a moment about the word empowerment. Rosabeth Moss Kanter, in *Men and Women of the Corporation* defines power as:

> the ability to mobilise resources to accomplish something . . . the ability to produce a change. . . . Power is the ability to do in the classic physical usage of power as energy, and thus it means having access to whatever is needed for the doing. The powerful are the ones who have the access to the tools for action.

These tools for action in the 1990s are knowledge and information and the ability to apply them. An example comes to mind: a man in his late 30s or early 40s named Jerry, who works for Scott Paper Company in southern Alabama and appears on a video made by the company, on one of our joint ventures. In this video Jerry is wearing a hard cap, and is standing in front of the equipment that he operates and talking about what it has meant to him to have that opportunity to go back to school and learn to read and write and improve his maths skills, and how he can earn twice the money on that job. He now talks proudly about how he can help his son, who is going to school, with the things that he needs to learn in school. Jerry has been empowered. He is not threatened by the future; he says he is 'preparing for the future'. Through his formal classroom learning and basic skills, combined with his experience of learning, Jerry now has the tools for action in a complex and changing workplace like that paper company, and in his community in Alabama as well. He may not yet be ready to undergo assessment of the experience of learning, but he intends to pursue a degree. His entire life has been transformed. This is like a dream come true, because whatever you learn, no one can take it away from you. When Jerry talks to you on that tape he owns what he knows, and he has control over his life and that is empowerment.

The company programme that Jerry participated in is called 'LEAPP' – the Life and Education Action Planning Programme. Like many of the employee growth and development programmes that CAEL manages, LEAPP has many components to it that we believe lead to empowerment for workers like Jerry.

Establishing the learning partnership

First, CAEL goes directly to the workforce, a face-to-face outreach, to talk about this programme, what it means to people, what it can mean to their work, their employer, and their families. We explain how the programme works and how it is not out of their reach, a key point. Our staff travelled in jeeps in the timberland and talked to the workers in their 15 minute breaks for their lunch or when they were back from work. We reached people in a direct and personal way, telling them what is possible. This I think is the first step to empowerment: we go to where they are. We bring the learning opportunities to them so that a bridge is built between them and the opportunities for learning. We do not simply send our brochure and announce a new idea and assume that they will build the bridge, we have to make it for them.

The second element in all our programmes like LEAPP is that we offer what is called 'Returning to Learning' workshops right where people work where they can overcome two other major barriers for adults: lack of information about educational options and lack of self-confidence about their own interests, skills and aptitude. Their interests lie in their personal history in their image of who they are and what they can do. We have designed the workshops so that they are experiential. They include both brainstorming and self-assessment exercises to help people realize that they have many more skills than they think and that their accumulated wisdom and skills are valuable, even though they have not gained them through formal education. Four hours of the twelve-hour workshop are devoted to the assessment of prior experiential learning. In addition we help them to understand the difference between work experience – what they do, and experiential learning – what they know. We also require them as a homework assignment to investigate a college by actually going there and asking a set of questions about courses and services and access. They do not talk about going to a college, they do not read college catalogues, they directly encounter one.

By the end of the workshop participants are highly motivated, much more aware of their strengths and they are also much more aware that these skills are necessary for functioning in the jobs of tomorrow. In other words, they have the tools for action and these tools have been gained through an experiential learning process.

The Scott Paper Company allows employees to take the workshop in work time. The programme is voluntary, yet in this and most cases, 80 per cent of the employees have completed the workshop. Today over 35 per cent of the workforce is enrolled in a school or college; prior to the introduction of LEAPP less than 2 per cent were enrolled. The key is to find out what they need in a supportive and empowering environment to lead them to the right educational level and then to help them move along through the main levels of education. In some cases people are linked to literacy colleges and later to community colleges and then to four-year education. Others are led to agriculture, forestry, liberal arts, the whole range of programmes. But in every 'joint venture' we manage, whether in manufacturing industries, telecommunications, public sectors, food and commercial industry, whether unionized or not, we see an enormous participation of the work force as a result of their increased self-confidence because there has been a bridge to learning. We think this is a demonstration of the empowerment of adults.

Many companies we work with allow employees to engage in several hours of individual advising, educational advising in addition to this workshop I prescribed, and with the help of an advisor who is a real enabler and has knowledge of assessment of educational opportunities, the person can begin to make a career plan. These counselling services are designed to overcome lack of information and lack of self-confidence. All along the role of the advisor is to overcome hurdles that stand in the way of achievement for these adults.

Funding the programme
A critically important element in the LEAPP is funding and that represents the kind of shift in corporate policy referred to earlier. It is a dramatic change in the way that the company pays for this kind of education. We have redesigned corporate programmes so that all tuition and fees necessary for the programme are pre-paid for all employees; most large employers in the USA have had some plan to make teaching available, but they have traditionally reimbursed the adults after completion of the courses and never is their support for the fees that adults

have to pay for assessment of prior experiential learning. A large number of adults have not been able to take the basic course in reading because they cannot wait for six months to receive the money back from their employer; so as a result the average of those who have the eligibility for funds is only 4 per cent of the US workforce. With the staff programme we have 35 per cent of the workforce participating in further education; it is the prepaid tuition and assessment that makes the difference. We grant employees vouchers or 'letters of credit' and this allows a person to undergo assessment of prior experiential learning or involvement without any money. They simply submit the 'letter of credit' to the college or university which then bills CAEL as manager of the tuition funds for the employer and the person is free to engage in learning. We are convinced by our experience that without such systems in the corporate sector, only those who can afford to pay will be served.

Fostering a learning environment

The final component of LEAPP, and in some ways the most difficult, is beginning to work with supervisors and managers to foster a learning environment in the timberlands division. We are trying this with many other employers. This is a very early effort and I believe that it has real implications with respect to the work place of the future.

The chief executive officer of Scott Paper has said that he wants to 'unleash the full potential' of the workforce. Once large numbers of employees are engaged in learning it becomes very important for employers to re-examine their culture, their decision-making, their work structure, their approach to training and the link between experiential training in their workplace and productivity in the workplace. We believe that employers must begin to rethink how their managers and supervisors can become people who can facilitate and foster experiential learning and we are tackling this in the timberlands division.

From our work with companies it is becoming very clear that much corporate training is wasted because of the failure to apply it and build on it in a work place. In addition it is irrelevant to the work place because it does not emerge experientially from an analysis of the key problems in the work place. We believe that we must collaborate with educational providers and that we must reshape and revitalise corporate training in this way. The focus has been on the process of experiential learning for adults inside the institution. We are now realizing that we must focus on the process of learning in the organizations that we bring together in the joint ventures, labour unions, government, corporations, universities and colleges – and even CAEL itself.

According to Peter Senge's book, *The Fifth Discipline: The Art and Practice of the Learning Organization* learning organizations empower the individuals in them because learning organizations share a vision about the future of the organization. They encourage things like team learning, risk taking and experimentation. But even in organizations which do this they do it for their managers, not for the front line hourly workforce. In one of the author's accounts of how experiential learning works he talks about an organization and the environment there:

> 'When you are immersed in a vision', says Herman Miller's president Ed Simon, 'you do know what needs to be done. But you don't often know how to do it. You run an experiment because you think it is going to get you there. It doesn't work. New input. New data. You change direction and do another experiment. Everything is an experiment, but there is no ambiguity at all. It is perfectly clear why you are doing it. People aren't saying "give me a guarantee that it will work". Everybody knows there is no guarantee. But the people are committed none the less'.

This is an example of a situation where experiential learning and experimentation are rich, where both the individual and the organization can grow. We are a long way from achieving this goal of learning in organizations and this will require sustained efforts for many years to affect change in even a few organizations. I believe that it is learning organizations that we must help to build and it is the empowered learners who will thrive in these work places and make a difference in society.

Conclusion

Much remains to be done in the USA on this. In most places of employment, learning is not supported, training is not offered and there is no shared vision or team learning. Many employers are, in fact, taking the route of de-skilling jobs and paying lower wages rather than attempting to build a high-wage, high-productivity learning environment. Many colleges and universities do not recognize experiential learning from the workplace even when it can be demonstrated and do not offer a mix of experiential learning and classroom learning.

Our challenge then is to create a climate conducive to empowerment in spite of these obstacles. I believe that change in organizations and people can come about in spite of obstacles but it will require a long time to get there. It will take some strategies like joint ventures and changing public policy and corporate policy in order to allow individuals to become empowered. It will require boundary-spanning organizations to bridge the gaps between the corporate labour, government and education sectors to create a vision of the 'new work place'. It will mean that those of us in adult and continuing education will have to rethink our assumptions about the adults whose learning we assess so that we are truly moving in a new direction and not simply assessing their past. This will mean a new look in our institutions. Most of all it will mean living with some creative tension between our vision of what should be possible for adult learners and what the current reality is. Peter Senge says in his book that living with the creative tension between vision and reality is the discipline of 'personal mastery'.

Experiential learning, according to Senge, is not simply acquiring more information in a first-hand way. It involves expanding the ability to produce a result you truly want in life, recognizing that there are huge gaps between what we want and where things are now. It gives us, in Kanter's words, the tools for action.

References

Coleman, James S (1974) *Youth Transition to Adulthood*, Chicago: The University of Chicago Press.

Dewey, John (1938) *Experience and Education*, New York: Collier Books.

Dufrenne, M (1973) *The Phenomonology of Aesthetic Experiences*, Evanston: North Western University Press.

Goodlad, J (1983) *A Place Called School: Prospects for the Future*, New York: McGraw-Hill.

Hahn, K (1947) 'Training For and Through the Sea', address to the Honorable Mariners Company, Glasgow, February 20.

Kraft, R (1988) *Journal of the Association for Teacher Educators*, Vol X, No 2, Summer.

Nold, J (1977) *Man the Adventurer*, unpublished paper presented at Outward Bound Inc. Seminar, Colorado, USA.

Richards, A (1981) There is a little of Ulysses in all of us, *Recreation Canada*, Vol No 2, pp 38–41.

Roberts, K, White, G and Parker, H (1974) *The Character Training Industry*, Newton Abbott: David Charles (Holdings), Ltd.

Quinn, W J (1987) *The Essence of Adventure*, unpublished paper presented at Association for Experiential Education, Annual Conference, Corbondale, Illinois.

Walsh, V and Collins, G (1976) *The Exploration of the Outward Bound Process*, Colorado Outward Bound: Denver, Colorado, USA.

13 Cooperative Inquiry into Organizational Culture: The Wrekin District Council Experience

Judi Marshall

In February 1987 a colleague, Adrian McLean, and I embarked on a cooperative inquiry with a group of people in Wrekin District Council, an organization of 1200 people. Our purpose was to explore their organizational culture and arrive at a portrait of it. Our sponsors, the Local Government Training Board, wanted a model of 'good practice' to publicize. Managers in the Wrekin wanted to evaluate the effectiveness of cultural changes they had been trying to implement over the preceding four years. What other members of the group wanted was less clear at the outset. As initiating researchers, Adrian and I shared the LGTB's agenda, but with some reservations. The Wrekin was already being paraded as a model, and we wondered if their value as 'exemplars' would be undermined by people saying 'Oh no! Not them again!' Before describing our experience in the Wrekin, I shall set the scene by saying a little about cooperative inquiry as a philosophy and form of research, and by raising some question areas.

Some basic themes in cooperative inquiry

Cooperative inquiry is a loosely defined term for research conducted by a group of people committed both to exploring their experience and making sense of it. There may be an initiating researcher, but they are not expected to take full control of the inquiry. In the various phases of research, described for example by Rowan (1981) as 'being', 'project', 'encounter' and 'communication', collaboration and participation are advocated. Core sources on this form of research are Reason and Rowan (1981) and Reason (1988).

Cooperative inquiry is not just qualitative, it is post-positivist in its key assumptions. People are considered to be self-directing, capable of making sense of their own experience. 'Knowing' is taken to be multi-faceted, incorporating at least propositional, practical and experiential aspects (Heron, 1981). Knowing is generally seen as for and in action, incomplete if it is disembodied or separate from practice. Self reflection is vital to research in this mode. Participants need to develop 'critical subjectivity' to know and evaluate their own processes of knowing. There is no absolute truth, rather respect for multiple perspectives. Validity takes on new meanings (Heron, 1988). It is enhanced by engaging in repeated cycles of inquiry. Initially the interests guiding the research are surfaced and pursued. Later, tentative conclusions are explored, tested out, refined.

These hints at the realm of cooperative inquiry give some idea of how demanding such research can be, how personally challenging. Some people think it an élitist approach because of its injunctions for high quality personal awareness. There are also, in some writings, hints of ideal models. There are important tensions here, most to be lived with rather than resolved.

I do not believe that there is 'one true way' to do cooperative inquiry; there is a multitude of possibilities. At the same time I think choices need to be made awarely and with appropriate self-questioning. People who are fully engaged in cooperative inquiry are likely to be highly creative in the forms they choose for research. But I hesitate if people then think that 'anything goes'. I want to know that the research is rigorous, in some appropriate way, questioning its own process internally and externally. Systematic attention to both the emerging knowing of the inquiry and the process is valuable to prompt high quality reflection and action.

There are dilemmas of control and direction, which raise important issues of power. The experienced researcher may initially 'educate' other participants in the principles of collaborative research and its possible forms. This taking of power is often appropriate and models being powerful to others. If other participants never discover their own power, or by subtle means the initiator stays in control, however, this may be a degenerative form of education. These issues, and others, will be touched on below. I would now like to outline the story of cooperative inquiry in the Wrekin (see Marshall and McLean, 1988, for a fuller version).

Working with Wrekin District Council

The people we worked with were chosen to represent different organizational levels and departments. They were:

Joy Bailey – play leader
Terry Brookes – principal engineer

Danny Chesterman – personnel officer
Pam Edwards – housing welfare officer
Anne Hewitt – employment development assistant
Annette Lewis – print room supervisor
Gordon Little – street lighting technician
Mick Paish – bricklayer
Brian Piper – senior estimator/surveyor
Derek Shaw – housing centre manager
Tony Smith – area foreman
Brian Wright – janitor

The work of the cooperative inquiry group went through three major cycles of action and reflection. There were four main meetings, each a day long, at roughly monthly intervals. There was also a shorter meeting directly before the presentation of the research findings to the senior management team and the project sponsor. Adrian and I were also collecting data by interviewing people throughout the organization and by just being around, gaining an ethnographic appreciation of the culture. We fed this data and our emerging ideas into discussions with the group.

Cycle I: forming the cooperative inquiry group and starting to explore culture

Table 13.1 shows the main cycles of inquiry and the issues covered at each of our meetings. Adrian and I did extensive preparation for the first meeting in April. We made a long list of expectations and possible

Table 13.1: *Cycles of reflection and action in a collaborative analysis of Wrekin District Council's organizational culture, 1987*

CYCLE I: FORMING THE COOPERATIVE INQUIRY GROUP AND STARTING TO EXPLORE CULTURE

Initiators (Judi and Adrian) surfaced possible issues; planned first meeting; consulted with Postgrad Group at Bath.

Meeting 1: April

Introductions and expectations
Base groups on what people wanted from the project
Input and discussion on organizational culture
Input and discussion on cooperative inquiry
Planning first data collection
Checking individual commitments and problems
Evaluation of the day

Initiators tape-recorded reflections on first meeting; consulted with postgrad group.
Data collection through interviews and self-reflection.

Meeting 2: May

Reviewing activities since last meeting
Feedback to Adrian and Judi on draft workbook
Subgroups generate lists of emerging themes
Whole group discussion

CYCLE II: LOOKING AGAIN, AND MORE WIDELY

Meeting 2 continued: Planning further data collection
Initiators tape-recorded reflections on meeting; consulted with postgrad group.
Data collection through interviews

Meeting 3: June

Process review and agenda negotiation
Subgroups generate lists of emerging themes
Whole group discussion
Evaluation of project so far

Initiators tape-recorded reflections on meeting; consulted with postgrad group.

CYCLE III: DRAWING THE PORTRAIT TOGETHER AND COMMUNICATION

Initiators analysed accumulated data and drew out key cultural themes; drafted report

Meeting 4: July

Detailed feedback and discussion on draft report
Plans for presentation

Initiators revise cultural portrait

Meeting 5: September

Presentation of findings to senior managers and project sponsor
Celebration of work done

---

problems; for example whether our academic perspective would be seen as inappropriate by others. We decided to take clear control in this meeting. Our purposes were to introduce other members to notions of organizational culture and cooperative inquiry (the focal aspects of the project) and prompt discussions about the purposes and processes of the research. We realized that we had expertise in such issues, and did not want to deny this in a falsely egalitarian approach. We also devised procedures such as base groups and asking questions about why people were part of the inquiry, and whether they wanted to continue to be, to encourage others to participate and start to contribute to decision-making.

We found, from our questions, that people thought it 'akin to an honour' to be asked to participate. They thought that the council has many positive qualities and were happy to help publicize them. They had reservations as well, things were not perfect, and welcomed an opportunity to incorporate this 'realism' in any portrait. Their main concerns were that they may not find time for the research because of heavy workloads.

This meeting was more 'successful' in several ways than we had dared to hope. From the outset, members of the group took an active, inquiring, reflective approach. In the first round of statements of how people saw the project, some noted that there were no 'cynics' ie, people who were not committed to Wrekin culture, in the group. They thought this exclusion could jeopardize the validity of the findings. Also, organizational culture as a perspective (looking at the taken for granted, the subtle processes of 'how things are done around here') seemed to fit well with the Wrekin. People seemed used to being aware of process, and had finely developed senses of style and how well things fitted with 'the Wrekin Way'. As we introduced notions of culture, other group members quickly used them and illustrated from their experience. We felt we were giving them frameworks and a language for ways of seeing they had already adopted. Further, the notion of working collaboratively seemed sympathetic to the culture. They were pleased that we did not want to use traditional methods of 'research *on* people', and liked our ideas of 'research *with* people'. Within the group collaboration had been noteworthy. Everyone had contributed to the day; there had been little sense of hierarchy and no pattern of deference. At the end of the day we reviewed how things had gone. Again group members brought up issues to do with research process and validity. Monitoring the inquiry already seemed a shared endeavour.

In this open atmosphere of exploration, Adrian and I reviewed our plans as we went along. We realized that we had been too ambitious in thinking that the group would now be ready to go out and ask other people about the organizational culture. Also, in this plan we had overlooked the group's own expertise. We proposed instead that we circulate a draft workbook which we were in the process of writing and which included exercises for surfacing one's appreciation of culture (McLean and Marshall, 1988). Group members readily agreed to this plan. In the month before the next meeting, people mainly worked individually; some also started exploring issues of culture with co-workers.

Researching as multiple conversations
My image of this project is of multiple arenas for conversation. The Wrekin is an informal, discussion- rather than memo-based culture, and much debate went on there. Two other arenas Adrian and I used were very important for our abilities to reflect on the research process and on our actions. At times we took questions posed in one of these arenas and shared them with the inquiry group.

We were members of a staff-student postgraduate research group at the University of Bath, with our friend and colleague, Peter Reason. At various stages we discussed the project with this group. They were both challenging and supportive, helping us reflect on decisions we were making, and particularly on how collaborative our relationships with those at the Wrekin could be said to be. At the outset they were, for example, particularly suspicious about whether we were controlling the agenda too much from our own research needs.

We also found it helpful to tape-record conversations after each day of meeting with the Wrekin inquiry group. We usually did this back at the hotel, over a relaxing drink. We reviewed group process, challenged ourselves on issues of collaboration and validity, and reflected on what we seemed to be learning about the organizational culture. Doing the research together was, in itself, very helpful. We could relax and notice in a way that the solo researcher may find difficult. We could model dialogue whilst with the group, as we reflected openly on the process or debated interpretations of culture. We also found out, through this project particularly, that one of us is typically more sceptical, the other more accepting, and this gave us different perspectives to look from in synthesizing an appreciation of the culture.

Cycle I continued: sense-making
The second meeting, in May, saw several significant developments in group process. Adrian and I had done less direct preparation. We started the day inviting everyone to say something about what they had been doing in their life outside 'work' since we last met. There was a positive, relaxed and friendly feeling in the group from the start. We spent the first hour reviewing what people had been able to do in the month, what obstacles they had encountered, and with Adrian and I hearing back the other members' comments on the draft Workbook. This latter activity seemed in retrospect to have important implications for equality of power in the group. The comments were not all positive, although offered in a constructive tone. We felt vulnerable, and said so. The feedback was very helpful, and many of the ideas were incorporated into the revised version. That we were willing to be vulnerable, and the trust in the group it implied, seemed to set important markers for our process.

141

The rest of the second meeting was mainly spent going through the data on culture people had generated. Subgroups (the initial base groups) met to put together lists of emerging themes. This material was then discussed in the whole group. The emphasis was on exploration and entertaining 'tentative hypotheses', rather than on pinning down the meaning.

Cycle II: looking again and more widely

Towards the end of the day we planned a further phase of data collection. The group generated a long list of people whose views should be covered. They particularly wanted to include those at the bottom and periphery of the organization, and those in close contact with the public. They did not want a head office, senior management view of the culture to predominate. The question of cynics was addressed. As people took responsibility for contacting different groups, most decided to elicit the views of a possible cynic or two. The list also influenced the next phase of interviews that Adrian and I arranged.

The activity during the following month was impressive in several ways. People innovated in terms of their strategies for exploring culture. Some used workbook formats, adapted to particular audiences, others devised their own approaches. It is interesting how confident members of the group became about inquiring. We wrote: 'We felt that they had a fund of knowledge about how to do research which our presence was helping them to tap' (Marshall and McLean, 1988). A wide range of people, numbering well over a hundred, were contacted in some form or another. This spreading effect belies the image of qualitative research as necessarily small-scale (although there is no inherent fault in the latter). What did happen, however, was that approaches were tailored to the particular group contacted, allowing differences of perspective to speak through clearly.

We met again, for the third day, in June. By now Adrian and I were doing little prior planning. This meeting felt initially more haphazard. As we questioned this we realized that we were experiencing aspects of the Wrekin culture. People there are into action; a catch phrase was 'ready, fire, aim'. The group was feeling impatient to move on and look at implications of the research.

The mirroring of research content in the process

Throughout the inquiry we found that the form of the research mirrored the content (in this project organizational culture) in illuminating ways. For example, the other members of the group were sometimes impatient with questions (Adrian and I) posed about how the research process was going. But as issues became salient they *were* raised. The group returned often to the question of what claims we could make for the portrait we produced, whether it reflected all important parties' views, how sure we could be of the conclusions we drew. These are all key questions about validity. What we learnt was that they arose in their own time, and related to possible action. We found people engaging in *reflection in action* rather than treating these activities as separate. We identified the primacy of action as a key feature of the culture; we therefore paid continual attention to the balance of action and reflection in the research, noticing if action (as the culturally favoured mode) seemed to be taking over.

I think cooperative inquiry will often involve this mirroring of content in research process (it may be apparent in more traditional forms of inquiry too). I have certainly experienced it in other projects. The researchers therefore need to be alert to the possibility and willing to treat aspects of process as 'data' rather than issues for research management. This can offer a certain freedom. The group does not have to work 'correctly'; whatever it does is relevant and needs appropriate attention and respect. This attitude can, however, leave individuals vulnerable and could be an excuse for not addressing conflict. It is not, therefore, a licence for abdicating responsibility.

Cycle II continued: sense-making

Despite our lack of planning, Adrian and I clearly had aims for the day. They were to review the further material collected by group members and move towards an overview of the culture. Other members of the group were initially very reluctant to set aside their previous analyses and look at the new material. They thought nothing significant would emerge. We persisted in this suggestion, working from a commitment to research cycling, expecting that further analysis would generate richer appreciations. Also, the rest of the group were now impatient to hear what ideas we had on the culture. We had all previously treated Adrian and my speculations as equal in worth to those of Wrekin members, but now they wanted to hear from us more clearly. Each sub-group accepted the other's strong insistence. This meant that Adrian and I needed time to pull our ideas together. We repeated the format of the previous meeting. Small groups generated lists of themes and illustrative examples, and then we discussed the material in the whole group.

As I now write about these dynamics, there are obviously expressions of difference. I do not, however, remember these discussions being difficult; rather there was a sense of honest confronting. My main concern was that the ideas Adrian and I generated might seem more important than those of other group members and might become an over-valued reference point. We did not discuss this possibility explicitly, rather I carried it as a prompt to noticing into the next stage of the meeting.

Adrian and I spoke first, but our views were not accorded particular power. The rest of the group were surprised that their new analyses took their understandings of culture further. That day we seemed to be getting to grips with some of the conflicts and paradoxes of the organization's culture; we looked in detail at the shadow side of some of its more impressive characteristics. At the end of the discussion, members of the group questioned, and sought to re-balance, the more negative tone of our conversations. (A key cultural injunction in the Wrekin is 'be positive'.)

Except in this important respect, we did not achieve a synthesis of all our data on the culture. This seemed far too difficult to do in the group at this stage. Adrian and I volunteered to take the available material away and produce a first draft of the case study for discussion. In this we departed from a collaborative ideal, and perhaps tacitly colluded with the group when they attributed us with more expertise than them in this area. We accepted this role, however, only on the understanding that they would discuss the draft fully with us and add further sections themselves if they chose. In retrospect this decision still seems appropriate given differences in past experience, time available and types of commitment to the research.

To close the day the group evaluated the project so far. The Wrekin members were satisfied with the validity of the process and with the power they had been able to exercise, but pointed out that they could not yet judge the product.

Cycle III: drawing the portrait together and communication

The third cycle therefore started out with Adrian and I going in detail through all the sources of data we had and meeting to surface core themes in the culture. We also felt that there were some metaphors appropriate to the Wrekin, ie, that it was like an adolescent and had a right-brain way of acting, which might be worth exploration. We subdivided the writing and produced a draft report.

It is worth noting that we had not seen most of the 'research data', such as interview notes, generated by other members of the group. We did have their flipcharts of emerging themes, and we had taken copious notes of all discussions and examples from our meetings. We felt relatively comfortable with this, but appreciated how much it departed from the traditional researcher image of 'capturing' all the data. The mutual trust involved in proceeding in this way challenges the initiating researchers' needs for control. Part of our sense of security came from having interviewed people ourselves and having lived in the organization over a period of time. We had grounded appreciations of the themes we had discussed in the group on which to draw.

The fourth group meeting took place at Bath University. We wanted to repay some of the Wrekin hospitality. We went page by page through the draft report. This process was less relaxed than previous meetings. The group generally endorsed the cultural portrait we presented, but wanted to clarify and qualify many points and to open up some issues to further debate. They were particular sensitive about any mention of local government political matters. We agreed that Adrian and I would revise the portrait and check it with the group before the presentation of findings scheduled for September. This we did, to the other members' satisfaction. We had identified a web of ten themes in the culture, each with a positive and a potentially degenerative aspect. Achieving this balanced appreciation was important to us all. The Wrekin is an impressive organization in many ways, but it is not without its shadow side.

Adrian and I had initially been sceptical that any organization could live up to such a positive image. As we came to know the Wrekin, we became increasingly impressed by the organization as a whole and by the people we met. We liked and respected them; we felt very 'at home' when there. There was a danger that we would not want to explore the negatives, that we would become acculturated, co-opted. As we felt ourselves aligning with those at the Wrekin, we therefore maintained a critical awareness about this. Seeking distance and detachment would have been a parody of being 'objective'. We preferred to work with our ability to be critically subjective in the midst of the inquiry process.

Adrian and I led the presentation. The whole group was present, and other members spoke to many of the issues in the discussion. We were all pleased with the work we had done. There was a sense of completion, satisfaction, pride and celebration. The feedback was congratulatory, thoughtful and challenging. The Wrekin managers felt that cultural change had been achieved in the last four years, and, characteristically, started posing questions for the future.

Further developments, and an evaluation of outcomes

The culture work in the Wrekin did not stop there. The Culture Club, as they have become known, continue to meet. I hesitate to use the word (as it appears in the volume title, it may be wearing thin), but the group seems 'empowered' through the conceptual and practical languages of culture and research that the inquiry process introduced them to. They negotiate specific projects with the chief executive and directors and pursue them using cycles of inquiry. They then produce frank and challenging reports and presentations. Their role has survived a change of chief executive. The group has deliberately rotated its membership and key roles to maintain its abilities to take fresh perspectives and to stand outside the culture when necessary. Sometimes themes from the original 1987 report prove illuminating. The adolescent metaphor seems particularly to have resonated and lasted. In Spring 1990 the group contacted me again, and I occasionally meet with them to provide an outside perspective to their work. That this process could be sustained is further testimony to its 'fit' with the Wrekin culture.

That is one outcome. The research process paper (Marshall and McLean, 1988) is another. From the feedback we have received, it seems a useful contribution to the literature. Adrian and I have drawn on the resulting portrait of the Wrekin in our training, consultancy and teaching work. Some people in local government were reluctant to hear, yet again, about this much-publicized organization. I have become better at telling the story in inoffensive ways, or raising awareness of the process of rejection. I still use the Wrekin as an example of an open, responsive, largely egalitarian, 'can do' and continually learning organization – also noting that every theme has its potentially degenerative aspect.

The original aim of circulating the Wrekin portrait more widely was never achieved. It often happens that cooperative inquiries generate action and enlightenment and change the lives of participants, but are not as adequately portrayed in writing and publication. The final portrait we produced (McLean and Marshall, 1989), was 91 pages long, and therefore unsuitable for general release as a Local Government Training Board publication. At the time, Adrian and I did not feel able to produce the requested 'slim version' because the richness of the picture seemed irreducible. Then our lives moved on to other projects. The portrait is available, on request, but has not achieved the circulation its model of possible organization really deserves.

I am used to judging this 'project' a success. In writing this chapter, I note with interest that I had not carried major regrets about this lack of dissemination, although I now feel some. The continued living of the inquiry in the Wrekin and in myself has seemed more significant. I notice that wider publication was an initial prime, and contracted, commitment for Adrian and me, which we did not fulfil. Instead we produced a document which has been useful to the Wrekin itself and to some others willing to take an in-depth look at the dynamics of a particular culture. It seems our allegiance had shifted towards the Wrekin and away from our sponsors; it would have been worth questioning this movement more clearly at the time.

In this there is another typical lesson from cooperative inquiry. Groups tend to start out with multiple, diverse, interests. Part of managing the research process is the negotiation of interests, with due attention to issues of power. There are also multiple, often unexpected, outcomes. Sometimes the original 'purpose' of the inquiry, such as writing a PhD thesis, gets left behind in the life-learning people do. Any criteria for 'success' identified in advance may become inappropriate – but reflection on this issue, too, requires critical subjectivity.

References

Heron, J (1981) 'Experiential research methodology', in Reason, P and Rowan, J, op cit.

Heron, J (1988) 'Validity in co-operative inquiry', in Reason, P, op cit.

McLean, A and Marshall, J (1988) *Cultures at Work: How to Identify and Understand Them*, Luton: Local Government Training Board.

McLean, A and Marshall, J (1989) *The Wrekin District Council: A Cultural Portrait*, Luton: Local Government Training Board.

Marshall, J and McLean, A (1988) 'Reflection in action: exploring organizational culture', in Reason, P, op cit.

Reason, P (ed) (1988) *Human Inquiry in Action: Developments in New Paradigm Research*, London: Sage.

Reason, P and Rowan, J (eds) (1981) *Human Inquiry: A Sourcebook of New Paradigm Research*, Chichester: Wiley.

Rowan, J (1981) 'A dialectical paradigm for research', in Reason, P and Rowan, J, op cit.

14 Police Probationer Training: Resistance to Writing as an Aid to Reflection in Experiential Learning

J. A. Bartrop

Seven years after the first major disruptions to inner city peace for many years in England the police service is attempting to steer the training of its police officers towards a more experiential, student-centred approach to learning. This movement has resulted from extensive research and subsequent recommendations made by working parties and review teams (Police Training Council, 1983a; Macdonald *et al*, 1987). The movement does not only relate to police probationer training but is intended to form a developmental training structure throughout the service (Police Training Council, 1983b). This change process is being developed by the staff at the Home Office Police Central Planning and Training Unit, assisted by numerous academic bodies, including the Centre for Applied Research and Education at the University of East Anglia. I have been involved in the process as a change agent.

The training process through which police trainers pass should be a model of the courses which they will eventually teach, and the police trainer's role should now be very much an enabling one. He or she should aim to elicit ideas, perceptions and views from students through a facilitative process, but above all enable them to learn from their policing experiences.

It was just such a course which was going to train me as a change agent and introduced me to the learning how to learn process. My recollections of the precise questions I received during an interview for a place on this course are vague, but one such question remains with me and has caused me some disquiet and due reflection. The question was 'Do you consider yourself a revolutionary person?' My immediate thought was of verbal battles, political causes and whose side will I be on. I saw the situation that police training was in, not as a revolutionary cause, but as needing innovation and an evolutionary process in order that the police service could become a more caring profession which allowed officers to display their true selves rather than a 'John Wayne' facade. As a change agent in an organization traditionally opposed to change, how true I have now found that statement to be, with my newly acquired 'innovatory and evolutionary procedural principles' often being frustrated by verbal battles, political causes and my cognitive dissonance of 'whose side I am on'.

My learning how to learn experience started on 13 January 1986 with a group of 22 police officers on a trainers' directing staff course at the Central Planning and Training Unit. During this course I was blind and insensitive to what was happening in the classroom. I was screaming out for organization: flow charts, diagrams, information, facts and new teaching methods, but the staff were not telling me. They tried to emphasize a shared responsibility for learning, but my colleagues did not seem to be able to help me either. I could not concentrate in the evenings on reading the masses of paper that were handed out, as my previous understanding of learning was to read every document from first to last word. That was a massive block to learning, as were my consistent efforts to 'take flight' from the active learning opportunities offered to me. The eight hours in the classroom were constantly taken up by discussion, but I wanted things my way. I wanted the tutors to give me *their* ideas of what 'the ideal group' was, or tell me of their experiences: how I could use a 'buzz group' or 'brainstorm', or *explain* to me what 'role play' was like. I also had visions of instant change but now realize that it takes time. After all I have learnt through experience all through life, it is only now that I am learning the subtleties.

I am still sceptical about the application of all this in police work. Do they see me as a revolutionist, if so they've still not given me any bullets to fire at instructors. Most of it's talk going above my head and at this stage I can see I'll have to sit down at the end of the course and do my best to translate it. Why can't *they* do that? (Extract from my Course Diary, 27 January 1986).

The group's trainers were often attacked. Attacking the trainer can give the group its first sense of common identity.

Negative feelings, often very strong ones, are aroused. At first they are not expressed because one does not 'talk back to' or correct the teacher, but as tension mounts some bold soul outbursts 'I think we're wasting our time! I think we ought to have an outline and follow it and that you ought to teach us. We came here to learn from you, not to discuss amongst ourselves.' (Rogers, 1951, p 173).

Little was I to know that it would soon be me as a trainer attempting to cope with the same attacks from students.

I wrote many of these frustrations in a diary which was given to me as an option to assist me in understanding the process through which I was going. It is only in hindsight that I can now see how diary-keeping assisted me to learn how to learn; how to interpret and measure the quality of a situation or encounter. The diary assisted me to re-construct what the experience was like at the time. It assisted me to record a personal account of my observations, feelings, reactions, interpretations, reflections, hunches and guesses; just what it was like to be there participating; how I saw others and how they affected my values and judgement. It helped me to keep on target (and find a target at times!) thus developing my self-awareness. The changes were slow for me as a result of this interpersonal skills training and although I kept my scepticism I tried to keep my mind firmly open.

> The first thing I noticed was that everyone had put their chairs back into a formal 'U' formation, waiting for a new part of the course to begin. The tutor spent a while setting out the next 7 days. Some good questions came from the class (I am glad *they* asked them!) which showed their concern as well, but typical of policemen, we all laughed it off – 'Are you going to take my brain out?' and 'It's like waiting to see the dentist' were some of the jibes. I couldn't help feeling this was true because the trainer kept emphasising 'You may not like what's going to happen.' 'You must win them over' seemed to be his philosophy. Fine, he's a pro, but how good will I be at winning them over when I start as a trainer? To do that I'll have to be fully committed but at this stage I am still sceptical. He says you can do it, I'm saying I am not sure. (Diary entry, 23 January 1986).

I have since found this diary to be my greatest evaluative tool during my task as a change agent at district police training centres, force training departments, as a course tutor and now as researcher. It assisted me to cope with the verbal battles (which, of course, were never aimed at being personal!), the political arenas in which I found myself and to realize whose side I was on and that I was aiming at the statement of intent which had been set out by the Police Training Council and the Central Planning and Training Unit:

> The actions of the Police Training Council are ultimately directed towards helping police officers develop the knowledge, understanding, skills and attitudes required to meet the need of policing present and future. (Police Training Council, 1985).

Diaries and introspective projects

Probationer constables are introduced to writing as an aid to reflect on at the commencement of their training. Most of them participate whole-heartedly as positive encouragement from trainers and group reflective sessions give students the opportunity to share the entries they had made with each other. However, as their foundation course progresses, and just when reflection on operational experiences and pressures would be most beneficial, writing as a reflective aid decreases rapidly.

Operational officers often view the diary with cynicism, causing probationers to soon give up the idea.

> Tutor constable: 'When it comes down to the nitty gritty, it doesn't matter what policy is dictated by training. When it comes down here on a Friday night when training staff are all tucked up in bed. You know it's not reflected. You are just throwing men at the holes in the wall. That's what it boils down to really isn't it? The best laid plans. . . . It's like these probationers' red books (diaries) you've got out. They are valueless. On division they are treated as a bit of a joke really'

In an attempt to encourage probationer constables to use writing as an aid to reflection more after they had been involved in operational incidents, my action research motivated me to task probationers with a project on 'Barriers to communication', which aided the reflective process. This project asked officers to prepare an assignment identifying the barriers to communication which they had experienced between themselves as police officers and members of the public or other police officers with whom they had contact. The assignment was based on their own practical experiences rather than being a reproduction of the theories of communication. To gain the maximum benefit from their experiences, the need to reflect on what had happened was emphasized, this being an integral part of the learning process. They were encouraged to keep notes, diaries or portfolios, recording their experiences together with their own thoughts and feelings and including examples, stating why, in their own judgement, the various problems arose.

This is having a more beneficial effect on the reflective process, as this policewoman points out after submission of her project on her experiences of policing an inner city council housing estate:

> I am not sure what other people would gain from reading this piece of work, for as I stated in the title, it is entirely introspective; each section's conclusions being for my own benefit – to give myself a better understanding of what went wrong and why, of what barriers existed and how I could surmount them. (Pearce, 1989, p 30).

Yet reflective projects, in a hierarchical and accountable service, have many pitfalls which can demoralize the student. This student centred hers on women prisoners, which entailed her making many visits to the custody suite:

> I found that my study was very difficult to do, as the PCs were suspicious of my motives, just as much as the prisoners. The prisoners who did want to help thought it

was a good idea and something that could be looked into. There were a lot more weaknesses; one was the lack of the prisoners in while I was on duty, even if there were prisoners in custody you could not always get in to talk to them. If the custody suite was busy, they did not want any more staff down there getting in the way of the few who were working. Some prisoners were worried that if they talked to me it would hold up their release.

My last problem was that complaints (the Complaints & Discipline Dept.) kept appearing and because my number kept appearing on the custody sheet I was being asked to give a statement about what had happened, most of the time I did not know what had gone off (Diaper, 1989, p 27).

Probationers' entry into the behavioural world of police 'canteen culture' with its 'real' values and norms, which can also mean exclusion, will constitute a great personal challenge to them and an even greater personal challenge to those who advocate a different set of values from those which the organization seeks to instil. It has been recognized that officers of high rank must now acknowledge a new training philosophy and decide which set of values they will endorse and which set of values they will actively discourage (Shepherd, 1984, p 299). In order to work their way through this minefield, probationer constables will need every aid to reflective and critical thought; diaries and introspective projects are a sound basis from which to start.

So how do we overcome the resistance of police officers to the keeping of diaries or portfolios as an aid to reflecting on their experiences during training? Do we need to overcome resistance, or is this part of their learning process?

Adult learners are renowned for wanting activity, instant success, and relevance of any learning to the work they are currently involved in. If this is so then surely they learn more effectively by keeping reflective notes. How do trainers encourage them to do so? This is the conundrum.

References

Diaper, N (1989) 'Women prisoners', Barriers to communication project, Leicestershire Constabulary Training Dept, unpublished.

Macdonald, B et al, (1986) Final Report of the Stage II Review of Police Probationer Training, London: HMSO.

Pearce, C E (1989) 'Taming the beastmaster': A policewoman's account of policing the Braunstone Estate, Barriers to communication project, Leicestershire Constabulary Training Dept, unpublished.

Police Training Council (1983a) 'Police probationer training working party report', unpublished.

Police Training Council (1983b) 'Supervision and management working party report', unpublished.

Police Training Council (1985) Police training strategy document, unpublished.

Rogers, C R (1951) Client-Centred Therapy, Boston: Houghton Mifflin.

Shepherd, E (1984) 'Values into practice: the implementation and implications of human awareness training for the police, Police Journal, LVII, p 286.

Learning to Learn

This section focuses on experiential learning processes from a variety of different perspectives.

Richards draws on the adventures of Ulysses for his model of the experiential learning cycle. Boud and Walker describe how their model of experiential learning evolved over the years and identify further avenues for development. Knights focuses on the development of reflective processes, while Mulligan explores the function of seven internal processors in experiential learning. Henry highlights similarities between the development of creative capability and experiential learning. Hooper-Hansen gives an overview of an accelerated learning process called 'Suggestopedia'.

Papers in Section 5 have considerable relevance to this theme and also Bartrop (Chapter 14) and Marshall (Chapter 13) in Section 3, Hull (Chapter 11) in Section 2, Ranjan (Chapter 6), Mak (Chapter 3) and Saddington (Chapter 2) in Section 1.

15 Adventure-based Experiential Learning

Anthony Richards

Introduction

Experiential education appears to be a 'throw back' (Coleman, 1974). Since the beginning of time humans have learned through direct experience, particularly during early childhood when much of the skill developed seems to be based on trial and error. However, as the amount of knowledge has increased exponentially, it has become too time-consuming to learn from first-principles every time and even impossible to learn everything. The education system or schooling has become selective in what is taught, and more important, has become selective in how it is taught. In the name of efficiency schools have evolved to become buildings that house several hundred children with 35–40 in each room. Each of these rooms has one adult teacher and rows of desks. The content is divided into 40-minute segments. The learning is evaluated by tests which measure the ability to regurgitate what the teacher says and thinks. It may be that the physical structure of the school buildings may have to be challenged.

It is not the purpose of this chapter to put down the evolution of the school system, which has become preoccupied with the acquisition of knowledge, but rather to look at the roots of learning through direct experience, the advantages of learning experientially and the outcomes of this kind of learning. If there is such a thing as an experiential education movement it would probably trace its roots back to Rousseau's *Emile* or the Progressive Movement of the 1930s in North America. More recently it has become fashionable to analyse the role of experience in learning because of the failure of contemporary schools to meet the needs of large segments of the youth. In North America the percentage of drop-outs, push outs, and alienated youth is increasing, particularly in urban centres (Kraft, 1988).

So many of the reports on education have recommended changes. The problem is that most of these changes have been cosmetic rather than systemic. Still the acquisition of knowledge is paramount because it provides the best predictor for completion of university education. The school curriculum is designed and delivered based on university preparation not preparation for active living in the real world, even though 50 per cent of the population do not attend university.

Of course the debate will go on as to the merits of education for life or education for more education. Most of the decisions will be based on political whim and the relative success American children have with their Japanese counterparts. President Reagan's National Commission on Excellence in Education entitled *A Nation at Risk* (1983) was myopic in its recommendations. In order to improve it suggested more homework, longer school days and an extended school year. Unfortunately more of the same does not guarantee a better product. John Goodlad (1983) advocates less teacher talk and more hands-on experience. He also dispels the myth that more contact hours produce better results. Whether the 'back to basics' movement or experiential learning methods will prevail is hard to predict. However, what is certain is that the power of learning through direct experience is significant, provided that the process teaches young people how to learn rather than concentrating on the assimilation and re-presentation of facts.

John Dewey (1938) reduces the philosophy of experiential education into rather simple concepts. These have been followed by many who have developed the ideas into a workable system of experiential learning. Dewey claims that there is an organic connection between education and personal experience. However, he does not equate experience and education. This is fundamental to the notion of experiential learning. The teacher must help the learner make the connections. Unless the principles of continuity and interaction are carefully facilitated an experience may be considered to be mis-educative. By continuity Dewey means that there is an experiential continuum. The other dimension of interaction refers to the teacher making the student aware of his/her immediate environment; in other words, taking the learning outside of the classroom both physically and metaphorically.

The focus of control for what is learned has shifted from the learner to the examination board, the curriculum supervisor or the teacher. This is not to suggest that these people do not have a vital role to play in the process, but the learner must have ownership of his/her own learning. Direct experience will help to facilitate this process. Thus, in the 1990s it will become more important to learn experientially so that the relevance of what is learned becomes apparent in adapting to a rapidly changing society, and there is an ability to live and function in today's world. Finally, there is the belief that young people should be educated in such a manner as to maximize their personal development in the context of others. It is this last phrase, 'in the context of others', which sets experiential learning apart from the solitary learning in the more traditional contexts.

In the 1930s Kurt Hahn was asked to put on a compelling demonstration of the Salem method of education which he developed in Germany, based on the need to prepare boys to be active citizens. He did this by creating Gordonstoun School. The methodologies and techniques that he used to deliver this form of education were considered weird at best. However, his basic philosophy was simple and quite effective. Even though, at first glance, Gordonstoun School is perceived as élitist, Hahn was always striving to include the local people from the town of Elgin. He promoted service to others as being paramount in a young person's education, and the measurement and evaluation of academic content was secondary to the evaluation of the student's growth in areas of self-discipline, fitness, enterprise, tenacity, sense of justice, ability to deal with the unexpected, manual dexterity, etc.

Hahn's philosophy of education paralleled that of John Dewey but there was never any recognition by either man that the other existed. The creation by Hahn of the Outward Bound movement in 1941 was intended to promote his education philosophy and make it much more accessible to working-class boys in England. Whereas the Outward Bound schools were moderately successful they were used for ends that were not perceived as educational but more closely aligned with training. In fact it was the beginning of the 'character training industry' in England (Roberts et al, 1974).

In 1962 the first American Outward Bound school was established in Marble, Colorado. With the transfer across the Atlantic of instructors and British methodology, the American Outward Bound was destined to fail. There was a much different environment, let alone different culture in the United States. Partly due to the lack of residential facilities and partly due to American arrogance, the Outward Bound standard course was changed to become a mobile 28-day course. In retrospect it has been seen that the basic Outward Bound curriculum and Hahn's philosophy were robust enough to handle the transatlantic crossing and the subsequent drastic reshaping of the programme. In many ways the advantage the American school had was that the education philosophy of the programme was reduced to its essentials and rebuilt into a very unique American Outward Bound process. This process has been analysed and described in many forms but essentially it has formed the basis of a philosophy of education in North America known as adventure-based experiential learning. The Outward Bound programme has been copied, adapted and moulded to fit a variety of clients and settings. There are courses for delinquents, drop-outs, substance abusers, women in mid-life crises and sex-offending priests, to name a few. This chapter will not dwell on programmes for these 'special populations' but rather consider the generic model or paradigm which has emerged and can be applied to many mainstream educational settings.

Adventure-based experiential learning model

By implication the term 'adventure' separates this philosophy of learning from many other forms. However, most forms of experiential education may have an element of adventure without deliberate intention. The model described here has as its basis one of the earliest adventurers, namely Ulysses. It is this story which depicts a man of action who is continually driven to seek out new adventures. With each encounter he learned new things which he used as experience to create and handle new adventures. The spirit of adventure is generated with a desire or a drive to experience that which is hidden or unknown (Dufrenne, 1973). Ulysses was empowered by the discoveries resulting from his new experiences and the challenge of the elements. He went further than the physical objective nature of these challenges and experienced spiritual, emotional and intellectual spheres of personhood (Quinn, 1988).

By analysing the stories of Ulysses a pattern emerges which seems to be transferable to a number of adventure settings. When this pattern is applied to the process of learning it helps to describe not only the experiential learning process but a unique form of experiential learning, namely adventure-based experiential learning.

There are four distinct phases in this cyclical process: *separation, encounter, return* and *reincorporation* (see Figure 15.1). It is important that all four of these phases occur otherwise the process is incomplete and does

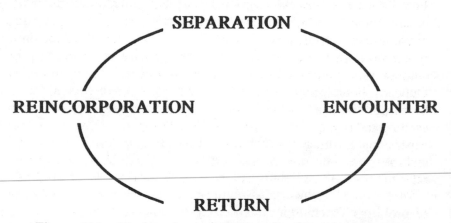

Figure 15.1 *The four phases of adventure-based experiential learning*

not provide the continuity that Dewey deemed so important. The time devoted to each of these phases varied and no ratio of times emerges in the model. In fact Ulysses spent several years in the encounter phase and relatively short periods of time in the separation phase. The appropriate duration for each phase will become more evident when the model is applied to generic educational settings.

Separation

When planning an expedition or trip there is considerable preparation for leaving the comfort and security of home as well as the leaving behind of loved ones and friends. In the education context it is necessary to be willing to leave behind old ideas, experiment with new ones and generally be open-minded. This is what Plato may have referred to as taking the lid off to allow the vessel to receive the knowledge. Unless the learner is willing to shift there is very little that the teacher can do. However, a good teacher will also be a skilful motivator and challenger. In adventure-based experiential learning it is important to be able to prepare the learner and the environment so that learning has a chance. In the description of the Outward Bound process by Walsh and Golins (1976) it was assumed that by placing the learner in a unique physical environment and a unique social environment, the 'separation' phase would be complete. However, when adventure-based experiential learning is applied to more generic settings than the wilderness or mountains, a greater challenge is posed; how do young learners prepare themselves for learning through a new challenge?

Encounter

Once the learner has willingly separated him/herself from the comfort of convenience and tradition, the activity or events can usefully take place. For Ulysses these were the great battles and the adventure of surviving the oceans' tempests while clinging to pieces of his wrecked ship. Physical challenges of this sort form the bread and butter of an Outward Bound programme; they are certainly the most photogenic aspect. In fact, without photographs of rock climbers, sailors and river rafters, the Outward Bound organization would be hard pressed to produce a brochure! There is little doubt that this phase of the process is the most exciting and engages the learner fully. The limitation in adventure-based experiential learning is that the encounter phase may be the only phase and the educational opportunity is diminished, if not lost. Dewey would refer to the preoccupation with adventure activities as mis-educative.

In the more formal setting the encounter phase is comprised of a series of problems which have to be solved. It is the challenge of solving problems and the concomitant uncertainty of outcome which creates the adventure. Therefore, presenting a library/research assignment which is designed for maximum discovery of new facts rather than verification of the teacher's already presented ones, can be an adventure. Some basic principles are necessary when creating the problems/adventures which need to be solved: ownership of the solution must rest with the learner; each problem should include some of the following characteristics: they must be organized and prescriptive, incremental and progressive, concrete and recognizable, manageable and solvable, consequential and worthwhile, and holistic.

Naturally, when creating adventurous situations and experiences there is an element of risk. Planning a first ascent of a mountain involves many unknowns and dangers. Most educators would not wish to risk the physical or emotional well-being of the learner. However, it is possible to create situations where the perceived risk is high but the real risk is eliminated. This form of risk management is essential to the successful creation of adventure-based experiential learning programmes. However, the ethical issue arises as to how much information the educator withholds for the sake of maintaining the perception of risk.

Another aspect of encountering the challenge is that the learner, through successful problem-solving, develops a sense of mastery. This is done by honing the coping skills and the relationship issues which occur when working in small groups. Whereas there is a guarantee of some level of personal development, the fact that it is achieved in the context of others places it squarely in the arena of adventure-based experiential learning.

Return

Joe Nold (1978) referred to an adventure being incomplete without the telling. Adventures come to life when retold to friends, written up in books or journals, or even when reflected upon by the adventurer. When Kurt Hahn asked a boy if he enjoyed the sailing trip from which he had just returned, the boy responded, 'Yes sir, but not at the time'.

It is the ability to reflect and consolidate the experience that makes the learning have meaning and appear to be relevant. The Outward Bound model includes processing or debriefing time for each activity. In addition there is a two- or three-day 'solo'. It is at this time that the student is able to reflect, consolidate and begin to make connections between the metaphors of the wilderness and life back home. In the school setting there is seldom time for children to be alone, least of all an expectation to reflect on experience.

Reincorporation

This is the phase which permits and leads the adventurer to pursue the next challenge or adventure. Ulysses spent little time on the 'return' phase recalling all his experiences to his wife Penelope. Much to her chagrin he would start talking of his next adventure before retelling the previous one. The Outward Bound programme is least effective in this stage. When Hahn was developing the programme he always tried to promote a 'follow up' to the four-week experience. Both time and money prevented this and it was hoped that the student would be sufficiently empowered by the process to reincorporate the metaphors into his/her life without special programming. The value of employing adventure-based experiential learning in the school setting is that there is often more time available to ensure that the reincorporation is occurring. That is, having successfully completed one adventure in learning, the student will be motivated to take on another challenge independently and use previous experiences to stimulate new ones.

The simplicity of this model permits it to be used in a variety of settings. It may be applied to a senior citizen macramé course, executive training, a canoe trip for youth or learning in a school setting. The principle is simple but the level of empowerment that is created for the learner is more complex. Whenever the learner has ownership or control of his/her learning there is a level of personal efficacy which does not seem to be present in the traditional learning environments. There is a greater chance of developing active citizens if the youth are empowered to feel that they can indeed make a difference. Through adventure-based experiential learning, which encourages personal development in the context of others, there is hope that young people will indeed be prepared to cope with the complex life of the next century. More important, they will feel confident and competent enough to be an active participant in that future.

References

Coleman, J S (1974) *Youth Transition to Adulthood*, Chicago: The University of Chicago Press.

Dewey, J (1938) *Experience and Education*, New York: Collier Books.

Dufrenne, M (1973) *The Phenomenology of Aesthetic Experiences*, Evanston: North Western University Press.

Goodlad, J (1983) *A Place Called School: Prospects for the Future*, New York and London: McGraw-Hill.

Hahn, K (1947) 'Training for and through the sea', address to the Honourable Mariners Company, Glasgow, February 20.

Kraft, R (1988) *Journal of the Association for Teacher Educators*, vol X, no 2, 38–41.

Nold, J (1977) 'Man the adventurer', unpublished paper presented at Outward Bound Inc. Seminar, Colorado, USA.

Richards, A (1984) 'There is a little of Ulysses in all of us', *Recreation Canada*.

Roberts, K, White, G E and Packer, H J (1974) *The Character Training Industry: Adventure Training in Britain*, Newton Abbot: David & Charles.

Quinn, W J (1987) 'The essence of adventure', presented at Association of Experiential Education Conference, Carbondale, Illinois. Unpublished.

US National Commission on Excellence in Education (1983) *A Nation at Risk*, Portland: USA Research Inc.
Walsh, V and Golins, G (1976) *The Exploration of the Outward Bound Process*, Denver, Col: Colorado Outward Bound.

16 In the Midst of Experience: Developing a Model to Aid Learners and Facilitators

David Boud and David Walker

Introduction

For many years we have both been involved in the design and conduct of learning activities in both formal award courses and in informal personal and professional settings. We are both committed to respecting and utilizing the experience of participants in order to move learning beyond the superficial. Even cognitive learning is severely restricted when no account is taken of the person – the learner. Although our backgrounds are very different, we have been struck by the similarity of issues with which we have been faced. Together with colleagues in the Australian Consortium on Experiential Education (ACEE), we have been trying to make sense of the messy reality which we face when we attempt to assist others to learn from experience. In this process we are confronted with the need not only to closely observe the learning of others, but also to take account of our own learning. Our purpose is to ensure that the conclusions we draw apply both to others and to ourselves.

In this chapter we outline some of the stages of our development during the past seven years and describe the main features of the models we have been evolving. The process has been one of progressive focusing and refinement to flesh out our hunches about what is important. In the final section we focus on those elements which require further elaboration to produce a more comprehensive model of facilitating learning from experience. While we have attempted to incorporate our understanding of the processes of learning from experience, the outcomes are still tentative and open for exploration. The models have the status of pragmatic frameworks which have value only insofar as they focus the attention of learners and facilitators on key elements of their own learning. They take on greater value when they are linked to particular contexts and practices.

We are not assuming that the elements of the models represent some external reality, nor that they purport to describe actual processes of learning; these processes are in general inaccessible to us. If the framework prompts learners to more fully engage with their own experience, and find value in working with this experience, our approach is successful. In describing the stages of our own understanding we are attempting to explain the progressive refinements of a framework for prompting reflection. Our description encompasses those elements with which we have become aware.

A first approximation

Over a period of several years, together with other members of the ACEE, we had been looking at ways of increasing the effectiveness of our own practice as facilitators of learning. While we explored a rich array of methods and techniques, which are informed by a variety of theoretical frameworks, we wanted to move beyond the particular. Our goal has been to examine the central features of learning from experience which operate in most learning situations. We took reflection by the learner on his or her own experience to be the central focus in learning from experience. The question we posed ourselves was: what are the key elements in encouraging reflection following a learning activity? In other words, if a learner was to direct his or her energies to some features of the experience, which would be, in general, the most fruitful?

Our view was that there were three clusters of reflective activity which might prove productive: returning to the experience – recalling and recapturing the experience in as much detail and richness as possible; attending to feelings – building on and utilizing good feelings about the experience and surfacing and dealing with negative feelings; and re-evaluating the experience – relating what has become known to what is already known, integrating new knowledge with old, mentally testing our understandings in new contexts and making the knowledge gained our own (Boud *et al*, 1985). These three clusters represented a shorthand description for what can be quite complex and demanding activities. Many different types of activity may be involved: writing, expression of feelings, creative responses in many other modes, are all ways in which learners can gain insights and enhance their learning through reflection. These activities might be solitary, or one-to-one or involve groups of people. We did not wish to imply any necessary link between any one of these elements and any particular learning outcome; indeed, what is counted as a positive outcome may itself be problematic, and the outcomes might vary markedly from individual to individual.

A second approximation

Reflection after the event is not enough. Clearly, reflection following experience is valued by many learners. We have had much positive reaction in our own teaching to the introduction of reflective activities such as the keeping of learning portfolios, debriefing sessions, guided reflection and periods of quiet contemplation following experience-based classroom activities. However, while we were satisfied that our first approximation had captured something important, there remained too many loose ends and matters which we believed needed further development. On the one hand, we were questioned for not giving sufficient emphasis to critical reflection, the questioning of taken-for-granted assumptions, or the entire socio-cultural-politico-complex which influences experience (by implication even in our own volume, cf. Kemmis, 1985). We saw some validity in this as we had not explored these themes. However, we believed our model did not deny them nor inhibited the incorporation of this perspective into subsequent revisions. On the other hand, we were only too aware that at the simplest level we had not taken sufficient account of what precedes any given experience. What the learner brings with them to any event powerfully shapes and impacts on what they experience. Also, what the learner does to guide and influence the events in which they are involved contributes greatly to their learning. In general, the more actively engaged (though not necessarily overtly engaged), the greater the likelihood that the event can be a significant experience. Our next attempt over the past two to three years took the chronological stages of learning (preparation for the experience, the experience itself and subsequent reflection) and focused on what might helpfully be considered within each. The two additional elements, preparation and reflection-in-action are discussed below (see Figure 16.1 from Boud and Walker, 1991).

Preparation

Our assumption now is that greater use can be made of learning events if learners prepare beforehand. This preparation needs to focus on learners themselves, the nature of the event and what learners can do to utilize the potential of what is available to them. The elements to be considered in preparation include: Focusing on the personal, what learners bring to the event, what they want from it. Focusing on the context, what constraints and opportunities does the event provide. Focusing on learning strategies, how learners can get what they need from the given situation.

During the later phase of development of the model, we were continually confronted with the folly of underestimating the importance of the knowledge and experience which each learner brings with them to

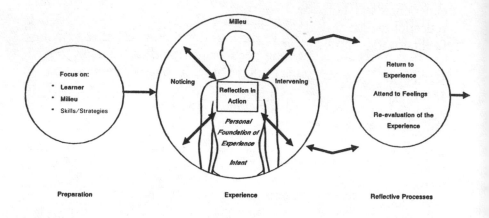

Figure 16.1

an event. The influence of what we termed the 'personal foundation of experience' is all-pervasive. The fact that different learners bring with them massively different prior experiences, even when apparently they might have a similar background, influences the knowledge which they can be assumed to have. It also profoundly shapes their entire approach to the enterprise of learning and their specific perceptions and interactions in any given event. When we are dealing with groups of learners, whose members may have widely different social, cultural and political assumptions, it becomes ludicrous to imagine that facilitators can be fully effective without taking account of these differences in their plans and the way they debrief activities. Learners bring with them 'intent', which may or may not be able to be articulated, and which influences their approach to the event. That is, they make assumptions about the possibilities inherent in the event, often with very little knowledge of what specifically they might be expected to do. This 'intent' can be such that it entirely cuts across the purpose of those who have planned the event. The result of such mismatches of intent and purpose can be behaviour which is perceived by either party as negative, disruptive or counter-productive. Recognition of learners' intent means that it is rarely possible to set up experiential learning events without either a good understanding of the nature of the participants or at least the opportunity for participants to influence, in ways meaningful to themselves, the nature of the activity. Acknowledgement of learners' (and facilitators') personal foundations of experience and both sets of intents, promotes critical approaches to reflection which take the actions and assumptions of both learner and facilitator to be problematic.

Reflection-in-action

In any experience there is a natural process taking place within the learner in which what is being taken in is processed, affects the learner and can provide the basis for action. It is possible to heighten awareness of this process so that the learner becomes more conscious of it and deliberately works with it to enter more fully into the experience to enhance the learning which comes from it. Schön (1983) uses the term reflection-in-action to describe what practitioners do while they are engaged in practice to monitor and adjust their own performance. Effective practitioners are characterized by their ability to utilize knowledge of the situation and ways of learning from it to improve their practice. We shared Schön's view of the importance of this concept and tried to build a consideration of reflection into the experience itself. However, this is much more challenging than it might at first appear. There is a fundamental tension between becoming fully immersed in an event and standing back to witness our own actions. The former is required if we are to be a full player in the event; the latter is implicit in the concept of reflection. We played with the idea of thinking of the interstices of experience using the analogy of the interstices of a crystal, the parts between the arrays of molecules. In this model reflection occurs within the interstices of experience. While this can be a helpful image, we cannot pretend that experience is not seamless. We experience as we reflect and we reflect as we experience. Nevertheless those elements which we had originally thought of as applying to post-event reflection also seem relevant within the event.

In practice, there are many opportunities for reflection within planned learning activities. Natural breaks in the flow of events, time-out activities, and exercises of a reflective nature can all be scheduled as part of the overall structure. However, when the event is poorly designed – or has not been planned specifically for learning, as for example in much clinical experience – learners have to develop their own strategies to incorporate reflection, often covertly, during the activity. In the context of many learning programmes it is possible to brief the learners on the value and means to do so. The reflective process, whether specifically catered for or not in the design of the activity, can be aided by assisting the learner to explicitly consider two key elements. We labelled these 'noticing' and 'intervening' (Boud and Walker, 1990). 'Noticing' is the act of learners becoming aware of what is happening in and around themselves. 'Intervening' is action taken by learners within the event which can affect the learning milieu or learners themselves (including learners acting on themselves). While there has been much discussion of perception and intervention in interpersonal situations (eg, Hargie *et al*, 1987; Heron, 1989), we believe that these notions can be broadened to describe sets of intentions and behaviour applicable to any context. 'Noticing', for example, can refer to the learner becoming aware of and noting any feature of the learning milieu and 'intervening' to any act in which the learner might engage, related to people or objects, which seeks to influence what is occurring. Noticing the outcomes of the intervention and planning further intervention completes the cycle of reflection-in-action.

Where to from here?

Our second approximation had broadened our appreciation of the role of reflection in learning from experience. We now encompass reflection in the midst of experience and the foundations on which learning builds. There remains much to be considered. While there is informal use of our approaches, as yet only one application is known to us in a research context – in pre- and post-clinical conferences in nursing practice (Chuaprapaisilp, 1989). Unfortunately, there is generally little tradition of research on experiential learning.

Clearly, there is the need to test our framework in a variety of settings. This needs to occur at three levels. First, there is the issue of whether a framework of this kind is of value to learners and facilitators and, if it is, how it is useful. Our own experience and that of colleagues suggests that such frameworks can be helpful at least to the extent that devices such as the Kolb/Lewin learning cycle (Kolb, 1984) have pragmatic value to teachers and learners.

Second, there is the need for refinement to suit different learners and circumstances. We suspect that modifications to suit particular contexts are needed to extract the most from this way of viewing experiential learning. For example, in the debriefing of groups, the stages of reflection are commonly translated into the three simple questions: What happened? What did I feel? What does it mean? While these phrases do not represent exactly the same range of ideas as are encompassed in our three phases of returning to experience, attending to feelings and re-evaluating experience, they can be more useful prompts at the time, and can lead into more intensive reflection processes.

Third, there is a need for a project to examine the actual experiences of learners in a systematic fashion to determine how an appreciation of the processes of learning can alter such a framework and take our understanding further. This is a major undertaking, but one which must be confronted by those of us who are concerned about developing a research base for experiential learning.

Acknowledgement

We wish to thank Elizabeth Leigh for helpful comments on an earlier version of this chapter.

References

Boud, D J, Keogh, R and Walker, D (1985) 'Promoting reflection in learning: a model', in Boud, D J, Keogh, R and Walker, D (eds) *Reflection: Turning Experience into Learning*, London: Kogan Page.

Boud, D J and Walker, D (1990) 'Making the most of experience', *Studies in Continuing Education*, 12, 2, 61–80.

Boud, D J and Walker, D (1991) *Experience and Learning: Reflection at Work*, Geelong: Deakin University Press.

Chuaprapaisilp, A. (1989) 'Improving learning from experience through the conduct of pre- and post-clinical conferences: action research in nursing education in Thailand', PhD thesis, School of Medical Education, University of New South Wales.

Hargie, O, Saunders, C and Dickson, D (1987) *Social Skills in Interpersonal Communication*, 2nd edn, Beckenham: Croom Helm.

Heron, J (1989) *The Facilitators' Handbook*, London: Kogan Page.

Kemmis, S (1985) 'Action research and the politics of reflection', in Boud, D J, Keogh, R and Walker, D (eds) *Reflection: Turning Experience into Learning*, London: Kogan Page.

Kolb, D A (1984) *Experiential Learning*, Englewood Cliffs, NJ: Prentice-Hall.

Schön, D A (1983) *The Reflective Practitioner*, New York: Basic Books.

17 Reflection and Empowerment in the Professional Development of Adult Educators

Susan Knights

Background

My work as a lecturer in the School of Community and Aboriginal Education involves teaching on academic programmes from undergraduate diploma to Masters level. All our students are working in some way with adult learners, either in formal classes or in the context of community organizations and projects where there may not be formal classes but adult learning is definitely taking place and is essential to achieving the aims of the organization. Many of our students, particularly the Aboriginal students, see their role as educators as one of empowering the adults they work with to take action to improve their situation in the world.

I do not find the concept of empowerment straightforward and I am uncomfortable about the implication of inequality implied by the idea of one person 'empowering' another. Nevertheless I have to admit that I would like the outcome of all our programmes to be adult education practitioners who are aware of their own personal power, free of self-imposed constraints and confident about taking action in the world. Empowerment seems a reasonable way of describing the process of achieving this.

The acquisition of knowledge and skills such as those required to organize and facilitate a workshop or present a public lecture clearly plays a significant role in enabling our students to enhance their confidence in practice. The knowledge and skills aspects of professional development have always been recognized as important. It is only more recently, particularly perhaps since the publication of Donald Schön's *The*

Reflective Practitioner (1983) that reflection has been recognized as an important component of professional practice.

Reflection in professional practice

Lee Shulman has described the way in which teachers use reflection as part of their pedagogic process:

> This is what a teacher does when he or she looks back at the teaching and learning that has occurred, and reconstructs, re-enacts and recaptures the events, the emotions, and the accomplishments. It is that set of processes through which a professional learns from experience. It can be done solely or in concert, with the help of recording devices or solely through memory. . . . Central to this process will be a review of the teaching in comparison to the ends that were sought. (Shulman, 1987, p 19).

Boud *et al* (1985) see reflection as having three components: returning to the experience (what happened?), acknowledging and dealing with feelings (how do I feel?) and thinking through the implications (what does it mean?). Both Shulman and Boud *et al* place reflection as something happening after the event. Schön is interested in the way different professionals act and reflect in action. He challenges the assumption that professional practice involves only the application of relevant technical knowledge to clearly defined problems, 'the situations of practice are not problems to be solved but problematic situations characterised by uncertainty, disorder and indeterminacy' (Schön, 1983, p 50). In order to make sense of these problematic situations practitioners use a process Schön calls reflection-in-action:

> Stimulated by surprise, they turn thought back on action. . . . It is this entire process of reflection-in-action which is central to the 'art' by which practitioners sometimes deal well with situations of uncertainty, instability, uniqueness and value conflict (Schön, 1983, p 50).

Reflection is clearly an important part of professional practice but it is also important as part of the learning process. As adult educators we espouse the idea of praxis, balancing action with reflection and often make reference to Kurt Lewin's model of the learning cycle. However, we seem to assume that the reflection and abstract conceptualization parts of the cycle are things that will take care of themselves, presumably in the learner's own time. Since, in the programmes I am involved with, we only admit students who are already working in adult education, the majority on a full-time basis, and who are all mature adults which usually means they have family responsibilities, the likelihood of their finding time for reflection unassisted is extremely low. Therefore, it seems to me, we need to address it and provide for it explicitly in our courses.

Including reflection in academic programmes

For the last five years I have been experimenting with different ways of encouraging students to take time for reflection. I now teach a one-semester course in the undergraduate diploma programme called 'The reflective practitioner', but in other courses related to teaching and learning I also emphasize the importance of reflection.

First of all there is the need to introduce students to the idea of reflection using the kinds of descriptions given by people like Boud *et al*, Schön and Shulman and inviting them to share their own perceptions of what reflection involves. This is a stage I tended to neglect or gloss over far too quickly when I began to try to introduce reflection as a process. I tended to move on to the 'how' and did not spend enough time on the 'what' or the 'why'. So, even when addressing the concept of reflection, I fell into the trap of not allowing sufficient time for learners to mull over and consider the ideas in the light of their own experience and understanding! Now I try to slow down and spend a reasonable amount of time introducing the idea and giving students time to reflect on it.

In terms of understanding the value of reflection, Schon's metaphor of the hard high ground of technical rationality and the swamp of real life practice seems to be particularly helpful and reassuring to our students. Since adult education is what Darkenwald and Merriam (1982) have called an 'adventitious' profession, something people usually fall into by accident rather than design, we are very familiar with the feeling of making it up as we go along, thinking on our feet, living with and through situations of uncertainty, instability, uniqueness and value conflict; in other words the swamp of everyday practice. We tend to feel, however, that *real* professionals are up there, on the hard high ground operating according to research-based technical knowledge, solving well-defined problems with elegance and ease. Stephen Brookfield has written about the prevalence of the impostor syndrome among adult students he interviewed: 'This feeling of being undeserving impostors who will sooner or later have their real, pathetically inadequate identities revealed is remarkably consistent' (Brookfield, 1991).

So it is immediately reassuring for practitioners who are undertaking academic programmes in adult education to hear that technical expertise and logical problem-solving techniques are by no means the whole story as far as good practice is concerned. Their survival so far has not been a lucky accident and, in this learning situation at least, no one is out to unmask them as impostors. Introducing reflection in action as a necessary skill which they are already using in their day-to-day practice gives it a firm basis in reality.

Moving from reflection in action to the more traditional reflection after the event, I see the journal or diary as an important tool. In some of our programmes students are asked to keep a journal which they write up at least once a week and in which they are asked to reflect on the course, their work and the connections they see between them. Making time to write a diary is not easy, even for those totally committed to the idea, so in the adult learning and programme development course for Masters students this year I kept five minutes at the end of each class for written reflection. This had a particular focus as I explained that their experience as learners in that course could provide important information to complement the input about adult learning they were receiving from me, from the literature and from discussion with other students. To ignore this first-hand experience and rely only on other people's theories would be foolish, so I present the writing of reflections at the end of each class as a way, in the words of the title of Boud *et al*'s (1985) book, of 'turning experience into learning'.

I also kept a journal and would write in it at the same time as the students. At the beginning of next week's class I would ask if anyone had anything they would like to share from last week's journal. Sometimes I would read from mine, especially if no other offers were forthcoming. After a few weeks where only one or two, often the same one or two, spoke, I remembered the value of a listener in assisting reflection and we then started each class with five minutes in pairs sharing reflections from the previous week. This led to a more vigorous general discussion, as I would have expected from the loosening up in the one-to-one discussion, but even if this had not been the case, the one-to-one time meant that everyone had the opportunity at the beginning of the class to reflect upon their experience the previous week and the implications of this for general theories about adult learning.

Providing the opportunity for verbal reflection is one of the reasons we have introduced tutorless study groups into our undergraduate diploma programme. These groups meet for one hour every other week throughout the two years of the course and are meant to provide an opportunity for support and self-help from student to student. Sometimes the focus is on information sharing but at other times people simply take the opportunity to 'think out loud' about issues connected with the course or their work.

Another way in which students are encouraged to think aloud about their work and their studies is in discussion with their academic adviser either following a teaching observation in their workplace or in discussing possible learning contracts. Learning contracts themselves may be based on the keeping of a journal, for example where a student wants to keep track of what is going on in a particular group they are working with or in a relationship with a colleague, supervisor or student. The contract might be to keep a diary over a period of time, re-read it and discuss the implications, develop and test out strategies to change the situation and record and reflect on what happens. The criteria for assessment, negotiated in advance, would include not only the effectiveness of the strategies but also the ability to record and learn from experience. Problems in the area of time management have often been dealt with effectively through the keeping of a journal.

Journals, study groups, one-to-one reflection and tutorial discussions are activities that can be used in any kind of course to promote reflection and consolidate learning. In the reflective practitioner course I have a whole semester of weekly two-hour classes in which to focus on the place of reflection in the practice of adult education. The purpose of the course is to develop skills of self-monitoring and self-assessment, awareness of hidden agendas and a critical questioning approach to practice and at the same time to develop the skill of assisting others in their reflection. We are working at the second and third levels of Van Manen's levels of reflectivity:

1. The first level is concerned with techniques needed to reach given objectives such as keeping pupils quiet and concentrating on their work. (This is dealt with in courses such as the theory and practice of teaching adults)
2. The second level is concerned with clarifying the assumptions underlying any action and assessing the educational consequences of different actions; this leads to a debate over principles and goals.
3. At the third level of reflection principles such as justice, equity and human concerns become the focus of reflection. (Van Manen, 1977).

In the reflective practitioner course we spend some time on journals and the variety of ways they can be used and also use class time for writing and sharing reflections. To help students in analysing their own interactions with groups and individuals I introduce them to Heron's six category intervention analysis (Heron, 1989) and encourage them to reflect on their own use of the different categories in different situations. This is also the basis for work on developing the skill of assisting someone else's reflection, an activity which requires the ability to use a range of interventions. During the course, students are required to carry out a self-monitoring exercise, identifying an area of their practice to monitor, setting goals, deciding on criteria for success and developing a technique for recording their progress. The planning stage is done in pairs with the partners practising the skill of assisting each other in reflecting aloud on the best way to accomplish their project. Once the self-monitoring period has passed, students report back to each other in small groups with the group members again taking the role of assisting the speaker to extract learning from their experience by asking questions, challenging and offering feedback. The process I am describing as assisting someone else with their reflection is often more familiar under the names of counselling, consulting or de-briefing but, for me, the idea of assisting with reflection is far more empowering as far as the person who is the focus of the interaction is concerned.

Over the four years I have been teaching the reflective practitioner course I have experimented with various ways of addressing the question of the social and ethical issues of adult education practice. What I am trying to do is to raise awareness in particular of the ways in which racism, sexism and classism can affect our practice. I have used literature, videos and policy documents to provoke discussion and reflection and in the last two years I have asked students to read the works of various adult educators from Tawney to Thompson and think about the implications of these theories for their own practice. Small groups of students give presentations about their particular theorist and each of the presenters speaks to the reflective questions, What have I heard/read? How do I feel? What does it mean? (for me as an adult educator). This process, factual presentation plus individual reflection, emphasizes the importance of not just knowing, in this case what someone did or said, but exploring the impact and implications of that for one's own life.

Empowerment

These are some of the ways in which I have tried, in my teaching, to encourage the habit of reflection and to recognize the importance of the learning which emerges from reflection. On what basis do I claim that the outcome of this is empowerment? My main evidence is anecdotal, the enthusiasm of some students and the grudging acceptance of others, the accounts I receive of actions taken as a result of deliberate reflection that would not otherwise have seemed possible. The wide variety of work on preferred learning styles would confirm my experience that students will have a range of responses to the idea of reflection. Some will carry out the exercises and leave it at that, others will find it interesting and useful at the time but not pursue it consciously once the course is over, others, at least a third of every group, will pursue it further, even perhaps complaining about its addictive quality. 'The most irritating thing about the concept of reflection is that it's such an irritating concept that I simply can't prevent myself reflecting about reflection' (first year Masters student). I will end this chapter with some quotations from end of semester reports from Masters students which give some of the flavour of the positive reactions.

First of all there is a refreshing resistance in some students to answering the questions I had posed when their own seemed more interesting:

> Faced with a set of questions about myself as a learner: 'What situations give me satisfaction as a learner', etc, my mind goes blank as the page in front of me. But there are things I want to say here, and these do relate, albeit somewhat loosely, to the set questions.
>
> Sue, the questions posed for the reflection task did not seem to facilitate discussion of the actual experiences and my interpretation of your statements was that you wanted some of this. My solution, to include extracts from my journal entries throughout the semester for your information, as background

The first student quoted above expanded on the differences between this course and previous higher education experiences:

> I feel confident, bold enough to deviate from the set questions because there is something else I want to say. I feel less afraid of criticism and less of a fraud than in previous formal learning experiences.

She relates this explicitly to the focus on reflection:

> What then has led to these positive feelings about this particular learning experience? Firstly, I have really enjoyed being allowed, indeed encouraged, to use my own reflections as a basis for comment and analysis. I value the absence of an artificially imposed delineation between 'study' and 'life'.

Another student was initially resistant to the idea:

> Initially my reaction was not too positive. The concept of reflection and its application to the learning process seemed a bit wanky. Reflection smacked of novelty and theoretical transience – it had a touch of the hula-hoop or the Bay City Rollers about it. Most of all the idea irritated me. Yet, over a couple of months, the sheer irritation of reflection snared me. As I mulled on the idea of reflection, I began to apply reflection to my attitudes towards training, training delivery, and my own learning process.
>
> Acceptance of the reflective process has allowed me to develop and apply conscious, self-monitoring, observational and cooperative criteria to my training involvement. That is in no way to argue that such skills were not previously utilized. The difference is that I am more conscious of the needs and benefits involved in using the tools of reflection.

He goes on to outline one specific outcome of his reflections:

> The reflection process has assisted my understanding of myself as a learner. I'm surprised by a drift towards a reactionary and somewhat conservative attitude towards change and new ideas and values. . . . On another level I'm surprised by how easily I accommodate technical change and innovation. . . . Reflection has sharpened my focus

on this tension and, without imparting any value judgement to the equation, I acknowledge the need for some adjustment to the balance.

Another student, who works in English language teaching, noted the discrepancy between his encouragement of his own students to take risks and his own unwillingness to do so:

> The exercise of reflection as a learner has been most useful and revealing. In at least two of my reflections I noted how I only contributed to class when the area under discussion was one where I felt I knew something or felt safe about contributing. As a learner I feel I am unwilling to take risks. It is curious as it is a well documented fact that risk-takers make the most successful language learners and we constantly encourage them down that path, explaining that errors are an important part of learning. As this is something I believe in, I will have to force myself to be more adventurous in learning situations.

So the process of reflection, built into a course design, has led to recognition of contradictions, confidence in personal judgements and reduced fear of criticism. These comments are typical of remarks made in more casual conversations with students over the past four or five years, comments which confirm my belief in the potentially empowering effect of reflection and my interest in developing more and more ways of incorporating it into our academic programmes for adult educators.

References

Boud, D, Keogh, R and Walker, D (1985) *Reflection: Turning Experience into Learning*, London: Kogan Page.

Brookfield, S (1991) 'Grounding teaching in learning', in Galbraith, M (ed) *Facilitating Adult Learning*, Malabar, FL: Kreiger.

Darkenwald, G G and Merriam, S B (1982) *Adult Education: Foundations of Practice*, New York: Harper & Row.

Heron, J (1989) *Six Category Intervention Analysis* (3rd edn), Guildford: Human Potential Resource Group, University of Surrey, Guildford.

Schön, D (1983) *The Reflective Practitioner*, New York: Basic Books.

Schulman, L (1987) 'Knowledge and teaching', *Harvard Educational Review*, 57, 1–22.

Van Manen, M (1977) 'Linking ways of knowing with ways of being practical', *Curriculum Inquiry*, 6, 2, 205–28.

18 Internal Processors in Experiential Learning

John Mulligan

Overview of model

People have a range of internal processors enabling them to live and learn. I call them processors because each one has different capability and can be operated intentionally. These processors – will, memory, thought, emotion, sensation, intuition and imagination – are often operating well below potential and, contrary to popular belief, can be significantly improved. Poor processor operation is a recipe for frustration, low self-esteem, or even failure and will almost certainly result in limited or ineffective learning. This is especially so in the case of experiential learning since all of these functions are utilized significantly more than in the traditional mode of learning through and from books. For example, the learner has to gather and make sense of the raw, and sometimes chaotic, data of first-hand experience rather than from the orderly structure of a textbook.

The processors are described in their dynamic form to emphasize their function as a learned process rather than as a static god-given or genetically defined talent or gift as often implied in statements such as 'I have a bad memory', 'I have no imagination' or 'I am weak-willed'. Each of the seven processors makes a distinctive contribution to the learning process. While it is important to clarify each both conceptually and behaviourally for teaching and learning purposes it is unusual to find such clarity in everyday life. It has been demonstrated that most individuals have different strengths among these processors and invariably have some which are highly developed and others which are functioning poorly or at an unconscious level (Jung, 1977; Myers-Briggs, 1980). However, it is through conscious discrimination and intentional use that the full potential of these processors will be at the disposal of learners and teachers for experiential learning.

The model has been developed through a series of workshops I presented at the Human Potential Resource Group over the past few years. I am indebted to many authors for their work on individual processors and these are acknowledged in the references, but as far as I am aware, the inter-relationship and significance of the full model has not yet been explored. A rich resource, however, is to be found in the works of Carl Jung and current writings on neuro-linguistic programming. It is beyond the scope of this chapter to give a detailed description of each processor; for those who wish to explore them in more detail the attached bibliography will provide a useful starting point. Here a brief outline of each processor will be given together with some ways of activating it during experiential learning processes.

Willing

Willing is central to all our achievement and self-development. It is more than sheer determination or strong will, a legacy of Victorian interpretation. Will underpins our capacity for choice, is affected by diverse motivations both within and external to us and can be used in both healthy or destructive ways. Willing helps us to take charge and responsibility for our lives and turn our intentions into reality. The 'I'll do it if it kills me' approach often creates internal and external resistance resulting in broken resolutions and stuckness or stagnation familiar to most of us both in life and within the learning process. From a holistic viewpoint willing is a function of the whole person and not the reserve of the conscious ego (Freud, 1960) or any one sub-personality (Assagioli, 1975). Willing in a broader definition, therefore, must take account of the unconscious dimension of our being including our unique seed or potential which may not be actualized as yet but which exerts such a formative influence on what we may become. Assagioli has suggested that our willing functions like the conductor of an orchestra, as a coordinator of the activity of our being as a whole. Similarly, as an internal processor, willing coordinates the activities of the other six to enhance the learning process as a whole.

In everyday learning situations this processor will be needed to organize and order the learning process; to balance the need to learn with other needs, for example to relax or play, thereby preventing apathy or exhaustion; to decide and engage the other functions as appropriate, for example the thinking function when analysis or deduction is needed, or holding attention on bodily sensations or internal imagery when being in touch with our emotions. Conventional, compulsive or otherwise inappropriate use of the processors, which most of us have both experienced and observed, can also be reduced by development of the various aspects of our willing. Skilful will, wise will, goodwill and so on are aspects of this processor which need to be developed for it to function effectively (Assagioli, 1974).

Remembering

Remembering is the key to past learning and how we came to be the persons we are. Surprisingly, most people have good memories but many believe they don't, usually because they don't know how to use them effectively. We recall easily those things that are important to us, those that are active, distinctive, exciting and meaningful and those to which we have given undivided attention. Some people remember names or faces easily, others figures and so on, and these propensities relate, among other variables, to the personality type or the orientation of the individual toward the world; for example whether you are predominantly a thinking, feeling, sensing, or intuiting, introvert or extrovert type of person (Myers-Briggs, 1980). Such personality typing indicates a value stance or position and we tend to remember what we value.

We store memories at different levels; in our bodies as reflex actions; in the form of sensory based images; through words, symbols and concepts. In addition, everyone has a primary storage and recall or representational mode which they use for accessing memories (Bandler and Grinder, 1979). For example, some are visualizers, others rely on their auditory and sound channel, others on their kinaesthetic (movement sensation) channel. Primary accessing through gustatory and olfactory channels is less common. Inputting and recalling memories using your strongest representational mode is likely to be most effective and it is common to use our secondary (second strongest) mode to check or confirm memories.

The analogy of a computer memory is helpful to grasp the necessity of coding incoming information correctly if one wishes to be able to retrieve at will in an orderly and predictable fashion. However, our storage system can also function like the uneven landscape of mountainous territory with its outstanding promontories (emotionally charged or outstanding memories) and its shadowy recessed caves or hidden underground passages (vague or repressed memories) which are often difficult to access at will but may be restimulated through association when we least expect it.

Most if not all educators appreciate the importance of a good remembering processor. Most good teachers and educational writers present what has to be learned in an orderly structure (headings, introductions, summaries) and/or a memorable way (one which creates an emotional or sensory impact on the learner) so as to aid the learner's power of retention and recall. In experiential learning, however, there are no chapter headings, emboldened letters or replays of key moments created by a knowledgeable editor to help the learner prioritize what needs to be remembered, much less feed it to the learner in an orderly fashion. It becomes all the more essential, therefore, for the experiential facilitator and, even more so, the learner to have both an understanding of and a competence in the various remembering processes. Otherwise we tend, for example, to remember the sensational but not the important, have our attention and therefore our remembering narrowed by anxiety, or be left with memories of content divorced from accompanying effect, none of which are desirable outcomes from a learning point of view.

Reasoning

Reasoning is the key to understanding and making sense of our world. I use the word reasoning instead of thinking because the latter word is often conventionally used to denote a range of internal processes which include what I describe as imagination, intuition and even feeling (cf. De Bono, 1988). I wish here to refer to a specific range of rational processes by which we manipulate, clarify, and order our experience into ideas, images, concepts and so on to describe, explain, predict, or interpret our world. This may be done at enactive, iconic or symbolic levels (Bruner, 1966) although it is more commonly identified as abstract reasoning.

Each person has a set of constructs, internal frameworks or models which reflect the way they understand the world (Kelly, 1955). These constructs may be helpful or inhibiting depending on the extent to which they reflect the reality which they represent. They reflect our theories and beliefs about what is true and how the world works. They embody our attitude and stance toward the world and form the basis, for example, of how we analyse, explain, interpret, predict and interact with the world around us. Becoming aware of the constructs or frameworks we use to think about ourselves and the world can help us modify those which are ineffective or inhibiting and begin developing ones which may be of greater value to us in adapting to and performing effectively in the world.

It is because reasoning uses such frameworks that it is said to be objective. However, most of us will have encountered thinking which was not objective or rational. We say that reasoning is subjective or incorrect when the constructs, frameworks or theories which were used in the reasoning process were unrealistic (did not match reality) or incoherent (internally inconsistent). Alternatively, it may be that the reasoning processes themselves were either defective or inappropriately applied. For example, a deductive process which did not follow the rules of logic, a categorization which only took account of some of the characteristics of the object or a conclusion based on false assumptions, could not be accepted as valid reasoning.

Experiential learners will need to be aware of the way in which their existing constructs, ideas or theories can predispose them to perceive events in a certain way. For example, if we believe that a person is competent we tend to pick up those pieces of information which confirm our belief even when it may be obvious to others that our belief flies in the face of available evidence. It may be that we do not have the thinking skills to submit our beliefs to the rigour of experiential testing but it is more common to find that it has not occurred to us that they needed testing. So it is that learning often means unlearning something that we have previously learned, or at least suspending our belief in what we know, or even that we know, in order to test the validity of existing knowledge and create the possibility of learning something new. Suspension of belief is just one of the many reasoning skills available to those with a developed reasoning processor.

Feeling

Feeling and its underpinning, emotion, is the key to personal satisfaction. It is our subjective way of judging the world. At its most undifferentiated level emotion is an extension of the pleasure/pain response and how we decide whether and to what degree we like something or not at a visceral level. It is a function of our needs. We tend to react with anger or frustration when choice is blocked, fear when understanding is blocked, and grief when love is blocked (Heron, 1979). When these needs are satisfied we experience well-being, joy, elation, delight and so on. From a learning point of view, all emotions, positive and negative, are valuable; it is what we do with them that helps or hinders. At times they must be controlled, at others expressed. Blocked emotion or distress can be awarely released, increasing vitality and intelligence or emotion can be transmuted into action or creative activity. Competence in all four ways (expression, control, catharsis, transmutation) of managing our emotions will be most effective (Heron, 1983).

It is regrettable that we live, here in England (though it is not alone among the developed nations), in a culture where the stiff upper lip has become a symbolic representation of the predominant national emotional characteristic; one of emotional inexpression and control, though some would say suppression. The result is that many are out of touch with their emotional response or have such a delayed response that they would be characterized as educationally sub-normal were the problem a cognitive one. Besides the difficulties which this lopsided emotional development creates in the area of interpersonal relating, experiential learners are without their early warning system which can tell them that their needs are not being met. This often results in states of mental indigestion, confusion, and even physical exhaustion or worry which are counter-productive from a learning point of view. At worst the learner is in danger of engaging in meaningless learning or brainwashing once they have been conditioned compulsively to override or ignore the emotional feedback system.

It may sound strange that I have sometimes to teach grown adults to feel again, but they have literally forgotten how, from lack of use of that processor. Feeling, often to their surprise, takes them a lot longer than thinking and requires the lowering of their attention to a visceral level and holding it there while they experience and make sense of the bodily response of which they become aware. Memory is often another casualty of emotional suppression or miseducation in so far as it depends on emotional impact to create a vivid and lasting memory. Emotional mobility is a necessary prerequisite for this to occur. The limiting effects that emotional distress and trauma can have on our beliefs, perceptions and thinking have been well documented (Heron, 1977) as has the healing and intelligence-liberating effects of abreactive and cathartic release of such distress (Freud, 1960). Basic client-centred co-counselling (Heron, 1979) techniques facilitate such release and belong in the domain of the feeling processor.

Sensing

Our five senses are the key to observation and contact with material reality. Sensing is our way of gathering and checking information about the world. How well our senses function will determine our level of awareness and ability to interact with our environment. Many people tend to rely on second-hand information (other people, the media) about the world and find it difficult to gather, trust or make use of the data supplied by their own sensory experience. This can seriously limit ability to test our beliefs and expectations and result in poor flexibility and adaptation to changes in our environment. Sharpening our senses will increase our ability to notice the subtleties of shape, tone, smell, movement and so on which contribute to the richness of our experience and directly underpin both memory and imagination.

It is not uncommon for people's beliefs and expectations to distort their perceptions as I have already mentioned. We often see what we expect to see, or what we think we should see, rather than what is actually there. Often too, we do not discriminate adequately between observed facts, our interpretations of them and our feeling reactions in response to them. In experiential learning it is essential that we make these kinds of distinction so that we can allow our observations to confound our treasured beliefs and theories, an essential component of such learning (cf. Piaget, 1970, on assimilation and accommodation).

Montessori (1967) realized the fundamental contribution which sensory perception contributes to our intelligence and based her educational philosophy on its development. Gestalt psychology and therapy as well as most art education has much to offer by way of refining of the sensing processor. Science itself is based on the pillar of empirical observation and has vastly extended some of our sensing powers.

Intuiting

Intuiting like sensing is a perceptual processor and another way that we have of gathering information from the world around us (Jung, 1977). Intuiting is the key to what is tacit, missing or hidden, and therefore to potential or what is unrealized in people and situations. A keen intuition can point where to explore for something or the direction development might usefully take. It is complementary to the sensation function but works in the opposite way, by defocusing on sensory detail and relying on an internal voice, image, hunch or felt sense to provide the necessary information. It would not be uncommon for an intuiting person to walk into a room and pick up a great deal about the covert undercurrents of relationship between people but be unable to recall anything about the more overt decor. A person may know something but not know how it is that they know it. Intuiting at its best would appear to be a form of direct knowing, difficult to explain but foolish to ignore. Many great discoveries are made in this way and only later confirmed or proved by sensory observation (Polanyi, 1966).

'Not able to see the wood for the trees' is an expression that is often used to refer to somebody who is unable to see the whole of the situation or take an overview of it. Intuiting requires us to take a holistic perspective rather than focusing in on the detail. This is an important ability in experiential learning as it can help us to appreciate the inter-relationships and emerging patterns in what we experience and thus help us to begin making sense of or giving some order to that experience. Many a valuable hypothesis emerges in this way. Of course most researchers will know the folly of not putting our hypotheses to the empirical test by using the sensing processor or even confusing hypothesis with fact. While intuitions are of undoubted value as indicators of starting points for inquiry, there is a danger that such intuitions may, if left ungrounded, turn out to be little more than projection or even paranoia.

Intuiting, therefore, can help us quickly disregard the irrelevant and go to the core of the matter by prioritizing what is important, a valuable asset to the experiential learner in the unsignposted territory of life. Allowing such intuitions to form, however, does not occur by dint of wilful effort but rather by being in a state of passive-receptive expectant attention ready to catch the fleeting image or sound when it occurs. This attitude and stance may not be easy for busy, goal oriented, will-powered learners impatient and hungry to learn. Vaughan (1979), Gendlin (1981) and Goldberg (1983) offer much to help us understand and develop this generally undervalued processor.

Imagining

Imagining is the key to the future and to what has not yet been realized.

It is the precursor to creativity and action. It can reproduce or recreate past and present and envisage how things might be. It helps us transcend current experience of reality and combine the possible with the impossible. It underpins the creative arts and existentialist theorists would say the day-to-day recreation of ourselves implicit in learning and play. Neuro-linguistic programmers say that if you can imagine yourself doing something you can probably do it, or at least that you're more likely to than if you can't imagine it, and they demonstrate the truth of this maxim by helping people to learn activities as varied as golf and fire-walking.

Imagining entails the formation of images and, as with memory, these can be visual, auditory, kinaesthetic, and so on. Images can be created externally as well as internally. By practising your ability to create, sustain and develop images you can significantly enhance your powers of imagination. It is usually the case that some people have aspects of their imaginations more developed than others and one can use that aspect to develop others. Buzan (1984) has also demonstrated the importance of imagination to memory in the creation of memorable images to retain important but lack-lustre information. Houston (1982) has demonstrated how one can become one's own internal teacher through the use of imagination and how this technique can accelerate the learning process to an extent one would not have believed possible.

For the experiential learner as for the playful child the ability to imagine otherwise or to pretend allows us to engage in the impossible, to become someone or something else and in so doing become capable of experiencing an event, as it were, from many other perspectives than our own. This seemingly simple act enables us to gain a multi-dimensional view of an event or experience which encourages substantially greater depth in our learning than if we were trapped in the prison of our everyday point of view. It allows us to try out new roles and behaviours without having to become committed to them; it is the basis for empathy and also allows us to explore a new situation at an internal imaginal level without a high risk of personal exposure to the real-life consequences.

Conclusion

In this chapter I have tried to give some idea of the potential of this model for enhancing learners' ability to learn from experience as well as a flavour of each of the seven processors. It is suggested that learners can be greatly empowered in their learning and living by developing both discriminative clarity and behavioural competence in the seven internal processors outlined above. It is, however, necessary for teachers and facilitators to possess such discrimination and competence themselves if they are to model and activate the processors to enhance the experiential learning competence of their students. The challenge is not a small one.

References

Assagioli, R (1974) *Act of Will*, Wellingborough: Turnstone Press.
Assagioli, R (1975) *Psychosynthesis*, Wellingborough: Turnstone Press.
Bandler, R and Grinder, J (1979) *Frogs into Princes*, Utah: Real People Press.
Bruner, J (1966) *Towards a Theory of Instruction*, New York: W W Norton.
Buzan, T (1984) *Your Perfect Memory*, New York: E P Dutton.
De Bono, E (1988) *Six Thinking Hats*, Harmondsworth: Pelican.
Freud, S (1960) *Standard Works*, London: Hogarth Press.
Gallwey, T (1982) *Inner Game of Tennis*, London: Bantam Books.
Gawain, S (1976) *Creative Visualization*, California: What Ever Publishing Inc.
Gendlin, E (1981) *Focusing*, London: Bantam Books.
Goldberg, P (1983) *The Intuitive Edge*, Los Angeles: Jeremy Tarcher Inc.
Heron, J (1977) *Catharsis in Human Development*, Guildford: HPRG, University of Surrey.
Heron, J (1979) *Co-Counselling*, Guildford: HPRG, University of Surrey.
Heron, J (1983) *The Education of the Affect*, Guildford: HPRG, University of Surrey.
Houston, J (1982) *The Possible Human*, Los Angeles: Jeremy Tarcher Inc.
Jung, C G (1977) *Psychological Types*, collected works, vol. 6, Bollingen series XX, New Jersey: Princeton University Press.
Kelly, G (1955) *The Psychology of Personal Constructs*, vols. 1 and 2, New York: W W Norton.
Kolb, D (1984) *Experiential Learning*, New Jersey: Prentice Hall.
Montessori, M (1967) *The Montessori Method*, Cambridge, Mass: Bentley.
Myers-Briggs, I (1980) *Gifts Differing*, CA: Consulting Psychologists Press.
Ornstein, R (1977) *The Psychology of Consciousness*, New York: Harcourt Brace and Jovanovich.
Piaget, J (1970) *Genetic Epistemology*, New York: Columbia University Press.
Polanyi, M (1966) *The Tacit Dimension*, New York: Doubleday.
Vaughan, F E (1979) *Awakening Intuition*, New York: Anchor Books.

19 Creative Capability and Experiential Learning

Jane Henry

Introduction

Think of one person you know who you feel is creative. What do you notice about:

- the kind of person they are, their character and the way they relate to people;
- how they set about their work; and
- what they produce?

In exercises such as this it generally transpires that the creative person is seen as imaginative, perhaps doing unexpected things, but generally also that they produce appropriate work of a good quality, work hard, are experienced in what they do and demonstrate perseverance in areas of interest to them; qualities that seem to have more to do with attitude, experience and motivation than skill.

A short leap through historical conceptions of creativity shows considerable change. Traditionally, exceptional creativity was seen as a matter of grace from the gods or muses. More recently, this quality has been reserved for individuals of exceptional ability – major and minor geniuses, not something that we all do every time we perform a new act. The more cynically minded may prefer serendipity and the idea of accidental discovery as an explanation. Perhaps the most popular theory nowadays stresses the importance of association, where ideas from one field applied to another give rise to creative insight.

Much academic work in the 1940–60s was devoted to attempts to identify the 'creative personality'. The characteristics identified included mental skills like fluency of ideas, mental flexibility, problem sensitivity and redefinitional skills and it seemed reasonable to suppose that people's competence in these areas could be enhanced through training. More recently, evidence has been growing that creative behaviour is domain-dependent; experience and motivation also seem to play their part in creative endeavour.

Teaching creativity

The medium through which much creativity training takes place is creative problem-solving. There are a number of variants which all involve some kind of staged problem-solving process and include periods where imaginative and reflective thinking is encouraged and critical evaluation is discouraged.

Kolb (1984) and others have drawn attention to the parallels between the stages in problem-solving and the experiential learning cycle. Figure 19.1 relates the experiential learning cycle to the stages in creative problem solving.

Competency

Training in creative thinking draws on techniques designed to mimic the role the unconscious is assumed to play in serendipitous discovery;

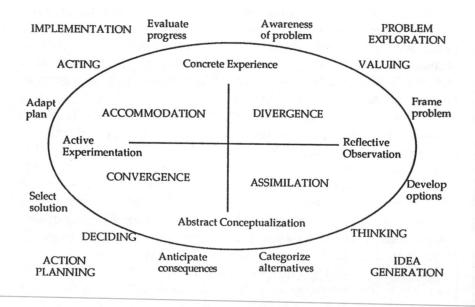

Figure 19.1 *Problem-solving and experiential learning cycles*

specifically, to associate ideas from one field with those of another through lateral or analogical thinking. Thus creative thinking employs an expansive mode which encourages divergence through the use of techniques like brainstorming, metaphor and reversal. Its practice stresses a principle of anything goes and encourages a state of dreaming and drifting and building on others' ideas. The assumption here is that quality ideas will emerge from the quantity of ideas generated. The distinguishing feature, however, is not just the use of imaginative thinking but rather that all judgement is deferred. The underlying principle is that this non-evaluative imaginative phase prevents premature closure, where the first possible solution is accepted, when further examination from different perspectives might have produced a different and better alternative.

To produce workable outcomes this kind of divergent thinking is set within a staged problem-solving framework in which the creative divergent thinking described above is alternated with the more traditional convergent thinking where the ideas generated are evaluated. Figure 19.2 shows such a process involving problem exploration, idea generation, action planning and implementation with an expansive imaginative or divergent phase followed by an evaluative or convergent phase at each of these stages as shown.

The problem exploration stage allows the problem owner to reflect on the nature of the problem and explore it from different angles. It is likely to involve some kind of reframing exercise which forces a re-examination from different perspectives. The idea generation stage encourages participants to consider many different alternative solutions to the problem. Brainstorming, lateral thinking, the use of metaphor, matrices and checklists are among the many approaches that can be used for this purpose. All develop a mass of ideas which eventually need sorting. Mind

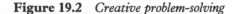

Problem exploration	Imaginative phase	Exploring different angles
	Evaluative phase	Selecting problem
Idea generation	Imaginative phase	Generating ideas
	Evaluative phase	Categorizing solutions
Action planning	Imaginative phase	Anticipating consequences
	Evaluative phase	Selecting option(s)
Implementation	Imaginative phase	Adapting plan
	Evaluative phase	Evaluating outcome

Figure 19.2 *Creative problem-solving*

Problem exploration
Awareness	Brainstorm issues, domain map
Mapping	Cause and consequence, tree diagram
Reframing	Redefinition, replacement

Idea development
Imagine	Analogy, metaphor, brainstorming
Analyse	Checklists, attribute matrices
Categorize	Mind maps, post it

Action planning
Anticipate	Other people's viewpoints, help and hinder
Select	Feasibility matrix, criteria, hurdles

Implementation
Organize	Schedule, review
Support	Map, check

Figure 19.3 *Developing creative problem-solving competencies*

maps offer an ideal way of categorising options within particular classes of ideas (Buzan, 1974). In deciding between options, participants may be encouraged to spend time, not just reflecting on their preference, but imagining the likely consequences and using this to inform their judgements as to the appropriate way forward. Finally, the chosen course of action needs to be put into practice and progress evaluated. Figure 19.3 offers an indication of the different capabilities associated with each stage of problem-solving and some of the approaches that are used to stimulate them.

The theory behind such procedures is based on the idea that creative competencies are transferable skills which can be taught and applied in diverse circumstances.

Attitude

During the last eight years I have run numerous courses on creative problem-solving for managers, civil servants and Open University students. These groups are student-centred in that the entire time is spent using various techniques to address issues and concerns brought by the student. The majority of work takes place in small groups, involving reflection, imagining and sharing, together with some grouping, evaluating and deciding. Such groups provide a non-threatening way in which to structure a process of reflection which incorporates imaginative thinking and the perspectives of others. The ideas and plans that result seem particularly fruitful where the problem-owner has been stuck or had great difficulty with the problem area chosen. Being forced to entertain possibilities they would not normally consider makes it easier to break the limiting mindsets and assumptions that have inhibited their thinking on that topic to date.

The real learning seems not so much the ideas that are produced but rather some kind of wisdom that comes from the process of engaging with a group of people reflecting on an issue in a procedure which subtly forces them to re-evaluate possibilities and prejudices. This produces increased personal and interpersonal understanding and a deep unconscious apprehension of the principles behind the techniques that has much more to do with shifting attitudes than learning skills. For example, through the process of reflection, imagination and evaluation students become clearer about what they want and what they are willing to do to get it. Some develop a determination to act and an increased willingness to undertake the consequent risks. Others realize that they are not willing to act, which can be an equally empowering experience. Another outcome is an enhanced respect for other individuals and an understanding of the value of different ways of approaching common tasks. The ground rules preclude judgement of ideas that might ordinarily be dismissed as silly or irrelevant and participants cannot help but notice when an idea they thought useless leads to the preferred solution. This appreciation of the value of different perspectives leads to greater tolerance and faith in others.

If one takes the view that we are all creative and it is largely the presence of barriers of mind that inhibits our creative efforts, creativity training should focus more on removing affective and perceptual barriers than inputting conceptual competencies. The group-based methods used were designed to teach transferable creativity skills. Ironically, their greater contribution may be in helping people to become more open to alternative perspectives and to develop greater faith and respect in the value of others' contributions, to know themselves, dare to risk and recognize which avenues they care enough about to persist through initial failure and which not. Advocates of the conceptual and affective block-busting approach to creativity training tend to assume that when these barriers of the mind fall, a fully competent and empowered individual will emerge, able to act creatively in many areas. However, studies by Belbin and others challenge the idea that creative capability is necessarily transferred from one area of life to another.

Experience

Experience in the field in question must also be reckoned with; chance, after all, favours the prepared mind. Studies of creative people in fields from music and management to mathematics conclude that long experience in the field in question precedes any exceptional creative output (Weisberg, 1986). Cognitive psychology shows us it is not just that 'experts' such as chess grand masters and others know more, but rather that they organize the knowledge they have in ever more efficient chunks, permitting readier access to the patterns contained therein. It may be that this organization of knowledge makes it easier for the expert to recognize the importance of a particular anomaly in a way novices would find difficult, as they lack the sophisticated knowledge to back up a capacity for apprehension that can recognize the critical problem. In this view, creativity becomes largely a matter of expert recognition and creative competencies domain-dependent.

Motivation

Amabile (1983) argues that creative actions emerge from a congruence of intrinsic motivation, experience in the field and creative mental skills. Her studies suggest it is the intrinsic motivation that allows the individual to demonstrate the persistence that seems necessary for creative effort. Thus we may conclude that individual competence, experience in the field, an open attitude and personal motivation all play their part in opening the gates to creative flow. Figure 19.4 summarizes the focus, assumptions and consequences for training embodied in each of these perspectives.

Climate

Studies of creativity within organizations suggest that the prevailing

	Skill	*Attitude*	*Experience*	*Motivation*
Focus	Process	Perspective	Preparedness	Play
Model	Transferable skill	Transferable skill	Domain-dependent	Domain-dependent
Competence	Mental skill (Knowledge and practice)	Attitude shift (Openness and risk)	Expert recognition (Perception)	Passionate play (Intrinsic motivation)
Training	Input skills	Remove affective and perceptual barriers	Gain experience	Nurture passion

Figure 19.4 *Comparison of training models derived from assumptions about the nature of creative competencies*

organizational climate is also an important variable and can do much to inhibit or release creative potential (Ekvall, 1991). These and related findings have generated considerable interest in the organizational literature on how best to nurture the kind of passion that might lead to the creative breakthrough whilst maintaining the day-to-day work of an organization. A climate of openness which affords the employee a measure of freedom as to how she sets about a task, accepts rather than punishes mistakes and generally builds up an atmosphere of trust is more likely to empower employees than a rigid bureaucracy that does everything by the book.

Thus setting becomes an important variable since culture and climate can affect the degree of engagement. Hence the environment in which the creativity is to take place at lasts joins the rather individualistic conceptions of creativity that have tended to dominate the field until recently.

Writers such as Reich (1987) contrast the West's long tradition of emphasizing the individual and idolizing the lone hero with the Japanese culture's greater emphasis on team work and acceptance of the part that teams play in creative effort. He argues that there are corresponding myths about the origin of creativity, with the West focusing on dramatic breakthroughs and Japan recognizing the large part played by incremental improvements. He and others believe an over-emphasis on the individual has led the West to stress the role of the inventor in innovation whereas most breakthroughs are the result of many people's contributions which in turn build on the shoulders of previous efforts. Some will go so far as to claim that this cultural difference partially accounts for the relative industrial decline of the West and the rise of the Pacific rim countries.

Style

Studies by Belbin (1981) and others have shown the different roles individuals can play in teams and further that certain combinations of personality types seem to work more harmoniously and efficiently than others. This work serves to emphasize the very great differences in the way people habitually approach problems. Kolb's (1984) learning style inventory can be used to illustrate this point. The inventory divides people into four types: divergers, convergers, assimilators and accommodators which map onto the four quadrants of the experiential learning cycle, as shown in Figure 19.5. The theory posits that individuals tend to favour tackling tasks in particular ways and have different strengths and weaknesses related to these preferences.

For example, someone who favours divergence is likely to be

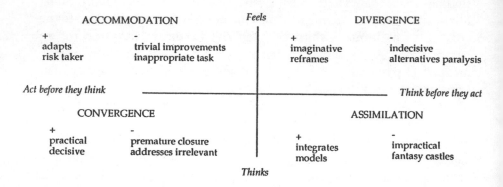

Figure 19.5 *Strengths and weaknesses associated with Kolb's (1984) learning styles*

imaginative and full of ideas, the classic creative person who is able to see beyond the obvious. However, being so aware of many alternative possibilities can lead to indecisiveness and a failure to complete. In contrast, the converger is much more down to earth and, being practical and decisive with a tendency to a one-track mind, can be relied upon to get things moving. The weakness of this sort of task-orientated attitude is that fundamentals are not considered and much effort may be directed to a sub-optimum or irrelevant exercise. The assimilator is epitomized by the academic who loves to think before they act, if they ever act at all. This type of individual is probably excellent at theorizing and pontificating but, isolated in their ivory tower, lacks grounding and may build fantastic but useless schemes. In contrast, the accommodator is more action-orientated and dares to take risks, the sort who gets involved. Less rigid than the converger, they are able to adapt plans easily, but may waste time spending a disproportionate amount of effort on the relatively trivial and unimportant.

There is anecdotal evidence that individuals with different learning preferences respond better to some creativity approaches than others. For example, divergers are often happier with the use of the provocative techniques typical of creative thinking. Both assimilators and divergers often respond to the use of metaphor and analogy whereas convergers are sometimes happier with more down to earth checklists and matrices. Hopefully we can look forward to a time when students are given more freedom to learn through an approach that suits their style.

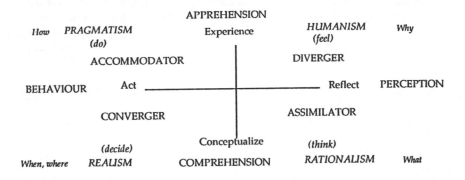

Figure 19.6 *Relationship between problem-solving preference and world view*

World view

It is possible to draw parallels between these preferences and an underlying world view, as shown in Figure 19.6. Divergers with their concern for people, the stress they place on values and sensitivity to feelings, clearly emphasize people, a position in line with a humanistic orientation. Assimilators spend much more time thinking things through logically with little thought to the personal concerns of others, playing out the rationalist position. Convergers are the realists who are more concerned with the practical realities of when and where things are to happen. The accommodator is the classic pragmatist who adapts to circumstances. (See Kolb, 1984, for amplification.)

Our rationalist culture has traditionally emphasized the skills of comprehension in educational settings. In the last 30 years that school of experiential learning that emphasizes personal development has made considerable strides in legitimating the area of affective competencies. Creative capability seems bound up with perceptual competencies and powers of apprehension, an area our culture has all but ignored for centuries and which is not well understood.

Conclusion

The strength of creative problem-solving programmes seems to lie in teaching the imaginative powers and multi-perspective skills of divergence. What it does not do so well is teach the naturally indecisive, the focus that characterizes convergence. I believe the forward-looking approach stressed in creativity ideally complements the processes of reflection stressed in experiential learning. The former opens up new possibilities and the latter enables the individual to focus on those that are relevant.

References

Amabile, T (1983) *The Social Psychology of Creativity*, New York: Springer Verlag.
Belbin, R (1981) *Management Teams*, Oxford: Heinemann.
Buzan, T (1974) *Use your Head*, London: BBC Books.
Ekvall, G (1991) 'A creative climate for the management of ideas', in Henry, J and Walker, D (eds) *Managing Innovation*, London: Sage.
Henry, J (1991) *Creative Management*, London: Sage.
Kolb, D (1984) *Experiential Learning*, New Jersey: Prentice Hall.
Reich, R (1987) 'The team as hero', *Harvard Business Review*, May–June, pp 77–83.
Weisberg, R (1986) *Genius and other Myths*, New York: Freeman.

20 Suggestopedia: A Way of Learning for the 21st Century

Grethe Hooper-Hansen

The word 'education' is derived from 'educare', to draw out. The ancient Greeks regarded the educator as a person whose job it was to draw out ideas already existing in some form in the mind of the learner (the Socratic method), rather than pour in information. Suggestopedia does pour *in* information, but it has to do more with learning than with teaching: learning how to engage much more of the whole being in the learning process, and having the exhilarating experience of tapping unsuspected potential, absorbing a huge amount of information very rapidly, without stress and with little conscious effort. Learning can take place two to three times faster than in the traditional way.

It is essentially an experiential method. In the superficial sense, it plunges the learner into a language 'bath' in which s/he finds him/herself 'swimming' or producing language as a result of unconscious processing rather than being told how to do it. But there is also a more profound experience of change of consciousness through the adoption of new patterns of response to stimuli. First, the learner becomes aware that s/he can tap much greater potential in him/herself which s/he has been blocking by negative expectations and beliefs. Second, that learning is mediated by the total organism of body-mind, not just the part of the brain associated with conscious thought. Thirdly, s/he is more inclined towards holistic perception in a formal learning situation, that is to say selecting wholes, patterns and inner coherence in what s/he receives. This perceptual change has very important implications for education, as we shall see.

Suggestopedia is the creation of a doctor and psychiatrist, Georgi Lozanov from the University of Sofia, Bulgaria. The method was developed in the 1960s after 20 years of therapeutic practice and research into hypermnesia, and began from an experiment to induce enhanced memorization in schools. Predictably, it makes use of behaviourist principles, albeit modified and refined: for Lozanov, the *inner* dimension of behaviour, that is the subject's own will and desire, is just as important as the external. But there is a basic assumption that the best way to produce more of a particular behaviour is to reinforce it. Psychologically, Lozanov makes use of four fundamental strategies to achieve his effects (these will be referred to subsequently as principles 1, 2, 3 and 4):

1. he has devised a systematic way of feeding information into highly retrievable memory in synchrony with the natural patterns of brain/mind functioning;
2. he has found a way of 'programming' the receiver for very high receptivity to that information;
3. he enables the learner to receive the information through different cerebral processes and in different states of consciousness so that it is stored in many different parts of the brain, maximising recall;
4. he manages to transfer the information very swiftly to active, creative use.[1]

He also consistently designs *mediate* learning activities. Luria pointed out in 1966 that the higher mental processes are essentially mediate structures, that is to say, they achieve their ends by indirect means. Luria's example is of a man who ties a knot in his handkerchief in order to remember something. The act of tying the knot appears to be unrelated to the task of remembering, but in fact this is the way in which memory is mastered. Lozanov has provided us with the technical means of making use of this insight; he has created a whole repertoire of sophisticated knots.[2]

From a philosophical point of view, this is a humanistic method, aiming at liberation from both inner and outer constraint and self-fulfilment within a cooperative social context. In educational terms, this is expressed as a gradual building of *learner autonomy*, with the teacher progressively giving up direction and control. Unfortunately, this aim has been widely misunderstood. As John Heron has observed in describing the evolution of counselling skills, a hierarchical framework may be necessary at the beginning, when learners are insecure and dependent; cooperative and autonomous behaviour must be allowed to emerge gradually.[3] Lozanov's initial authoritative stage has often been seen as representative of the whole process, so that he has been quite wrongly accused of authoritarianism.

Another problem has been the name 'Suggestopedia', which not only has an unfortunate connotation in English but is actively misleading, as will become apparent. In Germany, where variations of the method are widely used in business, are a subject of research in most universities and are gradually emerging in the state school system, it is often referred to as 'super-learning'; other variations are accelerated, enhanced and rapid learning. It can be applied in different ways to all subjects. It is, for example, the standard teaching method at all levels in the school system in Liechtenstein, but has been particularly developed by Lozanov and his collaborator and master teacher, Dr Evalina Gateva, for language teaching – and that is the context in which we examine it. We shall work through the lesson cycle, considering what is happening at each of the different stages and noting the principles and mechanisms which are in operation.

A thumb-nail sketch of the lesson cycle

Text: a comedy in 8 – 10 acts (1 act per cycle) c. 1000 – 1500 words per act, depending on level

Cycle: 8 – 10 hrs., parcelled as appropriate or feasible:

Presentation: Teacher (T) introduces story of act, using target grammatical structures and vocabulary. Learners (Ls) watch and listen. No written language.

1st Concert: T distributes text with translation, then reads the text very slowly aloud to the accompaniment of a piece of music (dramatic), segmenting sentences and varying the voice according to the musical phrase. Ls listen, read and follow the translation.

2nd Concert: T reads again to the accompaniment of baroque music, this time at normal speed and with normal expression. Ls listen, eyes closed, relaxed.

Elaboration: activation of target structures and vocabulary. Stage 1: Ls reading aloud, some translation and examination of text, games, songs, etc. Stage 2: transfer (putting language to own use): freer games, role plays, activities, drama, songs. Varied pace and activities; different group formations.

Primary role-play: each learner chooses (or is given) a name and profession in the target language and assumes this role for the duration of the course.

While the general appearance of the lesson is of happy, spontaneous, non-stop games playing, the teacher is in fact following a very rigorous and detailed programme which involves picking out all the necessary grammatical points, monitoring the learners' pronunciation and understanding and adapting accordingly, activating all the linguistic structures for visual, auditory and kinaesthetic learner preferences and always being extremely alert so that activities last long enough for understanding to be achieved but time is never wasted. The high-volume learning depends very much on teacher efficiency.

The Text
The text is enormously long by comparison with texts of any other method. This is because Lozanov is aiming at a different brain process from that normally stimulated in traditional education. We are all familiar

with the analytical approach: reduce ideas or information to basic elements and teach them clearly and simply one-by-one, achieving overall understanding by means of a gradual accumulation of knowledge. This meets our need for conscious analysis and logical coherence, a need which arises from that part of the brain which perceives information serially. However, the other half of the cerebral cortex and the subcortex process information in a parallel way, perceiving wholes, relations and connections rather than separate parts. They need a great volume of different kinds of stimuli in order to make inferences, and we are unconscious of their activities.[4]

So (principle 1), Lozanov bombards the brain with a great volume of information, which is received at a paraconscious level: that is, attention could be focused on any point at any moment but because of the flooding effect of quantity, the conscious mind is overwhelmed and remains passive, which encourages the unconscious patterning processes to do the work. The fact that the text is a play means that all information occurs in a context, and can be presented as a *gestalt*. In this dramatic form it is also more likely to stir affective responses.

Lozanov's aim is to keep the learner working globally throughout the lesson. In this way he is not only obliged to take in more information but he calls on many more parts of the brain, achieving simultaneous memory encoding in different areas, and at the same time better psychological integration. In traditional education, polarization towards conscious, analytic work (the serial processes) tends to make learning a rather stressful and arid experience, and also dampens other non-conscious forms of intelligence. Lozanov, by contrast, stimulates other forms of intelligence, particularly those associated with the limbic (emotional) brain, and provides a learning experience which is altogether more enjoyable and deeply satisfying.

In a 'normal' learning situation the presentation of a very long text could well reduce the learner to despair, but Lozanov has so orchestrated the environment that in fact it has the opposite effect, of being a positive suggestion. We shall consider the suggestopedic atmosphere after the discussion of the lesson cycle.

Presentation

This is standard language teaching practice: the teacher gives an overview of the text in order to set the learner's mind in the right direction and to activate appropriate memory circuits. There is also passive learning: the first memory traces are created in the brain. At another level, the psychological scene is being set: learners tend to mirror teachers and at this stage the teacher is 'acting out', perhaps even dressed up, playing with different objects, having fun.

First concert

At one level this is an extremely efficient way of inputting information: the learner has the opportunity to study the text with the double security of the translation and the knowledge that s/he will not be 'tested' in any way or required to produce language (principle 1). S/he enjoys the music and it engages his/her mind sufficiently to keep him/her both awake and relaxed.

The music is also performing several other functions:

- it produces endorphins, chemicals in the brain which reduce pain and discomfort and make us feel 'better'; they also modulate stress and affect basic processes of learning and memory and boost the immune system;[5]
- it sensitizes the learner's acoustic perception, encouraging him/her to listen more actively and with greater discrimination, to notice more clearly intonation and undertones, and to classify and order his/her acoustic experiences better;[6]
- by relaxing the learner, lowering his/her threshold of vigilance and stimulating the emotions, it helps to make the mind more receptive to new material and the whole personality to new ways of thinking and approaching learning[7];
- it assists memory by encoding information with emotion.

At the psychological level, the first concert is a ritual adapted to change expectations, similar in effect to the consultant's round in a teaching hospital.[8] Lozanov's fundamental and best known tenet, derived from his study of hypermnesia, is that the human brain has enormous reserve capacities which are held in check but which can to some extent be made available. One of the main obstacles blocking these reserves is our unaware acceptance of 'socio-suggestive norms' on which we largely base our whole set of beliefs about ourselves and the world.

We are all familiar with the idea that we develop only a small percentage of our brain potential and that this gross underuse is in part due to limits that we have imposed on ourselves. We have grown up with certain expectations of what we can and cannot do and in our behaviour we unawarely meet those expectations and thus reinforce them. The extent of self-limiting thought is enormous and it has catastrophic consequences for learning.

Before Lozanov can set a positive attitude for accelerated learning, he has to work on 'de-conditioning' these negative attitudes, and he does this by persuading the learner to hold his/her negative beliefs in abeyance for long enough to have the *experience* of accelerated learning. This is one purpose of the ritual; it makes him/her *expect* to succeed (principle 2).

Lozanov found that hypermnesia 'is the result mainly of a suggestive or autosuggestive set-up directed towards the memory potential',[9] in other words, expectation of success. At this stage authority is essential: like the medical specialist, the teacher must have sufficient presence to inspire in the learner confidence that he/she will succeed. This is authority in the sense of professional prestige rather than authoritarian behaviour (as critics have sometimes assumed it to be).

Second concert

This demonstrates the principle described by Pavlov as that of 'inhibition – activation': the inhibition of the conscious mind, will and intellect, in this case through music, relaxation and reduction of stimuli (eyes closed, body still, auditory sense occupied by the music), leads to an activation of other functions such as feeling, emotion, imagination and intuition as well as the unconscious patterning processes. Lozanov calls this state, in which mind and body are both relaxed, with inhibitions at minimum but also vigilant, 'concentrative psychorelaxation'.[10] The speed of brain activity is reduced typically to the alpha rhythm (though Lozanov has found that more than 25 per cent of learners do not produce alpha waves); in fact each individual is different and achieves a state which is peculiar to him/her.

Lozanov is now using principle 3, and the learner is achieving state-dependent learning, which is extremely durable but tends to be retrievable only when the same state is reached. It provides a third opportunity for memory traces to be established and encoded in a different way. The use of largos from baroque music is significant: the slow beat helps to maintain the 60-cycles-per-second alpha rhythm and the very regular, mathematical nature of baroque music helps to regulate bodily function and synchronize body rhythms,[11] giving a feeling of harmony and well-being. It has also been pointed out that this rhythm is similar to that of the human heart and may trigger the sensation of being in the womb. Be that as it may, learners emerge from the second concert feeling relaxed and refreshed in spite of considerable learning.

Mental fatigue is associated with high production of beta waves, typical of normal problem-solving activities,[12] but little or no fatigue is experienced when learning is accompanied by alpha waves. It is important to note that Lozanov designed this system to be psycho-hygienic, to be conducive, both in the short and long term, to health and well-being.

Elaboration

Up to this point passive learning has been taking place and it has occupied about one sixth of the total learning time. Building *active* knowledge requires practice and repetition, which aims at eventual automation, or speech which no longer requires the conscious control of the speaker. Practice and repetition are provided (and disguised) largely by games, activities, role plays and drama, and singing songs.

However, Lozanov's method is not one of pure 'acquisition' (as some critics have wrongly interpreted it): while in first-language learning, practice and hypothesis-testing alone seem to be sufficient, with a second language there are problems of interference from the first language method, and the mature learner also has conceptual needs and expectations. Thus, at this stage the teacher does provide grammatical analysis and explanation of logical connections. However, explicit grammatical teaching occurs in very short bursts, so as to be encapsulated within the global structure, and points are never fully elaborated, leaving material for the unconscious patterning processes to work on.

There are two parts to the elaboration:

- the first part is more mechanical, involving reading aloud (training speech muscles) and going through the text, with interruptions of brief grammatical explanation and activities, games, songs, etc;
- the second part is freer (principle 4), using games, activities and drama in such a way as to require the learner to put the language to use *in his/her own way*.

All suggestopedic interactions observe the 'communicative' principle, which is that attention is directed to informational content and thus diverted from linguistic construction, so that stress, if it occurs, is not associated with language production. Also, all games and activities appear to arise 'naturally' and spontaneously and language occurs within a realistic context, an important factor in maintaining globality. There are two sources of games and activities: first, the text itself, which is rich in possibilities. Second, the primary role-play: the learners have assumed a role for the duration of the course, a character (in the target language) which will be built up during the different activities as the course continues. This alternative self provides a disguise or shield for the personality and at the same time the possibility of heavy self-investment in all the activities. It protects to some extent against mistakes, it allows new behaviours to be sampled and very often an 'ideal self' is chosen, which brings various psychological advantages. The primary role-play also makes use of the principle of 'acting as if', which is so important to psychosynthesis, the inner game technique, neuro-linguistic programming, etc. By acting as if he/she were already a fluent speaker of the language, the learner engages powerful energies to help him/her in his/her endeavour.

The suggestopedic atmosphere

As already noted, the overall atmosphere is crucially important. In his research on hypermnesia, Lozanov found that the way to achieve access to the reserve capacities is through suggestion rather than direct communication with the conscious mind. Suggestion works through 'non-specific mental reactivity' (NMR),[13] and the particular target is paraconscious perception of peripheral stimuli. NMR factors, such as voice intonation, facial expression, gestures and bodily movements, because they are normally below the level of conscious attention, often betray emotions which are concealed by conscious processes such as the wording of a verbal message. Although consciously unnoticed, they play a significant role in determining actions, emotional attitudes, decision-making, etc. This is the dimension of influence demonstrated by the 'Pygmalion effect'.[14]

Lozanov makes use of what he calls 'double planeness' or conveying suggestion through as many different channels as possible simultaneously: the classroom itself, its colours, decoration, possibilities for physical comfort as well as the many posters on the wall conveying information visually; then the activities undertaken with their suggestion of enjoyment, spontaneity and self-expression, the mutually supportive group behaviour, and most important of all, the behaviour, voice, appearance and beliefs of the teacher. Lozanov teachers are always cheerful and friendly, playful and humorous, and radiating confidence that their highly interesting and intelligent students are learning extremely fast! (We are now back in principle 2.) There are also many important guidelines for non-directive behaviour, including minimal and always disguised correction, non-verbal rather than verbal praise, minimal question answering and invitation to, rather than insistence on, participation in the various activities. In addition, the teacher progressively abnegates control, while carefully observing and nurturing the learners' emerging autonomy.

Lozanov's use of suggestion has led some critics to accuse him of manipulation. There are three points to be made against this criticism:

- first, remembering the Pygmalion effect, can we really say that teachers are more responsible when they are not aware of the consequences of their behaviour? The same problem arises over the issue of psychological competence;
- second, Lozanov insists that teachers confine themselves to teaching the *subject matter* according to his guidelines for 'positive' behaviour and never to stray into areas (such as the psychological) which are beyond their professional competence. He is absolutely opposed to

the use of what he calls 'hypnotic techniques' in the classroom. Lozanov's guideline No. 1 is 'Non nocere'; this is applied in never making learners tired, never hurting learners' feelings, never invading learners' personal space and never attempting to manipulate;

- finally, suggestion has only a 'placebo' effect, that is, it lulls the learner's critical faculties for long enough for him/her to *experience* his/her own vastly accelerated learning, and it is this experience, and this experience only, which provides long-term motivation and change of attitude.

Lozanov does not believe that suggestion can work over the long term; it is simply a temporary measure. He has found that his method in fact makes people *less*, not more, suggestible, although they are more aware of the power of suggestion and the great importance of what they 'say to themselves'. But ultimately the psychological learning by this method is *experiential* in that it depends on the inner experience of tapping the reserves of the mind and not on any form of autohypnosis. Thus, the name 'Suggestopedia' is actively misleading; it might have reflected Lozanov's intentions in the early days, but the method has now evolved far beyond this.

The importance of Lozanov's method is twofold:

- first, it engages and develops forms of intelligence other than the conscious/rational, which is too often the sole focus of traditional education. This not only results in much higher achievement by a much wider range of learners, but it makes the learning process both more enjoyable and more conducive to psychological and physical health.

In this way, it can also draw out ability and intensify motivation in the so-called 'non-academic': if a learner is weak in analytical skills, then the best way to develop them is likely to be through the things that s/he is good at, not a direct approach through what s/he already knows s/he cannot do:

- second, it encourages global or holistic learning. In his Sigmund Freud Memorial Lecture at London University in 1977, Richard Sennett spoke of the Anglo-Saxon tendency to particularity, with its concomitant passion for statistical measurement and rejection of non-statistical realities.[15]

Traditional education not only reflects this tendency but perpetuates it by favouring analytical skills, encouraging observation of the world in terms of linearity and cause and effect, and not recognizing validity in the nonmeasurable world. As a result we tend to ignore or negate feelings and emotions, which are then repressed. Intellectual consequences are fragmentation of thought, which results in difficulty in observing hierarchical relationships: missing the wood while examining the trees, attaching excessive importance to trivialities, etc. Psychological consequences include dissociation of thought and behaviour, which exacerbates problems such as the 'hidden agenda'. At a macrocosmic level there is the danger of excessive individualism, excessive competition, nationalistic aggression, etc.

Lozanov's insistence on global presentation of information, global elaboration and constant stimulation of the senses, emotions, feelings and intuition makes the learner aware that learning is mediated by the whole organism, and encourages him/her to seek for patterns and relationships in what s/he experiences. In addition, Lozanov's method involves a great deal of work on group cooperation and sharing, which raises awareness of interdependence and encourages group-oriented rather than individualistic behaviour. This is very much in keeping with the post-Einsteinian scientific view of the universe as a series of interpenetrating hierarchies united by a principle of reciprocal causation. A major problem of education is how to influence habits of thought based on a Newtonian view of the universe as consisting of separate elements united by the principles of time, space and cause-and-effect.

Of course, this is not to deny the validity of serial thinking; on the contrary, we need to work constantly to improve our rational and analytical skills. But if we are to develop the *whole* mind, then we must not pursue one process to the exclusion of others. The ideal is harmonious interaction, though obviously each person has his/her own preferences and his/her own particular pattern of brain dominance. For those who are weak in analytical skills, the best way to improve is likely to be by approaching them through existing strengths.[16]

The operation of the mind is to a large extent conditioned by what it *does* and the evolution of the brain by its activities, the 'routing instructions' it follows, the circuits it creates. Thus, in education the *manner of teaching* can have more influence on the learner than the information that is conveyed; learning is essentially experiential. In the words of Marshall McLuhan, 'the medium is the message'. Lozanov offers one possibility for effecting a radical change of thinking behaviour by reinforcing holistic learning.

References

1. For these observations I am grateful to Dr W Wender of the Institute of Visual Thinking, Gaithersburg, MD.

2. Luria, A R (1966) *Higher Cortical Functions in Man,* New York: Basic Books.
3. Heron, J (1989) *The Facilitators' Handbook,* London: Kogan Page, p 18.
4. See, for example, Gazzaniga, M *et al* (1978) *The Integrated Mind,* New York: Plenum.
5. See Davis, J (1984) *Endorphins,* New York: Dial Press.
6. Lehmann, D (1988) *Music in Suggestopedia,* translated by Sigrid Gassner-Roberts, Department of German, University of Adelaide, available from the latter in English, or in German from Dr Lehmann, Musicology Department, Karl Marx University, Leipzig.
7. See Lehmann, p 28.
8. For a discussion of ritual, see Lozanov, G and Gateva, E (1988) *The Foreign Language Teacher's Suggestopedic Manual,* London: Gordon & Breach, p 125.
9. See Lozanov, G (1978) *Suggestology and Outlines of Suggestopedy,* London: Gordon & Breach, 1978, p 9.
10. For a full treatment of this subject, see Lozanov, 1978, p 223.
11. For a discussion of musically-induced body harmony, see Seferis, F (1978) *Une Revolution dans l'Art d'Apprendre,* Paris, p 125.
12. See Lozanov 1978, p 223.
13. See Lozanov 1978, pp 160–63.
14. In the 1960s American researchers Rosenthal and Jacobson tested the effect of teacher expectation on student performance in secondary schools. It was announced that the schools would examine the effects of streaming by ability, and so examinations were given and classes streamed according to the results. What the teachers did not know was that the exams were a smokescreen and the streaming was in fact completely arbitrary. At the end of the year a second exam was given, this time genuinely, and the results were found to correspond significantly with the fake streaming. Conclusion: students live up to their teachers' expectations. See Rosenthal, R and Jacobson, L (1968) *Pygmalion in the Classroom,* New York: Holt, Rinehart & Winston.
15. Sennett, R (1981) *Authority,* New York: Vintage Books, p 9.
16. See the work on education for the right-hemisphere dominant, eg, Vitale, B (1986) *Unicorns Are Real,* New York: Warner Books.

Principles into Practice

This section presents examples of teaching and facilitation methods for experience-based learning currently being used.

Marshall and Mill demonstrate how the needs of learner, employer and educational institution can be addressed through the use of learning contracts. Anderson and McMillan evaluate a 'practice-centred learning' approach within nurse education. Higgs details a problem-solving simulation method currently in use for developing clinical reasoning skills with occupational therapists. Anderson shows how group-based and problem-solving approaches can be effectively integrated in technology education. Taylor explores the outcomes and implications of a project-centred, interdisciplinary group method.

These chapters present case studies of teaching and facilitation in a range of contexts: professional practice, project work with young people, learning contracts in education/industry partnerships, technology and so on. What all of these diverse settings have in common is that they call for new kinds of teacher/learner relationships and new concepts of role such as facilitator and mentor. The methods appropriate to facilitating experiential learning can vary quite widely and involve roles for people working in industry or the community as well as for those in traditional education settings. Several chapters in this book argue the need for staff development as a condition of implementing experiential learning modes and the chapters in this section have much to offer by way of example and practice.

These chapters also illustrate the range of individual and group approaches to learning that may equally incorporate experiential work but which entail quite different kinds of empowerment for learners. Learning contracts, for example, empower learners by means of cooperative assessment schemes; group projects enable learners to experience inter-disciplinary approaches to real-life problems; action-based learning enables learners to develop their own concepts of good practice, and so on.

Whether in an individual or a group contract therefore, facilitation is primarily concerned with balancing the expertise and authority of the facilitator with the autonomy of the learner through critical reflection on their practice. These chapters offer fine examples of, and reflection on, good facilitator practice.

Papers in Section 4 are relevant to this theme as are Heron (Chapter 5) and Barber (Chapter 4) in Section 1, Hull (Chapter 11) in Section 2 and Marshall (Chapter 13) in Section 3.

21   Learning Contracts: How they Can be Used in Work-based Learning

Ian Marshall and Margaret Mill

Introduction

To be aware of the rate at which new information about every conceivable subject is available to learners requires that teachers consider different ways of helping learners learn.

One approach is to see the learner as a resource, to be involved as much as possible in determining:

- where they want to learn (timing, frequency, duration);
- how they want to learn (modes of learning, for example lecture, seminar, project, reading, work-based experience);
- what they want to learn (that is, learners can define what constitutes learning to them).

All of this may be constrained by the resources available to the learner and by particular organizational policies. With colleges, polytechnics and universities, learners will have to take account of levels and standards which have to be achieved for the award of particular qualifications.

This approach taps into intrinsic motivational factors, and is consistent with Maslow: achievement, recognition, participation and personal growth. If the prospect of each individual learner choosing to learn in their own way and in directions other than that chosen by their classmates is disturbing to the teacher, then perhaps that teacher hasn't been aware of what happens in class currently!

A useful aid which holds things together in a reassuring way is the 'learning contract'. The term 'learning agreement' is closer to the activities engaged in by learner and assessor, but the term 'contract' is well established in the literature.

At the date of writing, there is little experience in Britain when compared with North America. What experience there is appears most often in the field of management education (see Boak, 1990) and in work-based learning. As an example of the latter, a pilot project looking at the learning achieved by undergraduates from their sandwich placement is currently under way at Napier Polytechnic in Edinburgh. The experience gained to date of using learning contracts to underpin student-driven learning which would gain academic credit is offered as a case study of the process.

Process

When people undertake responsibility to learn something on their own authority, what they learn may be learned more deeply and retained for longer than what they learn by being taught (Knowles, 1980). In part, this philosophy underpins the placement element (in North America this is called 'internship') of sandwich courses. However, the weakness in planning for existing internship/sandwich placements provision can result in inadequate learning by the student, particularly when they fail to recognize valuable learning opportunities. One way to make the learning objectives of the placement experience clear and explicit for learners and teachers is by means of a student-driven, three-way negotiated agreement which is referred to here as a learning contract (see Figure 21.1).

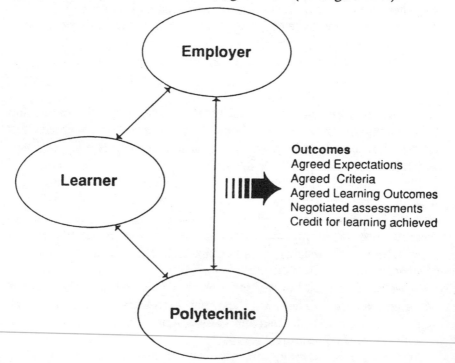

Figure 21.1 *Learning contract*

For the students, the process of identifying and agreeing appropriate goals for learning that are appropriate in a workplace setting is a significant responsibility and one that can engender powerful ownership of the proposal and strong commitment to the achievement of the goals agreed. The experience of using initiative, taking responsibility and assuming one's own authority can contribute to developing enterprise as a value system for the individuals involved. For the host employer, the negotiation of agreed learning outcomes may encourage an active role in helping students learn and an awareness of new possibilities in the students' potential contribution. For academic staff, engaging in the process of negotiating appropriate learning goals with students can result in a clearer recognition of the significance of work-based learning as an effective activity and may lead to its wider application.

The entire process of developing a learning contract and assessing it is shown in diagram form in Figure 21.2.

The various participants in the process are described as follows. The term 'learner' refers to the person who is expressing a willingness to add to their existing repertoire of knowledge, skills and attitudes. The term 'project staff' refers to staff involved in an action research capacity and to staff from the departments involved in supporting the students while they were preparing learning plans. The polytechnic staff who would have the

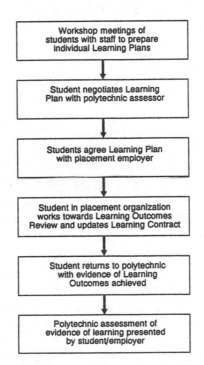

Figure 21.2 *Model of work-based learning process for students*

task of assessing the learning outcomes achieved by the student, here referred to as 'assessors', would normally be members of the departments supporting the course and at this stage of the development of the project were nominated by the students concerned. An advantage of this approach (where it is possible) is that the criteria for assessment can be explicitly discussed between 'assessor' and student. The term 'mentor' refers to the member of the employing organization's staff who is responsible for supervision of the learner during the placement.

A description of the theoretical model as it was applied to a higher diploma course at Napier Polytechnic might help others to make connections with opportunities in their own situation. Sandwich courses, or other courses which provide a work-based learning element, are particularly well suited to a learner-driven learning contract. The first pilot group of students were undertaking a higher diploma course in the hotel and catering studies department. During the second year of the course, before most students had found placements, the idea of a learning plan was introduced to the students and the classes were divided into workshop groups. The workshop had the purpose of assisting the students in preparing their learning plans and is the essential foundation of the process. In these workshops, consisting of 10–12 second year students, the director of the project and a member of staff seconded part-time to the project from the host department addressed the issue of what might be learned from proposed placements, which, at the time of this project, took place in the third year of the higher diploma course. This was accomplished by encouraging the students to consider *how* they learn and to anticipate the kinds of learning they would wish to achieve from their sandwich placement. Lists of learning outcomes were produced which were the result of discussions with departmental staff. The major consideration for inclusion in the plan was that a learning outcome should reflect the aims of the course being undertaken. This plan was to be the basic framework which, however much altered or extended during the placement, would reflect the learning achieved.

It came as a complete surprise to many students that one of the goals of education is to encourage the individual to move from a position of dependence towards greater independence. Where it was recognized a number of students voiced enthusiasm at the prospect of having a measure of control over their situation. Students were encouraged to use their learning plan as a personal agenda in interviews for placement jobs.

The role of mentor to the student in the company is of central importance to the learner, as it is often with the support of the mentor that effective learning takes place. To date, however, the mentor in the company is a learning resource which is all too rarely used. There are a number of reasons why this is the case; for example, students in placement are sometimes loath to recognize the mentor as a resource, a point which can be strongly made in the workshops when preparing students for placement. The person selected as mentor may not have given a great deal of thought to this task, and often appreciates some guidelines. The role of mentor may move to different people, so the task of maintaining very close links with the current mentor is an ongoing activity for polytechnic staff. In our experience, where mentoring is less than well done it is because the active cooperation of the mentor has not been negotiated. When employers understand what is being attempted, they are generous with their support.

A mentor in the company should be someone with whom close contact is possible. This is usually a line manager who is in a position to contribute to the final assessment. Towards the end of the placement he/she will be asked to complete an 'assessment grid', containing the student's learning outcomes. The student is encouraged to use the mentor as a rich resource in developing his/her learning contract. It is sometimes evident, even in situations where mentors were enthusiastic about the learning contract model, that they lacked the necessary information to enable them to understand the different needs of the student. There is an important role for visitors to students on placement to establish contact with the mentor and set up clear lines of communication. In situations where employers understand the approach, students feel more confident in entering into negotiations about their learning contract.

On the students' return to the polytechnic, it was agreed that they would bring with them their evidence of such learning as had occurred for discussion with staff and subsequent assessment by staff. During the placement the students were encouraged by the project director to assemble material to present for assessment on their return to the polytechnic. They were also asked to nominate and approach an assessor. When they returned to college and before they submitted their evidence of learning for assessment, they were offered an individual meeting with project staff. The purpose of these meetings was to review the students' experience with them, to see what they had brought back, whether notes or a report, and to encourage them to produce a final report. They were offered help if they needed it and asked to nominate and approach an assessor if they had not already done this.

A number of learning outcomes emerged as appropriate for assessment. The specific learning which the assessors were looking for varied from student to student, depending on the placement and the person involved. In some cases they were looking for breadth, in others depth. In addition to the general features of learning described previously, there were some specific learning outcomes mentioned by assessors:

- accomplish the tasks involved in the placement job;
- recognize operational problems within the work situation;
- suggest a strategy to overcome identified problems;
- communicate with others as opportunities arise;
- acknowledge the role of administration in the organization;
- develop skills of working with people in groups;
- take responsibility in a group;
- identify the features of the customer;
- analyse customer needs;
- identify management skills from observing role models;
- control resources within area of responsibility;
- develop personal effectiveness;
- react to an unpredicted situation in accordance with the policy and procedures of the organization.

It is interesting that the learning outcomes indicated can be seen as overlapping a number of management competencies which have been evolved through the National Forum for Management Education and Development (1989).

Conclusions drawn from assessment meetings

These conclusions are not in any order of priority.

- Self-assessment is one of the skills which the use of this model is designed to improve. This is seen as a life skill which assumes increasing importance as the student moves out from the educational environment into the world of work. The process of weaning the student from dependence upon the authority of polytechnic staff is a difficult one for both sides and it is believed that where there is a greater degree of mutual respect and self-confidence between student and staff, the transition from total dependence towards a measure of independence will be easier. Whilst it is acknowledged that there may be difficulties of a different kind arising from students having some say in the choice of their polytechnic assessor, it is judged at this stage to be worth attempting to bring together those staff who wish to work in this way and those learners who wish to work with them.
- Assessment requires very skilful handling of the material submitted by the student.
- Particular aspects of a placement should not be concentrated on simply because they are easily predicted or readily assessed.
- The learning that is specific to the placement experience and most valued by the students requires time and skill to tease out.

- Improved preparation of students before placement is necessary. The changes include:
  - exploration of 'learning as a process'
  - more information about what particular jobs involve
  - matching of learning outcomes to the placement so that a placement's potential can be realized.
- Students *do* learn a lot on placement.
- Submitting the learning for assessment clarified for most students the extent of that learning.
- Sympathetic and skilled assessment takes time. The assessor requires time to read and think about the portfolio of evidence submitted by the student in order to prepare for an oral with each student lasting about an hour.
- Contact between the assessor and the student before the assessment meeting is valuable.

When students were asked what suggestions they would have for students starting their preparation for placement *now*, there was strong advice that they make early contact with employers about their placement. Students also suggested there was a need to make contact with the people they would be working with as well as the *formal* contact person within the organization. The other advice which emerged was that students should try to think realistically about the tasks which they would be required to do during their placement. As this was something students found difficult because they didn't know what these tasks might be, an early contact with the employer is implicit in this advice.

All the assessors felt that they themselves had gained from the exercise and mentioned the following benefits:

- a gain in confidence from undertaking a task and completing it successfully;
- a revival and 'brushing up' of knowledge of the industry;
- a new (unexpected!) insight into the problems which can exist for students employed in the industry;
- feedback about the relevance and value of course work offered to students ('we usually have to wait till post-diploma to get feedback about this');
- a clearer knowledge of what and where the gaps in the course are.

The process of assessing the student's placement learning had prompted one lecturer into thinking about what kinds of things students *can* learn and made him question the role of the placement. In the past, students

217

had been sent on placement and when they returned they slipped back into the polytechnic-based role, which is often a rather passive one. He now feels that their experiences while on placement are more important than he had previously thought. In the light of this he now intends to try to involve students more in their learning within the polytechnic and to draw on their experiences during class work.

This carry-over into the polytechnic-taught element of the course was touched upon by an assessor during an assessment meeting. While one student claimed she had gained confidence in her own abilities while on placement, he asked her whether there was a way she could use this new confidence now she was back in college. She thought not – 'it's completely different here because I have no responsibilities. There is no need to take decisions here so I can regress. I would like to have more responsibility, but how?' He agreed that the present framework meant that she had to decide whether or not to attend classes but did not involve her in any real decisions about her learning.

Another potential benefit to the polytechnic was touched on in the discussion of the positive outcomes the assessors had attributed to the project, ie, the identification of strengths and weaknesses in the present course structure. These aspects could now be clearly identified and acted on from a solid base of evidence rather than intuition.

All the students said that they felt they had been given the opportunity to discuss, clarify and defend their reports and several said they enjoyed the assessment meetings. There was nothing about these that any of the students would change except to have these earlier in the term. All the students valued the assessment meeting and many of them said that it was the meeting itself which clarified for them just what they had learnt: 'You're learning more than you think you're learning at the time – the assessment meeting made me realize this'. The opportunity to discuss their learning rather than simply write about it was seen as very important and they liked the informal way in which the discussions were conducted. It was felt that this environment rather than a more formal one, or one where they had to make a presentation, was the most desirable.

As well as helping the students to realize what they had learnt, these meetings were seen as an expression of real interest by the polytechnic in the students' work-based learning. The students felt that more use was being made of their placement experience and that it was being linked more positively to the course content: 'It seems more worthwhile because it's linked to the course'. Not only was placement experience being used, but assessment meant that it was being valued by the polytechnic. One student stressed time and again what other students had also expressed, that to value placement was complementary to the value of course work and particularly appropriate in a '*doing* industry'. This approach was seen as more student-centred and appreciated by the students for the scope it gave them to follow their interests in learning.

Resource Implications

There are clearly resource implications in introducing learning agreements/assessment of placement learning into existing courses.
Project staff need to:

Prepare – students
          – mentor
          – assessors.
Support – students
          – mentor
          – assessors.

Assessors need time to:

Acquaint themselves with the project
Consider methods of assessment
Read the reports or look at other material presented for assessment
Meet students for assessment.

Other specialist departmental staff/assessors need time to:

Explore with students the particular nature of a placement in order that appropriate learning outcomes can be identified.

Discussion

From the very first learning plan preparation workshops there was a focus upon encouraging the students to reflect upon how they learn and to share that information with one another and with the staff involved. Points which consistently emerge from students include:

- the importance they place on being actively involved in learning;
- the need to see the relevance of material which is to be learned;
- the low value they place on the lecture as an aid to learning; and
- their wish to have some say in what is to be learned and in how they might learn it.

One consequence of repeated exposure to these staff/student workshops is that staff reflect upon their own learning methods and experiences and begin to re-examine the teaching methods currently adopted by them in teaching those same students on other parts of the course.

'Learning is necessarily a phenomenon of both teachers and learners. Teachers should not expect to remain unaffected by what they do' (Carr and Kemmis, 1983). However, not all staff are ready or able to work in this way, which raised the question of appropriate staff development. Where possible, staff should self-select into this system and be encouraged to identify appropriate staff-development opportunities. Many staff accustomed to the 'teaching' role will experience difficulty in adapting to a 'facilitating' role. It may be useful to pair an experienced facilitator with an inexperienced one, as a form of staff development.

Staff should be encouraged to develop closer contact with industry and commerce. As the model suggested here involves the students' placement host employer, this ought to be a natural development which emerges from negotiating the three-way agreement. Experience from the project suggests that:

- employers are likely to be attracted by students they perceive as enterprising;
- employers are likely to be pleasantly surprised to discover that educational institutions are prepared to involve them in three-way negotiated contracts.

Mentors should be involved as much as possible in the assessment of the students' work-based learning. It may be that existing employee appraisal systems can be easily adapted to encompass the learning outcomes/ competencies which the student is achieving.

Many qualities associated with enterprise such as taking responsibility, using initiative, coping with uncertainty, tolerance of risk and negotiating skills, are fostered by learner-centred methods such as Contract Learning. It should be borne in mind that in the future, employers will be competing for quality employees and colleges giving effect to models such as the one described here will be recognized as sources of competent and able people.

One of the aims of this project was to use the contract learning model to reduce the length of courses. In a credit-based system, the opportunity to obtain credit from sandwich placement allows the number of credits required for the award of a qualification to be achieved during a period which previously did not give academic credit, and can shorten the overall length of the course. Already, higher diploma courses have been reduced from three to two years, and models such as the one presented here provide a means of awarding credit for relevant learning outcomes achieved.

In degree programmes, the same opportunity exists to shorten courses which have a sandwich placement. However, the task will become easier if and when they are expressed in learning outcome terms. Students will then have scope for achieving these learning outcomes in a variety of ways, including work-based learning. Knowles (1986) makes the point that in the USA, 'Institutions of higher education are, without doubt, currently the most prolific users of Contract Learning'. On a recent visit to North America the Project Director found evidence of the widespread use of learning contracts in a range of educational institutions. At Empire State College, which is part of the State University of New York, most academic work is organized through learning contracts (SUNY, 1988/9).

So, the question being addressed is not the students' ability to learn by using a learning contract, but the ability of staff to devise systems and procedures which can support and assess learning which is relevant to the course of study being pursued.

References

Boak, G (1990) *Developing Management Competences*, London: Pitman.
Carr, W and Kemmis, S (1983) *Becoming Critical – Knowing Through Action Research*, Geelong: Deakin University Press.
Knowles, M S (1980) *The Modern Practice of Adult Education*, Cambridge: Cambridge Book Company.
Knowles, M S (1986) *Using Learning Contracts*, CA: Jossey-Bass Publishers.
Maslow, A H (1970) *Motivation and Personality*, New York: Mostrand.
National Forum for Management Education and Development (1989) *Certificate in Management Guidelines*, London: MCI.
State University of New York (1988/9) *Empire State College Bulletin*, p 15.

22 Learning Experiences for Professional Reality and Responsibility

Betty Anderson and Margaret McMillan

Background

The faculty of health is one of four faculties within the University of Western Sydney, Macarthur. It operates on two campuses, Milperra and Campbelltown which are about 30 kilometres apart in the south west of Sydney, Australia. This region, though on the fringe of greater metropolitan Sydney, is characterized by rapid growth and is encroaching on and absorbing what were formerly rural communities.

The school was established in 1984 and admitted its first students in February 1985 as a result of the New South Wales government's decision to transfer all nurse education out of hospital schools into the higher education sector. At the same time as the transfer, there was also a transformation in terms of how nursing practice was conceived. Instead of perpetuating separateness and the concept of difference by preparing nurses in separate educational programmes to practise by designated specializations, the new programmes acknowledged commonality. This commonality provides the generic basis for the discipline of nursing.

The course, as it is currently presented, requires 3 years of full time attendance. Three hundred students are admitted to the pre-registration course each year. Approximately 50 per cent have been mature entrants, many of whom have not completed the usual and mandatory final high school certificate. These students are admitted following satisfactory completion of a university admission test. In many instances, students have had less educational opportunities than most high achievers from secondary schools. They are frequently the first in their family to attend university but more than justify the chance given to them. The student population of the school is representative of the very diverse ethnic origins of the population of the region in general.

Organizationally, *all* staff representing various disciplines are recruited to the faculty in which a course is being offered, therefore there are not traditional servicing arrangements whereby nursing students are taught, say, science by staff from another faculty. Instead, science staff are recruited to the faculty of health. Most nursing staff of the school are involved in both classroom and clinical teaching. Teaching staff fulfil two major roles, that of learning process facilitator and that of specialist resource person, according to experience, skill and knowledge base.

Practice-centred learning

The specific educational programme with which this chapter is concerned not only results in an academic award but leads to registration as a (comprehensive) nurse with the New South Wales Nurses Registration Board. This in turn entitles the graduate to practise as a beginning professional nurse in most health care services. In order to address the questions of *empowerment* and *good practice* it is intended to focus on the kind of responsible and accountable practitioner to be developed by the educational programme. This focus will allow relationships to emerge among the learning process, its facilitation and the empowerment of the graduate to engage in good practice.

The context of practice has action of one form or another as its basis; it is dynamic in that situations, circumstances and conditions change, often very rapidly; it is invariably complex as many interactive factors combine to determine any one patient/client situation; usually one workplace is made up of a varying number of patients or clients at any one time. Finally, the outcomes of patient-nurse interactions have very direct and often serious consequences for the patient or client. In this dynamic action context the nurse practitioner must respond to situations by exercising judgement to initiate, manage and evaluate care or to refer the problem and/or to collaborate with other health care personnel in the interests of the patient. Any debate about nurse practitioners being 'other'-directed or self-directed, dependent, independent or interdependent in terms of the decision-making process must take into account the nature of the practice, the practitioner role and the practice context itself.

In the context of empowerment and good practice in nursing, an educational process must therefore reflect the demands of the practice as described and must allow the learner to develop a sense of responsibility by being responsible; the ability to initiate wisely and/or collaborate in management and evaluation of care, by 'acting out' these skills and to engage continuously in a meaningful learning process by carrying out the learning themselves. Further, it should enable graduates to adapt to the demands of reality (work versus academic environment) to respond to and be pro-active in respect of change.

It is intended now to illustrate the process of becoming the desired practitioner, as outlined above, through an examination of the learning process adopted by the faculty of health at University of Western Sydney, Macarthur. This examination will be followed by a presentation of outcomes, drawing on anecdotal evidence from and about students and graduates.

The learning process is consistent with the following six principles:

- A focus on learning rather than teaching or lecturing and therefore on a student-centred, self-directed approach. The students are to be actively involved in, and achieve ownership of, the learning, assessment and reflection processes.
- The action context and the reality of practice provide the stimulus to, and organization of, learning rather than traditional syllabus topics.
- The application of enquiry and processing skills to mediate learning in order that information, skills and values can be not only acquired but generated and used.
- An emphasis on integration in order that knowledge and concepts are structured in the way practitioners structure them when thinking and making clinical judgements in the action context.
- The provision of multiple and varied opportunities to experience and/or act out on the behaviours, knowledge structures and values of the profession.
- The provision of ongoing feedback inclusive of self-evaluation and reflection.

Learning through enquiry, reflection, evaluation and action

Whilst it is intended to focus on the learning process as the means of empowerment and developing good practice, it cannot be discussed without making clear that, in the context of our programme, the learning process is more extensive than the processes whereby new knowledge, skills and values are internalized and incorporated into learners' cognitive structures. The sequence of events set in train when students are confronted by a situation in need of improvement, represents an amalgam in which enquiry processes mediate learning, judgement-making, reflection, evaluation and culminate in action. These individual elements are intertwined and interactive and the relationships among them are circular, not on a continuum. Action-taking, though in one sense the end to which the learning is addressed, also stimulates more learning, enquiry, reflection and evaluation. In this way, the use of reality situations and the need to act provides a powerful motivation to learners when cast in the role of the practitioner.

The process of learning throughout a typical week on campus is stimulated by the need to know more about a given situation and to make all data or skills work for students as they act out the role of the professional in planning and/or carrying out intervention to improve the given situation. Both the need to know and to make judgements which determine action-taking are mediated by the enquiry process (see Figure 22.1).

Organizationally, students will meet on campus on average four times per week as a group: on three of these occasions the tutor acts as a facilitator of the enquiry process applied to the particular block of data with which students are working. On the fourth occasion, the tutor changes role and becomes a resource person providing sessions for skill development or content exploration if this material is not readily available to the students. What is planned for a resource session depends on what students identify as learning needs they cannot meet alone. With the exception of the resource sessions, students direct and own the process of enquiry, with the facilitator adopting a challenging and clarifying role. In between group meetings students carry out self-directed activities as individuals to set and achieve their own learning goals in respect of the current learning 'package'. A learning package is most frequently presented via print media, though combinations of print and audio-visual and computer packages are being tested. The situation presented is based

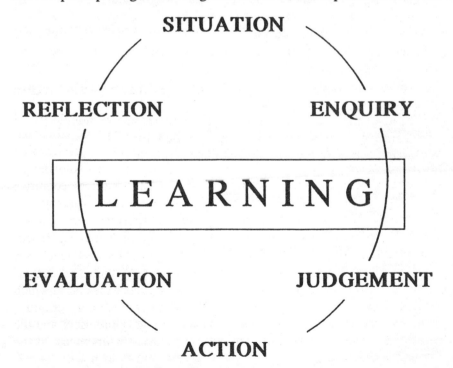

Figure 22.1 *The enquiry process*

on an actual case and because in reality, patient situations change, the blocks of data are introduced so as to develop sequentially the situation and cause students to respond or adapt to change and therefore be caused to modify intervention plans.

However, the clinical experience, especially selected for its relevance, challenges learners in the context of the real world. Students individually are allocated patients to act out the same process but in this instance to implement care also. A nurse academic accompanies the students (1:8) to facilitate learning and care-giving.

Assessment

An essential feature of sound educational practice is that most students are able to recognize that the assessment system in a programme reflects the real objectives. Often those who advocate the use of process-oriented curricula simply revert to the more traditional assessment strategies which tend to examine what students have learned when the emphasis should be on whether or not they can apply what they have learned and whether they have a capacity for critical analysis of concepts, issues and personal behaviour.

The learning outcomes in the Macarthur programme are as individual as the student using the self-directed, enquiry process. However in general terms, a situation improvement summary (SIS) will result; one which incorporates not only the process adopted to achieve the plan, but the learnings from all the discipline and practice areas which have contributed to the students' understanding of the situation and therefore influenced the judgements made.

The assessment and evaluation stages therefore are an integral part of the learning process, one which is enriched by reflection and self-evaluation and during which time students consider:

- what they did and with what result;
- whether they would do it differently next time;
- if so, how;
- the role of other members in their subgroups; and
- their own self-evaluation of their overall performance using set criteria.

The Macarthur faculty therefore focused on developing assessment strategies which monitored the students' use of knowledge in the clinical context, assessed the individual's clinical reasoning and capacity for self-direction, facilitated student reflection on both self-directed and cooperative learning ventures and reflected the reality of professional practice. A student can expect explicit feedback on two elements of performance, first, from faculty, judgements about performance as specified in the published criteria, and second, from self correction and critical analysis. Students themselves become adept at using (and later devising) criteria to assist their own evaluation, supporting their conclusions about personal performance by citing incidents to justify their claims.

Feedback derives from both on-campus and clinical practice experiences; students are encouraged to reflect on a critique of their behaviour from faculty, peers and themselves but also from clients (both simulated and actual) and health care personnel. Faculty are encouraged to model evaluative behaviours which demonstrate critical thinking and to provide a rationale for decisions made about students' work.

An evolutionary process of development

Whilst criterion-referenced assessment was always advocated in the Macarthur curriculum, bringing both staff and students to a level of functional understanding of its application has been a gradual process. Originally in 1985 an American tool, a critical incident technique, was used but did not incorporate the two crucial elements of problem-solving and skills in self-direction. During 1986, cross-checking of the technique with the profile of the graduate from the Macarthur programme and the Australian 'Standards for Nursing Practice' enabled faculty finally to identify five performance categories which were consistent with the course objectives and from which performance criteria and their indicators could be developed. Faculty believed that this insured not only a good and safe practitioner but demonstrated responsibility and accountability on their part as educators.

During 1989 it became evident that the criteria could be used to assess students' performance both on campus and in the clinical practice setting, thus acknowledging the importance of integration of theoretical and practice-oriented activities. The criteria also allowed for the use of a variety of assessment items, including essays to monitor the student's capacity for critical analysis and academic expression in, for example, the documentation of the process of package exploration, in modified essay examinations or completion of personal profiles. Interactive processes and application of enquiry and problem-solving could be monitored by the use of group and individual vivas. A form of integrated assessment, the objective structured clinical assessment (OSCA), which in itself can utilize a range of assessment strategies, is also an invaluable assessment strategy which reflects the school's contention that assessment should be a learning process.

Evaluation

Faculty at every stage in course development and implementation have reflected on outcomes. Evaluative exercises undertaken encompass both formative and summative, informal and formal approaches. For example, when adopting competency-based assessment, formative evaluation efforts were evident in the cross-checking of course objectives and student outcomes with the national standards for practice.

At the informal level, feedback has been received, recorded and reported to the various committees and to the teaching teams for appropriate action. Team members have frequently recorded both positive and negative student and group outcomes and sent these to the Dean. Staff members are encouraged to use facilitator feedback forms which reflect the process orientation of the course.

At a more formal level the nominal group technique has been used for feedback purposes and subsequent decision-making on future course directions. Year teams report to each other on progress/problems encountered within their implementation activities. Panels of students have met with staff to seek clarification of reported difficulties experienced with the course.

Evaluation of assessment strategies

Another example of efforts to demonstrate sound educational practice by the use of reflection was a study, funded by the New South Wales Nurses Registration Board, undertaken to monitor the validity and reliability of the OSCA. The OSCA was chosen as an assessment strategy because of its potential to reflect the reality of practice and the desirability of accommodating a mix of the actual and practice-oriented concepts in an integrated way.

It was a contention of the faculty that the OSCA could emphasize a range of health-related foci, as well as represent nursing roles and functions of a comprehensive nature. The assessment process, as always, incorporated the use of self-assessment and because of the use of simulated clients, provided opportunity for feedback from them as well. The OSCA could include any one or all of the performance categories of practice, enquiry and processing, application of knowledge and concepts, demonstration of professional values, and attitudes and self-direction in learning/practice.

The research methodology included the use of questionnaires directed to students with follow-up interviews, a panel of experts and an analysis of statistical correlation between the students' results in the OSCA and in another area of assessment. In relation to validity, interest focused on the students' and panel members' perceptions of the faculty's contentions about the OSCA.

The panel of experts was used because of their heightened awareness of the parameters of professional practice and the likelihood of identification of problems related to contemporary issues. They examined the written information provided to students, viewed videos of student performance, reviewed the organization of the OSCA, interviewed students on completion of the assessment task and had informal conversations with faculty, simulated clients and students prior to undertaking the assessment. They were able to provide formal written feedback to the researchers as well as engage in a summative group discussion on the exercise. The latter was taped for analysis which suggested that overall the OSCA appeared to reflect sound educational and professional practice because of its simulation of the real context.

Course evaluation

The entire course was evaluated prior to the adoption of the totally integrated programme. Stufflebeam's adaptation of a decision-making model incorporating the Stakeholder approach was used. Attention focused on:

- context: needs and feasibility of the programme within the community;
- input: design of the programme;
- process: actual implementation of the programme; and
- product: graduates and their fit with intended goals.

The findings and recommendations played a significant role in the redesign of the course, now in its second year of implementation. The project was reported in its entirety and was published by the school in 1989.

Follow-up of Graduates

A comprehensive study has been undertaken by Associate Professor McMillan (1990) using the elements of the profile of the graduate as the basis on which to make judgements of the graduates. Data from questionnaires and follow up interviews with the graduates themselves were validated against data from faculty and the registered nurses with whom the graduates worked.

Feedback suggests that in relation to practice, the graduate is a competent and safe beginning practitioner who has good communication skills when working with colleagues and clients in either chronic or crisis situations. The client is viewed as an individual and provided with care which is goal-oriented in the context of the total person.

In relation to problem-solving, the graduate is able to adapt to novel situations and new technology. Co-workers say there is evidence of the graduate's using a particular strategy to identify people's needs, determine priorities, choose a course of action and reflect on outcomes. When dealing with the unknown, the graduate does not hesitate to seek more information and use a range of resources which include other members of the health care team and written material. They apparently do this in a less self-conscious way than their hospital-based peers who had an expectation that they should know it all.

In relation to conceptualizing practice, the graduates report that on reflection the integrated nature of the course prepared them well for bringing together information and seeing new relationships between concepts. Above all else they value the spontaneity of the practice arena and the potential for new concepts to emerge which can be linked to on-campus activities undertaken within the course.

Whilst acknowledging the constraints of 'the system', the graduates, once acclimatized and socialized into the world of work, appear to be less constrained about making decisions and taking actions on behalf of their clients. They are more autonomous in their practice. For example, rather than asking more senior personnel whether they should take a particular action, they frequently inform their colleagues of what they deem an appropriate course of action.

In relation to professional practice, feedback suggests that the graduates have a keen sense of awareness of legal and ethical issues and though inexperienced, function within legal bounds. They are judged to be aspiring to high standards of care and behave in a responsible and accountable manner. They are reported as accepting ongoing learning as desirable and necessary and seek enrolment in in-service and formal education courses. There is a high level of exchange with colleagues of verbal and written information related to patient care. This confirms a commitment to ongoing learning.

Self-reflection is a strong feature of the graduates. Colleagues report an expectation of graduates that feedback will be frequent and constructive. They want advice on strategies for improvement. The graduates report on daily reflections on their behaviour, feelings and beliefs and the outcomes of particular actions taken.

For them, appraisal is a part of routine practice but there is also an expectation that others provide a rationale when advising on a desired course of action. They have had to withstand confrontation because of the different levels of acceptance of the tertiary approach to the preparation of the nurse. Particular strengths include a capacity to be assertive and deal with conflict within the team. They attribute this ability to the group process they had experienced within the course.

Conclusion

We have suggested that practice-based learning can be justified in terms of good practice and the empowerment of learners in the process of becoming competent practitioners on both educational and professional grounds.

The principles fundamental to successful implementation have been discussed. A particular position has been adopted in respect of learning – one that recognizes that the 'situation' (ie, the learning stimulus) is as important as the enquiry process in learning. Similarly, action-taking, evaluation and reflection are integral to this learning process, with each of these elements interacting with the other in a dynamic way. The result is a graduate who can adapt to the ongoing demands of reality in an action context and respond to and be pro-active in respect of change, gaining power through owning the learning process. Insights into their practice-based approach to learning continue to unfold as research and reflection inform its implementation.

References

Anderson, B M (1978) 'A basic nurse education curriculum evaluation incorporating an investigation into the cognitive aspects of clinical judgment of senior trainee nurses', New South Wales College of Nursing, Sydney.

Barrows, H S (1985) *How to design a PBL Curriculum for the Pre-clinical Years*, New York: Springer Publishing Company.

Barrows H S (1986) 'A taxonomy of problem-based learning methods', *Medical Education*, 20, 6; 481–6.

Barrows, H S (in preparation) Reiterative, problem-based, self-directed learning: A powerful, well-designed species of problem-based learning.

Barrows, H S (nd) 'Problem-based learning', *CPD Monographs No.5*, Centre for Professional Development, University of Southern Illinois.

Barrows, H S and Tamblyn, R (1980) *Problem-based Learning: An Approach to Medical Education*, New York: Springer Verlag.

Bujack, E and Little, P J (1989) 'Integrated performance-based assessment in problem-based learning', in Wallis, B (ed) *Problem-based Learning: The Newcastle Workshop*, University of Newcastle, Faculty of Medicine.

Bujack, E, McMillan, M, Dwyer, J and Hazelton, M (1991) 'Assessing comprehensive nursing performance: The objective structured clinical assessment (OSCA) part 2 report of the evaluation project', *Nurse Education Today* 11, 248–55, Longman Group, UK.

Fivars, G and Gosnell, D (1966) *Nursing evaluation. The Problem and the Process: The Critical Incident Technique*, New York: Macmillan.

Hengstberger-Sims *et al* (1989) 'Report of the evaluation working party: Evaluation of the Diploma of Applied Science (Nursing)', University of Western Sydney, School of Nursing and Health Studies.

McMillan, M (1990) 'An evaluation of the use of Objective Structured Clinical Assessment (OSCA) within the School of Nursing and Health Studies at the University of Western Sydney, Macarthur', University of Western Sydney, Macarthur.

Parliament of the Commonwealth of Australia (1990) *Priorities for Reform in Higher*

Education: A Report by the Senate Standing Committee on Employment, Education and Training, Canberra: Australian Government Publishing Service.

Ryan, G L (1989) 'Problem-based learning: some practical issues', in Edwards H and Barraclough, S (eds) *Research and Development in Higher Education*, volume 11, pp 155–9, Sydney: Higher Education Research and Development Society of Australasia.

Ryan G L and Little, P J (in press.) 'Innovation in a nursing curriculum: A process of change', in Boud, D and Felletti, G (eds) *The Challenge of Problem-based Learning*. London: Kogan Page.

Saunders, K, Northup, D and Mennin, S P (1985) 'The library in a problem-based curriculum', in Kaufmann, A, (ed) *Implementing Problem-based Medical Education*, New York: Springer Verlag.

Schmidt, H G *et al* (1989) *New Directions for Medical Education: Problem-based Learning and Community-oriented Medical Education*, New York: Springer Verlag.

Stufflebeam, D (1983) in Worthen, B R and Sanders, J R, *Educational Evaluation Theory and Practice*, California: Wadsworth.

Wilson, B (1987) *Methods of Training – Resource Based and Open Learning Study Skills*, Carnforth: Parthenon Publishing Group.

Weiss, C H (1986) 'The stakeholder approach to evaluation: Origins and promise', in House, E R (ed) *New Directions in Education Evaluation*, London: Falmer Press.

23 An Experiential Learning Approach to Developing Clinical Reasoning Skills

Joy Higgs

Clinical reasoning in its broadest sense connotes the internal thinking and decision-making processes associated with clinical practice. In today's world of rapid technological advances and knowledge expansion, professional people within health science and other disciplines need to be skilled reasoners, decision-makers and problem-solvers. They need to be able to deal effectively with a mass of information which is complex and dynamic in a manner which is situation-specific, effective and accountable. Experiential learning as an approach to teaching and learning has much to offer educators and learners alike in the development of these skills.

This chapter examines the process and outcomes of an experiential learning course which enables postgraduate physiotherapy students to understand and develop their clinical reasoning skills (Higgs, 1990). The course is conducted at Cumberland College of Health Sciences, the University of Sydney. The students are physiotherapists who are enrolled in a postgraduate programme in manipulative physiotherapy. Following completion of this programme, graduates frequently work in private practice, which in Australia (as in a number of other countries) involves working as first contact practitioners. That is, members of the community may seek their services without referral from medical or other practitioners. Such a prerogative demands that physiotherapists are able to make accurate clinical diagnoses and plan, implement and evaluate appropriate clinical management programmes. Good clinical practice therefore requires effective clinical reasoning skills.

Educators also need to determine what is good educational practice when conducting programmes to help students develop these skills. In designing this programme we believed that good practice in relation to the development of effective clinical reasoning skills should involve the following:

- the employment of adult learning principles, such as active learner participation and the use of learners' past experiences;
- the promotion of skills and attitudes of self-directed learning, such as a commitment to ongoing learning, responsibility for one's own learning and self-evaluation;
- the use of experiential learning as a framework for the learning programme. In this programme the learners' experience of clinical reasoning is accomplished through role playing the clinician's role in clinical reasoning, simulating the patient's role and problems, and practising the skill of reflecting on their performance;
- integration of learning derived from this course with learning occurring in other courses in the postgraduate programme. In particular this refers to utilizing the background knowledge and skills gained in other courses (such as applied and medical sciences, physiotherapy theory and practice) within the clinical reasoning course and combining the learning from all of these courses in clinical practicums.

The course extends over two 14-week semesters. It aims to help the students to become aware of how they reason in relation to clinical problems, to understand the theoretical processes of clinical reasoning, to critically evaluate this theory in the light of their own clinical experience and to develop their skills as clinical reasoners.

The subject commences with presentation of an overview of the theories of clinical reasoning by the teacher. This is followed by an exploration of the students' thinking, learning and clinical reasoning skills via simulation exercises and discussion of students' scores on learning inventories.[1] These inventories are used to illustrate parallels between learning and clinical reasoning, to help students become aware of how they think in relation to an activity (ie, learning) with which they are familiar, and to help them to develop as learners (an essential element of being an effective clinician). In addition, students are asked to complete a self-rating instrument developed by the author to examine their perceptions of themselves as clinical reasoners.

The course

The major teaching/learning strategy devised for the first semester of the course is based on the following experiential learning activities: fish bowl technique, simulated patients/clients, a 'hypotheticals'[2] panel discussion and role play. The room is set up with most of the class acting as an audience (and later participating in open discussion) and with a semicircle of chairs – 'the fishbowl' – facing the audience. In this semicircle are three students forming the 'patient group', three or four students forming the questioning/therapist panel, one to three experts (applied scientists, experienced clinicians and teachers on the course) and the session manager. This strategy involves the following elements.

a) Preparation of the patient/client

A group of three students (on a roster system) is assigned the task of preparing in detail a hypothetical patient who is seeking assistance from a manipulative physiotherapist regarding the management of a clinical problem.

Preparation time allowed is several weeks and students are encouraged to consult with an experienced manipulative physiotherapist to ensure accuracy and appropriateness of the signs, symptoms, background and responses they have created for the 'patient'. During the session in which this patient is involved, one student role-plays the patient, one acts as an 'information source' about the patient and a third as a scribe, recording information and decisions made on a whiteboard.

The purpose of the session is to examine and develop the students' clinical reasoning skills. Skills such as history-taking, physical assessment and treatment are developed in other classes and in the clinical setting. The 'information source' student is frequently called upon to provide data on request, rather than the panel obtaining this at a much slower pace from the patient. This provides more time for analysis, synthesis and evaluation of the information received, ie, for clinical reasoning and for discussion of the process of clinical reasoning demonstrated by students discussing the case.

b) Discussion of the case

Each week two groups of three or four students act as a panel of physiotherapists who discuss the case. They are asked to use information obtained from the simulated patient or information about this patient to reason through the case and make appropriate diagnostic, treatment and evaluation decisions. The session manager is responsible for time-keeping, stage managing the broad activities of the participants and for promoting discussion on clinical reasoning. This role requires an understanding of clinical reasoning and the teaching/learning strategy being employed. It involves ongoing analysis of the situation in order to enable appropriate intervention and management of the session.

c) Time out for discussion on clinical reasoning

This activity runs parallel to the discussion of the case. The manager uses several methods to promote discussion or questioning of the students' clinical reasoning, knowledge base, conclusions reached and appropriateness of clinical decisions. These include the manager asking students to provide reasons for their questions or decisions (eg, What did you hope to gain from asking that question? On what do you base that decision/ conclusion?) and asking them to consider the information they receive in relation to answers they would have expected in the light of their knowledge and clinical experience. They are also asked to examine their questions, answers and planned intervention in relation to clinical reasoning activities and skills (eg, Does the information you have just obtained help you in formulating or testing a working hypothesis, in assessing the patient, in setting baselines for subsequent assessment or in planning treatment?). This type of question is more frequent at the beginning of the course. Towards the end of the first semester a broader question (eg, Why did you ask that question?) elicits this information without prompting, indicating that students have become more aware of their clinical reasoning processes and are not only planning their questions and investigations meaningfully but are also monitoring their thoughts. That is, they are employing metacognition.

The expert panel also participates in this questioning. In particular the panel members seek to challenge the students' knowledge and their use of knowledge and clinical inquiry strategies and to engage students in exploration of the relative advantages of different inquiry methods, investigation techniques and intervention strategies. Of particular concern is helping students to evaluate the validity of their own knowledge and to critically review their clinical assessment and evaluation strategies.

These classes also seek to address 'people concerns' such as the relevance of the patient's (or client's) environment, background and preferences, the place of interpersonal skills in the therapeutic process and the role of the patient in cooperative decision-making and self-management.

d) Reflection on the class
At the end of each class, time is planned for general discussion with the audience. This deals with clinical management and clinical reasoning issues raised in the class and the experiences of the participants during the class.

e) Individual reflection
Apart from reflection during the class, students are asked to prepare written assignments which involve reflection on what they have learned about the process of clinical reasoning, what they have learned about themselves as clinical reasoners and ways they could improve their clinical reasoning.

f) Feedback

During the class, students' performance is assessed. Students in the therapist group are assessed on their clinical reasoning skills and knowledge base. The patient group students are assessed on their level of preparation and their understanding of the case presented. Individual feedback to students is provided after the class in order to promote the development of their clinical reasoning skills.

g) Implementing clinical reasoning in practice

The whole course is designed to promote integration of students' learning from different subjects and experiences. Running parallel to the clinical reasoning subject are therapeutic skills and applied science classes and clinical education sessions. All subjects aim to promote transfer of learning between subjects. Students further develop their clinical reasoning skills in the clinical education sessions.

h) Peer teaching and learning

In the second semester of the course the students are responsible for designing and conducting classes which enable themselves and their fellow students to further develop their clinical reasoning skills. This segment of the course has resulted in an exciting variety of highly innovative and effective learning experiences, including simulated court room dramas dealing with the legal implications of clinical decision-making, 'quiz shows' and debates, where competition and good fun combine to make clinical reasoning a challenging and enjoyable topic and a stimulating part of the students' overall learning experience.

Critique of the teaching strategy

The above teaching/learning strategy has been used effectively in several states in Australia, in New Zealand and in Hong Kong, with physiotherapy students and multidisciplinary groups. It is constantly evolving and being improved upon, and the author as well as students and teachers in the course are continually finding new applications for this method. The greatest identified benefits of this strategy are its ability to empower the students by stimulating their interest and enjoyment in clinical reasoning, by enhancing their confidence in and ability to use reasoning skills and by encouraging transfer of these skills to clinical practice. In addition, the course has encouraged these clinicians to empower their clients by sharing the decision-making role and by encouraging the clients to take a greater responsibility for their own health and well-being.

Notes

1. These are a) The Lancaster Approaches to Studying Inventory (Entwistle and Ramsden, 1983); b) Kolb's Learning Style Inventory (1976).
2. Refer to Scott and Andresen (1988) for a discussion of this method.

References

Entwistle, N J and Ramsden, P (1983) *Understanding Student Learning*, Beckenham: Croom Helm.

Higgs, J (1990) 'Fostering the acquisition of clinical reasoning skills', *New Zealand Journal of Physiotherapy*, 18; 13–17.

Kolb, D A (1976) *Learning Style Inventory: Technical Manual*, Boston: McBer and Co.

Scott, G and Andresen, L (1988) 'The hypothetical: A new training resource for adult educators', *Studies in Continuing Education*, 10; 14–32.

24 Task and Reflection in Learning to Learn

Bruce Anderson

Philosophy and direction

For me the main goal of education is for people to become autonomous learners, and I feel that becoming skilled in this process is far more important than familiarity with any factual material. In technological subjects it is also an intensely practical matter because of the enormous rate of change and the introduction of new methods and ideas. The other goal in my own courses is for students to learn about software engineering, by which I mean to become effective at technical work in that domain. I am not concerned with 'book learning' isolated from active use of the information obtained, though students on my courses do more reading than most.

I believe that the key to learning-to-learn is an emphasis on engagement and reflection; engagement with the material, with others and with the self. I generally use carefully structured exercises, stress getting to grips with the material and make use of resources – books, experts, computers. The processes through which this is done are important:

- work in pairs and small groups;
- peer comment and assessment;
- public presentation of work;
- an atmosphere of trust and safety;
- honesty, openness and real attention on my part; and
- attention to the learning process itself.

Students work together and awarely take responsibility for their own learning. I am much more a facilitator than a lecturer, though a consultant too, ie, a technical expert. This means that I can work with large numbers, for example 100 students working as 25 groups of 4, all at once.

An example

Aim
To learn about some topic; to experience variety in solutions and approaches; to express judgements.

Method
Students worked in seven teams of about five members. I issued a set of five problems for each team, with each solution about half a page long. I asked teams to bring six copies of their solutions to the class. In the class I split the teams the other way, by problem, and each such group discussed five solutions to one problem. Then they chose the best solution, or created a composite and someone presented it to the whole class on an overhead slide.

This worked very well: most teams solved most problems, and there was a good solution to each problem. The group discussions were active and constructive. The problem choice helped: they were interesting and not too difficult once the students understood the topic, but did require detailed knowledge. To my surprise and joy, each presentation was applauded – but the students had worked hard to gain an understanding which allowed them to appreciate the solutions.

I used my own expertise to devise the structure, to choose the problems, to suggest reference material, to run the classroom session and to comment (minimally in this case) on the final solutions. The students worked in two phases: initially, with books and the computer system to understand the domain and solve the problems with the help of others in the team; later, to compare and choose solutions with a different group of students. I was a facilitator and consultant, while the students were actively engaged with the material and each other, learning about software and learning to learn.

Engagement and Empowerment
The process of becoming a mature learner involves the development of critical skills and the development and valuing of personal theories and opinions. I believe that some of the value of an education in the humanities comes from the central role of this development: a first-year's own theory of *The Tempest* may be unsophisticated but it is valuable for discussion, and an opening to further work. There is 'something to talk about', and this talk (even to oneself) is important to learning. In technology, maths and science things appear to be different, so that , for example, Miller's theorem (in circuit analysis) is to be learnt, and at this level is not a topic for critique. What is there to talk about? Too often the

teacher's (and thus the students') assumption is 'nothing', so that after presenting the theorem and its proof, students are sent off to solve problems, returning to view the worked solutions. Engagement, and often learning, are minimal. My own approach is quite different – Millering is something you do, the theorem is to be used, and this provides the arena for development. After doing some using, learners can, for example:

- compare analyses they have done;
- look for alternative solutions that don't use Miller;
- create heuristics for the applicability of the method;
- formulate their own 'guide to Millering'.

This interaction and involvement is both a learning and a learning-to-learn experience. Well-structured reflection leads to conscious learning; seeing oneself learn means recognizing oneself as a learner, which is heartening and motivating. This is the beginning of the aware practice that is the hallmark of the skilled practitioner (Schön).

The need for science and technology students to do some creative/discursive work is often recognized, but my approach is quite different from asking students to write essays on 'The social implications of microelectronics', an activity for which they are generally unprepared and which splits off personal involvement from technical activity and denies its intellectual and personal challenge. I think this is how the gap between Snow's 'two cultures' is maintained.

Although students in traditional laboratories and problem classes do engage in practical work, the learning outcomes are often very limited; too often students just 'follow the script' and 'write it up', or 'have a go at the problem' and 'look at the worked solution'. Teachers often tell me, 'our course has a large laboratory element already' or, 'yes, I use a lot of practical exercises too', but though the method may be the same on the surface, the nature of the interaction is quite different and leads to a quite different experience.

Planning and working

How can we go about thinking about this kind of problem-centred work, and planning to use it? In my classes students work in a cycle of five steps: preparation, task, reflection, feedback and consolidation (Lewin, 1951; Boud *et al*, 1985). The last three of these are the most difficult to organize for people new to experiential learning, so here I present some notes and checklists to help teachers with organizing these steps. They are abstracted from a forthcoming book (Anderson).

Reflection

This the step where we look at the content or the process of the doing of the task, and analyse or measure it. This needs to be conscious, ie, more than just doing the task and organized, ie, more than saying 'reflect on this'. Almost any reflection step can catalyse learning, but usually I choose something that relates back to the stated aims and objectives, for example:

- results: values measured, conclusions reached, system designed, diagrams drawn, reports made;
- process: steps taken, methods used, difficulties encountered, errors made.

Reflecting on process is more difficult but vital; it takes time for anyone to learn how to watch themselves in the doing of something and it is essential at the beginning to use structures that encourage this safely.

You may want your students to reflect alone, with other learners or with experts. My own philosophy is generally to encourage students to work with each other, and to use scarce (and expensive!) experts only when really useful. I use various resources and stimuli to help students to look at their work:

questions, checklists, standard results, and other learners' work. Of course these can be mixed; for example a checklist used to compare a student's written report with a model one provided by a staff member (or last year's students!).

I often stress the production of some concrete output: a piece for further reflection, a lab report, a short writeup, an oral report, or an interview. Reflection outputs require the students to have good communication skills, so this way of working provides both motivation and a location for their teaching.

Feedback

Feedback may be any useful information: we include assessment, which uses some scale(s), and which may be formal, ie, count towards some classification. As with reflection, we need to pay attention to the details of being conscious and organized.

The topic and focus can be either the results or the process of a class. My own practice is to provide a concrete framework for all this, using documents and concrete products of the work where I can. The student, other learners or the experts do the job. As with reflection, I encourage peer interaction where I can.

With instruments of feedback and assessment, I make clear boundaries for the assessment process. In particular I often choose a checklist, a form or a table.

The feedback phase is a good time for students to assess the class – the script, the work/reflection cycle, the assessment process, the demonstrators and the equipment.

Consolidation

This is the stage of placing the work in context; linking to other ideas; making the new skill or knowledge explicit. Even after reflection, feedback and assessment, there is a further specific opportunity to aid students' learning, an opportunity to take stock at a greater distance from the task itself.

Further reflection is on the whole process so far, the task, initial reflection and feedback/assessment. It can sometimes be formulated as advice to others. At this stage of trying to be explicit about the bigger picture it can be useful to use some kind of map or tree or taxonomy to express this on paper.

A good way to consolidate new understanding is to use it – extend it, incorporate it in a new exercise and fit it explicitly into some larger knowledge structure. You can do some reflection work at the bench, but it may be necessary to use a classroom session or tutorial to get the necessary time or the right kind of space.

My experience so far

In presenting my work to others I have found it valuable to talk about my own experience, and of course this is vital to me in my own learning-to-teach. In this section I collect some of the things that seem most important.

Beginning

My main initial difficulty was seeing how to apply the student-oriented methods I was told about on courses, and read about in generic teaching literature, eg, UTMU (1976), to technical material. Teaching was generally described in terms of school work, or of arts/social science study. Eventually I was able to adapt the structures I read about (Habeshaw *et al*, 1987), but once I started doing things this way new ideas started to come. I have a lot of sheets of paper headed 'Next time'! I found out that it is OK to proceed fairly mechanically – many of these structures work themselves provided you are sensitive to what is going on. So starting off doesn't mean you have to be a brilliant and experienced groupwork facilitator!

Structure

A non-lecture based approach needs careful prior organization – bits of paper, forms, times, formats – especially in the beginning. Tasks must be specified precisely. Not 'Read this paper', but 'Read this paper and list the three points you found most novel; summarize it in 200 words; describe how you would use the ideas to . . .'.

Timing is important – I announce before any specific activity how long there is for it; occasionally it finishes early or I give a specific extension. Room layout is also important – I don't hesitate to move the tables about. Sometimes I stand at the front, but sometimes I just sit round the table as an equal participant. Students can work in fours in a lecture theatre if half of them sit on the desktops and face backwards. There will be some resistance to this initially.

Distribute the responsibility – for example if essays are to be passed around then get the students to make the multiple copies needed.

Presence

Take part! Students love to evaluate staff work. Trying the quiz for yourself may be quite illuminating.

Step back! You will be needed to help individuals or pairs with some of the activities. Let it run! Sometimes the students will get into a bad place but often it is best to let them get right into it and find out for themselves, rather than keeping them out by intervening too early.

Be flexible! Sometimes things don't work out.

Feelings

You have to want to do it; this way of working is too threatening for many people to use; you are closer to the students and their difficulties. Students may dislike it too, and say they are lost. I point out that if I gave a conventional lecture and they took conventional notes, then they would just get lost when I set them a problem sheet – but they would be lost in private, which is somehow more bearable, though often less productive. This approach is more creative for teachers. Is that what you want?

The key point for students is to get to grips with the material, to have something to do and something to talk about. The key feature for teachers is to provide a well-defined, perhaps even rigid, structure in which flexibility is allowed so that this can happen.

Vision and effectiveness

The approach I have outlined offers a practical alternative to the usual lectures and problem classes in that courses can still have a syllabus and students can still take examinations, though the limitations of both become clearer to all concerned. This approach could be fully exploited only in an institution which encouraged its adoption rather than permitted its presence; for many people, both staff and students, this would involve not just a change in technique, but a real shift in values. I am more interested in encouraging this shift than in measuring effectiveness on conventional scales.

My own vision is of a learning community, of people getting together to learn as a natural activity, an activity familiar from early in life and continuing until death. Educational institutions would still matter, but only as part of a web of resources to be used by learners. But I work in a university with rules and standards that are quite different from this. I use those standards to assess the students and their work; I am guided by peer assessment, and I give marks for contribution to the class, but basically I stick to the rules. If I feel strongly about it then I tell the students how hard I am finding it.

The way I teach is effective for students in the conventional sense that they take exams and pass them and they produce work which my colleagues respect. In terms of resources it is effective for me: some effort is needed, though I think that overall it's not more work, it's just more skilled and strategic work. However, I do need more time for a topic, because it is really being worked on, ie, work is being done in the classroom that is normally done elsewhere, or not done. Once staff and students can work this way, more staff time is not needed because the students do a lot. Staff can concentrate on facilitating and on showing real expertise in the domain.

However, for me the real effectiveness, the part that is not present in lecture-based teaching, is in empowerment; when students 'get the idea' they see what I am doing and why and they see that they are learning. After graduating, they tell me they see even better. However, at the time, the contrast with other courses is puzzling and sometimes even distressing.

I still have not made the move to truly student-centred learning, where they take responsibility for the exercises and their content. I do not believe I could have provided such a 'liberating structure' (Torbert, 1978) without more institutional support. However, my experience is that most professional software engineers are no more ready to be in such a structure than first-year students are. The difficulties are to do with the structures of our society as a whole, not just our universities.

Acknowledgements

Grateful thanks to the many people who have encouraged me in this work, especially Angela Brew, Steve Cook, Trevor Habeshaw, Benedict Heal,

Terry Wareham, Sue Knights, Richard Horobin and Max Clowes. And to all the students who have helped me to learn.

References

Anderson D B (forthcoming).

Boud, D, Keogh, R and Walker, D (1985) *Reflection: Turing Experience into Learning*, London: Kogan Page.

Brandes, D and Ginnis, P (1986) *A Guide to Student-centred Learning*, Oxford: Basil Blackwell.

Gibbs, G (1981) *Teaching Students to Learn: A Student-centred Approach*, Milton Keynes: Open University Press.

Habeshaw, S, Habeshaw, T and Gibbs, G (1987) *53 Interesting Things to do in your Seminars and Tutorials*, Bristol: Technical and Educational Services.

Lewin, K (1951) *Field Theory in Social Sciences*, New York: Harper & Row.

Rogers, C (1983) *Freedom to Learn for the 80s*, New York: Charles E Merrill.

Schön D (1983) *The Reflective Practitioner*, New York: Basic Books.

Torbert, W R (1978) 'Educating towards shared purpose, self-direction and quality work', *Journal of Higher Education*, 49, 109–35.

UTMU (1976) *Improving Teaching in Higher Education*, London: University Teaching Methods Unit.

25 Encouraging Experiential Learning: Lessons from the 16–18 Curriculum Enrichment Programme

Ian Taylor

Background to the development of the enrichment programme

The programme began when teachers in a girls' comprehensive school in Wallasey, north-west England, responded to the need to enhance existing 'sixth-form' provision by giving students opportunities to develop problem-solving and communication skills by having them work together in small groups to solve a project problem. To develop suitable projects, the teachers built upon informal links they had already established with the University of Liverpool and with industrialists at Unilever research.

The potential of such projects was recognized by the University of Liverpool and, funded by the (then) Training Agency, a two-year programme of development has been undertaken. Progress has been monitored and directed by a steering committee whose members include representatives of the university, local industry and schools.

The results of this programme have been to produce a series of project briefs and accompanying notes for teachers which is now available nationally. In these projects, the emphasis is on the development of skills rather than the acquisition of knowledge. A small group of students pool their resources in an attempt to solve a real problem. The projects are interdisciplinary in nature so that students with different subject specialisms are encouraged to work together. Each assignment is time-tabled alongside existing studies and requires between two and two and a half hours per week. During that time, students are encouraged to make contact with, and seek advice from, external sources (eg, local industry, higher education). They keep a log book of activities and, at the end, produce a written report. They also give a formal presentation of their findings to an invited audience. On completion of the project, a Record of Achievement in group project work is awarded to each student. This RoA is awarded following formal negotiation between the student and the teacher responsible for supervising the project. (For a more detailed description of the enrichment programme, see Taylor, 1990; 1991 a; b).

By placing these projects alongside 'normal studies', the programme is acknowledging that a combination of experiential learning and learning in more formal settings is necessary if individuals are to be capable of realizing their full potential. By posing problems which are real, open and interdisciplinary in nature, the programme also operates to forge links between the established bodies of knowledge which are already part of the formal curriculum.

The learning is experiential

The enrichment programme draws on a number of traditions but basically it represents a fusion of two. Embedded in the programme are elements of both a group-centred approach and a problem-centred approach to experiential learning. Much of the activity proceeds within the context of the group: members referring to others for support, feedback and, indeed, for validation of the enterprise. Much learning occurs from interaction between group members. There is an emphasis on considering different points of view and on collaborative decision-making.

The programme also adopts a project-centred approach, ie, the project itself gives meaning to and characterizes the enterprise. Although individual students exercise initiative and engage in individual learning in association with these projects, it is the goals of the particular learning situation which are central and these will tend to override the special interests of any one member of the group.

Descriptions of the project-centred approach (see, for example, Boud, 1985) point to one of the limitations of this form of learning: namely that the problem itself will define (and limit) the area of possible learning. But these projects are 'open' and the problems to be solved are interdisciplinary. What is to be learned is not prescribed; instead, the groups are given the opportunity to proceed through the problem in their own way. Important features of the projects include the following.

a) There are sequences of learning

Experiential learning is often described in terms of the sequences of learning that can take place (see, for example, Kolb, 1984). Certainly there is evidence (Taylor, 1989) that a number of aspects of learning associated with these sequences are present in these projects. Students, for example, undertake observation and reflection. They attempt generalizations by sorting or puzzling things out (Boydell, 1976; Kilty, 1982) and also undertake active experimentation.

b) Multi-dimensional learning
Clearly, these projects are developing much more than cognition. There are attitudinal and value-related elements and aspects to the learning that is taking place. Students must develop a sensitivity and respect for the others in the group and a desire to support each other and communicate effectively. They must also learn to access information and actively develop problem-solving skills.

c) Learner control
The projects provide opportunities for self- and group-directed learning. Contact is made with the 'outside world' because students themselves have identified areas where help is needed. Those associated with the development of this programme feel that if students are to gain a more accurate perception of the 'outside world', then it is the students who need to interact with it, when they feel the need to share with and relate their problems to others.

d) Relevance to activities in the real world
The link with the 'real world' is made easier because of the nature of these projects. The learner is active in a real context. What is learned is embedded in a larger setting – one which is encountered in real life. Participants are gaining an early insight, for example, into the research process: learning how to approach a problem and what kind of questions to ask, and experiencing the frustrations of going down blind alleys and of repeated apparatus failure.

Some outcomes

Details of the research findings are available in a series of evaluation reports (see, for example, Taylor, 1989). Three important outcomes are considered below.

Students participating in these projects regard as most important the benefits they have gained from working in a group. As described earlier, these projects replace the competitiveness associated with much of our formal schooling with the need on the part of the students to cooperate to solve the project problem. Damon and Phelps (1989) point out that collaborative learning can occur in a variety of ways and that each affords a distinct opportunity for students to learn from one another. (They

249

distinguish, for example, between cooperative learning, peer tutoring and peer collaboration.) The evidence from the evaluation is that the students, when working on these projects, get the chance to learn from all the ways listed and also have the opportunity to take on leadership roles.

Recent research evidence has emphasized how important the ability to work in a group is to the 'world of work'. In a recent survey of 200 of the country's leading industrialists (Taylor, 1991c) this ability was placed top of the items in a list of 10 attributes and was considered as 'very important' by 71 per cent of respondents. In a recent survey of 17–18 year olds conducted for the CBI by Gallup, 72 per cent of respondents felt that team-work skills would be of 'most importance' to future employees (Tysome, 1991).

Teachers acknowledge that the projects develop inter-personal skills and, as a result of the group work, point also to the dramatic improvement in communication skills which results, not only from having to talk to one another and to external consultants but also because the group must produce a final written report of its findings and make a formal presentation to a 'live' audience.

Conversation also provides opportunities for learning. All too often, experiential learning is conceived of as an interaction between the individual and the environment. Far too often the transaction between people as a constitutive element to learning is not considered. The importance of conversation as part of the learning process has, however, been stressed by a number of writers (Berger and Luckman, 1985; Freire, 1972). Conversation fulfils a number of functions (see, for example, Brookfield, 1985; Giroux, 1985) and the enrichment programme provides the context in which these can emerge.

The potential of the enrichment programme to provide experience 'across the curriculum' is being realized. There is evidence that the students gain an increased appreciation of their partners' abilities and perceptions and begin to understand that real problems rarely have solutions derived from one subject area.

Because of the inter-disciplinary nature of the projects, schools will often put together teams of students whose members are studying different areas of the curriculum. This means that, for some of their time, the participants must learn to cope with knowledge outside their own specialism. Some research has been carried out on undergraduates in this situation (Tobias, 1986) but not on students facing these problems in secondary education. There are early indications from these projects, however, that students specializing in different areas of the curriculum can have quite different perceptions of how to go about solving problems and can have different priorities when allocating 'project time'.

The enrichment programme – some implications

The University of Liverpool has supported institutions during the development phase in a number of ways. This has been documented elsewhere, along with a description of the philosophy which has underpinned its activities (Taylor and Derricott, 1990). In working alongside the institutions, the university has been able to:

- provide expertise to support the students in their projects;
- carry out an ongoing evaluation of the programme, which has encouraged participants to reflect on the process;
- provide in-service training; and
- support the institutions.

This list neatly identifies the important needs which need to be fulfilled whenever any institution embarks on the enrichment programme. Two of these are considered in more detail below:

The need for INSET

Teachers who take responsibility for the supervision of project groups find that their roles change from those associated with traditional teaching. This is represented in Figure 25.1.

Our research confirms work done by Burgess (1977) that the most important roles of teachers in their new situation are:

- to provide support for the group while undertaking their project;
- to help provide access to learning resources;
- to provide, on occasion, critical feedback to the learners; and

---

CONSULTANT

Informer/explainer

Instructor

ADVISER

Determiner of sequence

FACILITATOR/EXPEDIATOR

Teacher as fixer   ADVISER

Fount of all knowledge   ALSO LEARNING?

Figure 25.1 *The changing role of the teacher*

- to undertake responsibility for assessing the student (in this case, this involves working with the student for their RoA).

It became clear that teachers required opportunities to develop skills associated with facilitating group work and problem-solving activities and that some form of in-service was necessary.

In developing INSET programmes, the university recognized that:

- broadly formulated objectives and unclear expectations, imposed from outside, would not provide the necessary clarity;
- the input must enable participants to relate what was being considered to their own situation, ie, INSET must address practical issues;
- participants must be convinced that the changes being advocated would address a need. (In the case of teachers, it was accepted that what was on offer must fit with their perception of what their students actually need);
- too much training provision reduces participants to the roles of passive recipient. Teachers prefer active roles;
- the providers of INSET often underestimate teachers' ability to 'solve problems'. The university response was to provide situations where teachers would be working alongside others and were being encouraged to make a contribution based on their own insight and knowledge as experienced practitioners;
- the participant's effectiveness following any in-service training is also influenced by the characteristics of his/her workplace and a discussion of the constraints imposed by the institution is necessary.

Gessner (1956) pointed out that the way any INSET is organized will serve as a role model for those it attempts to influence. If, for example, it emphasizes paternalism, regimentalism, structuring of information and enforced dependence on those who are the providers of the service, the participants are unlikely to develop those skills associated with facilitating group work and problem-solving activities, no matter what material is presented. In providing INSET for this programme, attention must be paid to providing activities which reflect the situations for which the skills are being developed so that participants learn by their experience. The providers must be careful to include in their programme activities in which teachers are asked to collaborate (perhaps with total strangers) in their own problem-solving activities.

Supporting the institution

Introducing the curriculum enrichment programme into any institution represents change. Change is a process not an event. It proceeds through a series of stages, namely: initiation, implementation and incorporation. This process is not linear but two-way interactive. Various factors operate to influence each stage and it is a mistake to underestimate the problems associated with this process. Several authors, including Bolam (1978) and Hall and Loucks (1978), have stressed the limitations of any in-service training as a means of supporting clients if this is carried out in isolation. Clearly there must be some form of follow-up. As McLaughlin and Pfeifer (1978) point out, successful change is more a function of people and organizations than of technology or even money. It requires time and a willingness to support the people who are engaged in the process.

A major element of the university's commitment was the secondment of a member of the teaching staff to act as director. The responsibilities associated with this appointment have been many and varied, but one of the most important roles to emerge was that of providing 'moral support' to the schools when they were attempting to cope with the demands associated with introducing and running the enrichment programme. Much of the director's time has been spent visiting the schools to provide this support.

Outside support, however, is not enough and will not, on its own, ensure successful adoption of the programme. Our evidence is that those schools that have been successful in introducing and developing the programme have:

1. had active support from top management which has ensured that the programme has gained credibility within the institution and that adequate timetable provision has been made;
2. enabled the staff concerned to have a real share in the decision-making and provided them with opportunities to share their experiences and concerns; and
3. developed ownership of the programme so that teachers get opportunities to participate in the shaping of the change to the circumstances of their own particular school and go beyond being doers of other people's ideas.

The result of (3) above has been that an approach has been adopted which has permitted, at local level, some deviations from the original plan and has recognized grass-roots problems and the conditions of the school. Participants have also been encouraged to develop their own ideas for the projects and have been actively engaged in the development of the programme, most especially in the production of activities for the preparatory phase and in planning for the Record of Achievement in group project work.

As the programme has expanded and spread beyond north-west England, it has become clear that the role of the director will need to be undertaken by setting up local networks between institutions to enable further curriculum development along the above lines to continue.

Accrediting student achievement

At the end of their 13-week project, students negotiate with their supervisors to gain up to ten statements on an RoA. This RoA was not an original element in the enrichment programme; it grew out of evidence from the early trials and was developed in collaboration with participating teachers. The statements that have emerged are seen as being representative of the processes occurring as the projects proceed and do not attempt to reduce the educational process to a set of translatable skills and attitudes that lend themselves to accreditation. A further result of the collaboration has been the production of a set of teachers' notes to provide descriptors to accompany each statement and to outline what appears to be good teaching practice when introducing such an RoA and when carrying out negotiation.

Our research indicates that tensions can exist when an RoA recording individual achievement is introduced into project work which has group cooperation as its main feature. There is also a potential conflict between the teacher role as facilitator and that of being assessor. The evaluation indicates that, overwhelmingly, the teachers have striven to ensure students have directed their energies towards group maintenance and problem-solving rather than working towards personal gain. Research has also revealed something of the process of reflection and self-evaluation which must be undertaken by students in anticipation of their negotiation and of the use of personal diaries as part of this process (Taylor, 1991b).

One final point: we have been anxious to avoid some of the pitfalls associated with RoAs and to develop accreditation that will have credibility with future employers (and admission tutors in HE). The evidence from the industrialists' survey (Taylor, 1991c) is that, while employers welcome in principle the development of RoAs because they provide accreditation of achievements not normally recognized by the formal examination system, there remain serious reservations. It is clear, from the survey, that:

- respondents remained unsure of the reliability of RoAs. They need to know what evidence was gathered and how this was done;
- respondents doubt the validity of some RoAs. They need to know something of the accreditation procedures that were adopted; and

- the context in which the RoA is operating needs to be defined. Competencies are not neutral.

The procedures adopted and the documentation developed as part of the enrichment programme seek to address these problems.

Summary

This chapter has described the curriculum enrichment programme, a development that has built on much that excellent teachers already do. It has been directed and informed by its participants, with evaluation which has allowed them to reflect on their own practices, and with INSET which has encouraged them to share ideas and expertise, a development that has proved adaptable, so that institutions can use it to satisfy the demands of the current climate. But its most important feature is that it focuses on 'the group'. Concern has been voiced that education provision is becoming increasingly consumer-orientated with a corresponding reduction in the communicative domain. While developments on individualized learning and self-directed study (important strands of experiential learning) are to be welcomed, there is a danger that they place the individual at the centre of the value system and relegate the group to second place. One important consequence of adopting the enrichment programme is that it provides institutions with the opportunity to redress that imbalance.

References

Beder, H (1987) 'Dominant paradigms, adult education and social justice', *Adult Education Quarterly*, vol 2, 105–13.

Berger, P and Luckman, T (1985) *The Social Construction of Reality*, Harmondsworth: Penguin.

Bolam, R (1978) *Innovation in Inservice Education and Training of Teachers: Practice and Theory*, Paris: OECD.

Boud, D J (1985) *Problem-based Learning in Education for the Professions*, Sydney: Higher Education Society of Australasia.

Boydell, T (1976) *Experiential Learning*, Manchester: Department of Adult and Higher Education, University of Manchester.

Brookfield, S (1984) 'Self-directed adult learning: a critical paradigm', *Adult Education Quarterly*, 2, 59–71.

Brookfield, S (1985) 'A critical definition of adult education', *Adult Education Quarterly*, 1, 44–9.

Burgess, T (1977) *Education After School*, London: Gollancz.

Damon, W and Phelps, E (1989) 'Critical distinctions among three approaches to peer evaluation', *International Journal of Education*, 10, 1, 9–39.

Freire, P (1972) *Pedagogy of the Oppressed*, Harmondsworth: Penguin.

Freire, P (1985) *The Politics of Education*, London: Macmillan.

Gessner, R (1956) *The Democratic Man: Selected Writings of Edward C. Lindeman*, Boston: Beacon Press.

Giroux, H (1985) 'Introduction' in Freire, 1985, op. cit.

Hall, G E and Loucks, S F (1978) *Teacher Concerns as a Basis for Facilitating and Personalising Staff Development*, Austin: University of Texas R & D Centre for Teacher Education.

Kilty, J (1982) *Experiential Learning*, Guildford: Human Potential Research Unit, University of Surrey.

Kolb, D (1984) *Experiential Learning*, Englewood Cliffs, NJ: Prentice Hall.

McLaughlin, M W and Pfeifer, R S (1978) *Improvement, Accountability and Effective Learning*, New York: Teachers' College Press.

Taylor, I R (1989) *Experiential Group Work: An Evaluation*, Liverpool: N W Enrichment Programme, University of Liverpool.

Taylor, I R (1990) 'The curriculum enrichment programme', *PSSI Forum*, ASE, 2, October.

Taylor, I R (1991a) 'The 16–18 enrichment programme', *Science Teachers' Magazine (STEAM)*, 14, January.

Taylor, I R (1991b) 'Beyond formal qualifications: the Record of Achievement in group project work', *PSSI Forum*, ASE, 3, January.

Taylor, I R (1991c) *Employing Young People: A Survey of Industrialists' Perceptions*, Liverpool: N W Enrichment Programme, University of Liverpool.

Taylor I R and Derricott, R (1990) 'From enrichment to enterprise: the response of one university to the needs of its clients', paper presented at the 12th Annual European AIR Forum, Lyons, France, September 9–12.

Tobias, S (1986) *Peer Perspectives in the Teaching of Science, Change*, 18, 2, 36–41.

Tysome, A (1991) 'Students Hanker after Courses in Confidence', *Times Higher Education Supplement*, 21/6/91.

Index